A Functional Past

A Functional Past

THE USES OF HISTORY IN NINETEENTH-CENTURY CHILE

Allen Woll

Louisiana State University Press
Baton Rouge and London

Copyright © 1982 by Louisiana State University Press
All rights reserved
Manufactured in the United States of America

Designer: Patricia Douglas Crowder
Typeface: Linotron 202 Garamond #3
Typesetter: G & S Typesetters, Inc.
Printing and binding: Thomson-Shore, Inc.

LIBRARY OF CONGRESS CATALOGING IN PUBLICATION DATA

Woll, Allen.
  A functional past.

  Bibliography: p.
  Includes index.
    1. Chile—Historiography.   2. Chile—History—
1824–1920.   I. Title.
F3074.W64   983'.06   81-12411
ISBN 0-8071-0977-0   AACR2

To Myra

CONTENTS

ACKNOWLEDGMENTS

THIS BOOK ORIGINATED in an evening course at the University of Chicago on the philosophy of history taught by Karl J. Weintraub. Herbert Klein encouraged my early interest in Latin American history. Peter Smith, Thomas Skidmore, and the late John L. Phelan of the University of Wisconsin, Madison, provided diverse critical viewpoints which aided this manuscript considerably. Simon Collier of the University of Essex first introduced me to Chilean history, and he has read most of this manuscript and offered helpful suggestions. Charles Hale of the University of Iowa has expressed interest in this topic for many years. His comments, from the earliest days of the work to the final revisions, have improved this book immeasurably. I would also like to thank the Doherty Foundation for the opportunity to live in Chile during 1972 and 1973 and initiate the research for this book. Finally, I would like to thank my current colleagues at Rutgers University, Camden, for their continued faith.

Portions of this book appeared in the following journals: *History and Theory*, *The Americas*, the *Journal of Latin American Studies*, and the *Journal of the History of Ideas*. I would like to thank them for permission to reprint these articles in revised form.

A Functional Past

Introduction

DURING THE LAST YEAR of President Salvador Allende's rule in Chile, the government newspaper argued that historians were not performing a useful social function. It then proposed that the task of writing history be taken from the university professors and be given to those who were willing to use history to support Chile's incipient social revolution.[1] The charge that historians were socially irrelevant appeared surprising in a nation that has been called "the land of historians."[2] The importance of the historian to Chilean culture is immediately apparent to any visitor to Santiago. The countless monuments of historians provide a vivid contrast to other Latin American cities where statues of presidents and military men dominate the landscape.

Statues of Diego Barros Arana and Benjamín Vicuña Mackenna flank the National Library. José Victorino Lastarria sits regally in the lush Parque Forestal just a few blocks away. Standing alone, in the center of the Alameda, is a statue honoring the brothers Miguel Luis and Gregorio Víctor Amunátegui. These prolific writers face a monument honoring their mentor, Andrés Bello, situated in front of the University of Chile, which he helped to establish in 1842. Also close by are statues of Crescente Errázuriz and Ramón Sotomayor Valdés. Yet, these men are being honored for more than their contribution to Chilean historiography. Both Miguel Luis Amunátegui and

1. *La Nación*, September 21, 1972. All Spanish-language periodicals published in Santiago, Chile, unless otherwise noted.
2. Norman P. Sacks, "Some Aspects of Chilean Culture," *Topic 21* (Lexington, Va., 1971).

Vicuña Mackenna were presidential hopefuls; Barros Arana, Lastarria, and Sotomayor Valdés served as diplomats; and Bello and Barros Arana were perhaps the foremost educators of the nineteenth century.

The political activity of the great Chilean historians of the past century may seem surprising to one who is accustomed to current images of the intellectual immersed in thought in his library or archive. Indeed, contemporary definitions of intellectuals fall by the wayside when confronted with these extraordinary men. Edward Shils considered intellectuals to be "men vocationally concerned with things of the mind." Likewise, a recent study by G. Eric Hansen noted that the prime characteristic of the intellectual was "detachment as a commitment," while a politician was a person driven by "a passion to act, manipulate and make history."[3] Both conceptions are wholly inappropriate in the Chilean context since the man of thought and the man of action became one.

The Latin American *pensador* of the nineteenth century transcended all definitions which separate the activities of the man of thought and the man of action, since no incompatibility was seen between these two functions.[4] Lucas Alamán's activity as minister of state in Mexico or Vicuña Mackenna's senatorial duties offered no apparent incongruity with their vocation of historian. Indeed, some of the greatest intellectual leaders of nineteenth-century Latin America—Sarmiento, Mitre, Alamán, González Prada—were also among the foremost political figures of their nations.

Yet, as the *pensador* combined the supposedly opposing characteristics of the intellectual and the politician, prime requisites of each ideal necessarily had to be sacrificed. The intellectual's vocation demanded tranquillity and objectivity, while the politician's demanded action and commitment. The historian faced the dilemma of these conflicting tensions in a more acute fashion than his fellow artists. Whereas personal, political, and social convictions were not forbidden to the novelist, poet, or philosopher, the historian was bound by a more rigorous code. The historian's creed in the nineteenth cen-

3. Edward Shils, "The Intellectuals and the Powers: Some Perspectives for Comparative Analysis," *Comparative Studies in Society and History*, I (1958), 5–22; G. Eric Hansen, "Intellect and Power: Some Notes on the Intellectual as a Political Type," *Journal of Politics*, XXXI (1969), 311–28. See also Lewis Coser, *Men of Ideas* (Homewood, Ill., 1969).

4. For a discussion of Latin American intellectuals, see John Friedmann, "Intellectuals in Developing Countries," *Kyklos*, XIII (1960), 520. See also W. Rex Crawford, *A Century of Latin American Thought* (New York, 1961).

tury demanded objectivity in order that the past might be recreated *wie es eigentlich gewesen*, as Leopold von Ranke claimed, uncolored by present-day passions or emotions. However, as the century progressed, the historian concerned with the political affairs of his new nation found it increasingly more difficult to maintain the detachment that his intellectual vocation required. Politician or historian? Or both? These questions tortured Chile's historians of the past century as they were forced to reconcile the conflicting demands of their diverse professions.

The resolution of this problem wrought a revolution in Chilean historical thought which is the subject of this study. Two conflicting models of historical methodology were considered as Chilean historians began to establish the discipline in the new University of Chile. Andrés Bello, rector of the university, patiently attempted to institute the objective study of the past among his students. He argued that the historian must be concerned with the documentary and chronological approach to historical writing. He utilized all means at his command to encourage young historians to follow in his footsteps and avoid the modish European fad of the "philosophy of history." Nevertheless, José Victorino Lastarria, a young professor, and several cohorts abandoned Bello's methodology in the face of the political demands of the young republic. They argued that the arts, and especially history, had to be used to aid Chilean progress. European models—France in particular—pointed these historians toward a functional definition of their craft.

Throughout the rest of South America, the United States, and Europe, historians in the nineteenth century often utilized their craft as a tool in the attempt to accomplish social and political goals.[5] Thus one might expect Lastarria's ideas to be received warmly in Chile. Yet, according to recent studies, Chile appears to be an exception to this trend. Both Guillermo Feliú Cruz and Francisco Encina accord Bello a swift and thorough victory in these debates, and dismiss Lastarria's ideas as irrelevant. They argue that Chilean historians followed Bello's advice and consequently avoided the political controversy which affected the historians of other nations.[6] Two contemporary

5. See Stanley Mellon, *The Political Uses of History* (Stanford, 1958), and E. Bradford Burns, "Ideology in Nineteenth Century Latin American Historiography," *Hispanic American Historical Review*, LVIII (1978), 409–31.

6. Guillermo Feliú Cruz, "Andrés Bello y la historiografía chilena," *Mapocho*, IV (1965), 260, and Francisco A. Encina, *La literature histórica chilena y el concepto actual de la historia* (Santiago, 1935).

metaphors seemingly illustrated this notion. Barros Arana compared the historian in Chile to a judge, while Vicuña Mackenna painted him as a priest.[7] In this context political or personal passions had no place in historical writing.

This standard interpretation of Chilean historiography preserves two myths which this study attempts to revise. The first part of this work reconsiders the debates between Bello and Lastarria which are crucial to an understanding of the evolution of Chilean historical thought. Contrary to the assertions of Feliú Cruz and Encina, Bello's "victory" was neither quick nor thorough. Similarly, Lastarria's proposals were not wholly rejected, as is usually claimed. The resolution of this controversy provided a new direction for Chilean historical writing during the second half of the century, when it was considered among the best in the hemisphere.

The second part of this study endeavors to correct the apolitical interpretation of Chilean historiography in the period from 1850 to 1900. Far too often critics have accepted these historians' professions of impartiality at face value without examining the rationale for these statements. Despite their claims of objectivity, the historians who participated in Chile's political life, like their counterparts elsewhere, found history eminently adaptable to their needs. The proper interpretation of Chile's past might lend support to the fight for constitutional reform, the separation of Church and state, or Chile's supremacy in the international scene. Prominent educators discovered the social value of history and argued that it might teach Chilean youths to become patriotic and moral citizens. Still others found history a storehouse of knowledge that could reveal the existence of general laws governing human conduct, which might be used to plan the future of Chilean society. Finally, on a less exalted level, history could be used as a means of defending family honor and bolstering personal reputations.

The key to these trends in nineteenth-century historiography was *utility*, as the importance of Chile's future progress superseded any claims to intellectual objectivity. Thus, as intellectuals offered their services to their country, their works of art often followed suit, and history became as useful to the new nations as the historians themselves.

7. Carlos Orrego Barros, *Diego Barros Arana* (Santiago, 1952), 56–57, and Vicuña Mackenna, "Mi defensa ante el jurado de Valparaíso," *Revista Chilena de Historia y Geografía*, LXX (1931), 90.

Part I

THE ORIGINS OF HISTORICAL STUDIES IN CHILE (1830–1851)

DISCOVERY OF THE CHILEAN PAST

THE INTELLECTUAL RENAISSANCE OF 1842

EUROPEANS OBSERVING the young republic of Chile in the 1830s found it a model of stability when compared with its turbulent South American neighbors. However, this peaceful atmosphere did little to encourage artistic or intellectual endeavors. From the beginning of the Portalean era in 1830 until 1842, Chilean *pensadores* maintained a deadly calm. Few newspapers appeared, intellectual gatherings were rare, and drama and literature were almost nonexistent. Yet, suddenly, in 1842 an unprecedented flurry of intellectual activity awakened Santiago from its lethargy. The arts experienced an impressive revival, the University of Chile opened, and the youth flocked to join a literary society founded by José Victorino Lastarria. The society's members, honored as the "Generation of 1842" by Chilean critics, created works of history, literature, poetry, and drama which provided the cultural foundations of the new nation.

The year 1842 has become engraved in the minds of Chileans as the year of the intellectual renaissance of the republic, while the previous era has symbolized a dark age. The cause of this twelve-year hiatus in Chilean cultural life was a direct result of the lengthy and turbulent struggle for independence. Chile's liberty was not won quickly. After a few hopeful years of freedom from Spanish colonial authority, Chile succumbed to the Spanish Reconquest in 1814 as Royalist troops from Peru defeated the patriot army. The Spanish retained control until 1817, when the Army of the Andes under José de San Martín and Bernardo O'Higgins chased the army of occupation from Chilean soil after the Battle of Chacabuco. O'Higgins, as "Supreme Director," responded vigorously to the task of reorganizing Chilean life and erasing all remnants of Spanish colonial rule. He encouraged immigration and education, established new towns, and sought and received much-needed loans from the British. However, other aspects of his reform program were considered less welcome by the Chilean aristocracy, particularly his decision to abolish *mayorazgos* in 1818 and his tendency to meddle in internal affairs of the Church.

O'Higgins abdicated in 1823 after a revolt of the provinces and a conspiracy in the capital itself. A marked distaste for a strong executive dated from this period, and any favorable results of O'Higgins' rule became blurred before his image as a dictator. The reaction to O'Higgins' strong centralized government was inevitable, and his opponents favored federal schemes of organization modeled after the United States, and encouraged all attempts to limit the power of future chief executives. Yet, the federal experiments of 1824 to 1827 seemed as equally unsuitable for Chile as the reforms of the O'Higgins era. Regional revolts and military coups followed each other in rapid succession, the crime rate increased considerably, and the National Treasury was soon depleted as a result of the chaos.[1]

While President Francisco Antonio Pinto and the Constitution of 1828 attempted to moderate this intense reaction against a strong executive, a Conservative coalition used the disputed 1829 elections as an excuse to begin a civil war and seize control of the national government. Led by Diego Portales, a group of landed aristocrats (*pelucones* or "big-wigs"), dissatisfied with the anticlerical and antiaristocratic policies of the Pinto regime, along with former O'Higginists, hopeful of returning their hero to power, and the *estanqueros*, disappointed with the unsatisfactory climate for business and investment, sought to end the anarchy of the previous six years and institute a strong central government. Portales, who had opposed the Federalist governments since 1826, when his company's control of the state tobacco monopoly (*estanco*) was abolished, saw the forcible seizure of power as the only possible means to end the years of chaos and confusion.

Portales was not eager for personal fame in the new government organized in 1830. He never assumed the presidency, and only reluctantly did

---

1. Norberto Pinilla, *La generación chilena de 1842* (Santiago, 1943); Julio César Jobet, *Ensayo crítico del desarrollo económico-social de Chile* (Santiago, 1955), 31–35.

he fill the posts of vice-president and various ministries for short periods of time. Yet, as a private adviser, his personal philosophy dominated the government of José Antonio Prieto. He believed that "democracy was an absurdity in the new American states, where citizens lacked every virtue which was necessary for the establishment of a true *Republic*. For this reason, a strong centralized government, whose leaders shall be models of virtue and patriotism, shall set its citizens on the road to order and virtue."[2]

Portales' philosophy came to fruition in the Constitution of 1833, which, responsive to the perceived realities of Chilean society, survived the longest of all nineteenth-century South American charters. The Grand Constituent Assembly established firm powers in executive hands. The president could declare a state of siege whenever the Congress was in recess, and thus suspend the Constitution. He could also veto any law, which consequently delayed its reconsideration for at least a year. Similarly, he was able to control provincial aspirations by direct appointment of governors and intendants. Despite the ability of Congress to control the budget, the executive maintained strict control during this period.[3]

The Prieto regime used its ample powers to mute opposition of any type, a fact which limited opportunities for intellectuals to gather and discuss politics. The prime weapon for the quelling of dissent was a strict censorship law that stopped the multiplication of newspapers and periodicals, which had been commonplace since the first days of the Independence era. The Portales years (1831–1837) saw 75 percent fewer newspapers than the supposedly chaotic Federal period of 1824 to 1829.[4]

Exile was yet another tool for limiting criticism of the government. José Joaquín de Mora, a Spanish immigrant, who had actively supported the Federalist governments of the 1820s, had irritated Portales from the beginnings of the Conservative period. In response, the government withdrew all financial support from Mora's Liceo de Chile, and then established a competing institution, the Colegio de Santiago, in hopes of attracting students from Mora's school. Mora then attacked the legality of the *pelucón* regime in short-

2. Diego Portales, *Diego Portales pintado por sí mismo* (Santiago, 1941), 26.
3. Simon Collier, *Ideas and Politics of Chilean Independence, 1808–1833* (Cambridge, 1967), 346.
4. Compiled from Raúl Silva Castro, *Prensa y periodismo en Chile, 1812–1956* (Santiago, 1958).

lived newspapers such as *El Defensor de los militares* and *El Trompeta*. The sole result of his efforts was permanent exile from his adopted country.[5]

Despite expectations to the contrary, the rigid control of opposition politics and the press increased after 1835, when Portales considered the government as gravely threatened by external affairs. General Ramón Freire, a Chilean who led the rebellion against O'Higgins, launched a military expedition from Peru, again attempting to overthrow the government. As a result, relations with Peru decayed, and, still worse, Chile's neighbor to the north seemed about to enter into alliance with General Andrés Santa Cruz of Bolivia. The alliance was unusually one-sided, and, after a brief campaign against Peruvian forces, Santa Cruz declared himself the "Protector of the Peru-Bolivian Confederation." Portales viewed the new power to the north with displeasure, and considered it a threat to Chile's safety. The Congress authorized a declaration of war in 1836, and Portales, now minister of war and minister of the interior, sought to conquer Santa Cruz as quickly as possible. At first the war was unpopular as Portales, after declaring a state of siege throughout the country, obliterated all opposition and attempted rebellions with an unparalleled ruthlessness.[6]

José Victorino Lastarria, as a young professor at the National Institute, noted that intellectuals remained silent during this turbulent period since they felt threatened by the "1837 suspension of the Constitution, the mobilization for war, the political hangings, and executions without trial for committing treason or expressing seditious sentiments." He then expressed the intellectuals' dilemma: "If we reveal our ideas with a frankness that undermines the preoccupations and interests of the dominant political and religious groups, that criticism could be taken as an expression of public opinion, and therefore a violation of the state of siege, thus allowing the government to take measures against our attempt at intellectual development.[7]

This campaign of terror came to an end as a result of the assassination of Portales one morning as he arrived in Quillota to review the troops. The shock of Portales' death converted him into a martyr for the Chilean cause,

5. Miguel Luis Amunátegui, *Don José Joaquín de Mora* (Santiago, 1888). See also Carlos Stuardo Ortiz, *El Liceo de Chile* (Santiago, 1950).

6. Luis Galdames, *A History of Chile*, trans. I. J. Cox (New York, 1941), 269.

7. José Victorino Lastarria, *Recuerdos literarios* (Santiago, 1912), 111. See also Jacinto Chacón to Domingo Amunátegui Solar, *Atenea*, LXVII (May, 1942), 193–201.

and similarly quieted criticism as former opponents lent their support to the war. After the Chilean victory at Yungay under General Manuel Bulnes in 1839, constitutional rule was restored, and, soon after, dissenting political opinions were once again allowed in the press. Bulnes was elected president in 1841 and he promised further guarantees of individual liberties.

Coupled with the newly relaxed political atmosphere was greater economic prosperity. The new discoveries of copper and silver in the North and increased foreign trade eventually led to Chile's first balanced budget in 1845. Manuel Rengifo, minister of finance, further improved Chile's economic state by a renegotiation of the British debt and a complete reform of customs tariffs.[8] The end of the war, the new prosperity, and new guarantees of freedom of expression would have seemed to provide ideal conditions for intellectuals to gather, but no immediate issue spurred them to organize. A newly established literary society disbanded after its initial meetings in 1839, and a society of agriculture managed to enlist only twenty-nine members in its first year.[9]

Nevertheless, possibilities for future gatherings seemed hopeful since the paths of intellectual achievement in Chile were so few. Anyone with intellectual aspirations was channeled into an educational system which soon brought him to Santiago and placed him in contact with others of similar interests. If the student were one of the 10 percent of the Chilean children to attend primary school, he could then continue his education in one of the six national institutes of secondary education, where a few scholarships were available for deserving students of scarce means. Any further studies would necessarily take the youth to the National Institute in Santiago, the only school in Chile to offer higher education, where the student might be trained as a professor or lawyer. In this manner Santiago became the primary meeting place for all those with intellectual aspirations.[10]

While most of the youths who graduated from the National Institute

8. Francisco A. Encina, *Historia de Chile desde la prehistoria hasta 1891* (Santiago, 1948), XII, 59–69; Ramón Sotomayor Valdés, *Historia de Chile* (Santiago, 1876), I, 36–39, 201–25.

9. Gonzalo Izquierdo F., *Un estudio de las ideologías chilenas* (Santiago, 1968), 28.

10. Ana Guirao Massif, *Historia de la Facultad de Filosofía y Humanidades* (Santiago, 1957), 19; Raúl Silva Castro, *Don Andrés Bello* (Santiago, 1965), 41; Benjamín Vicuña Mackenna (ed.), *Historia general de la República de Chile desde su independencia hasta nuestros días* (Santiago, 1866), I, 105.

were children of landed aristocrats or businessmen, a few students of lesser means managed to obtain a higher education. One example was Lastarria, whose father had lost the fortune he had acquired as a businessman during the Wars of Independence. An education offered these youths a chance to rise in Santiago society, and one student optimistically foresaw the "decline of the colonial aristocracy and the rise of a new class based on the virtues of knowledge and talent."[11]

The mentor of the young Chileans was a Venezuelan expatriate, Andrés Bello. One of the few attempts of the Portalean government to improve the state of education and the sciences in Chile had been to attract illustrious foreigners to lend their expertise to the newly independent nation. Bello, who had served in the Colombian delegation in London, was lured to Chile by Mariano Egaña, who believed that Bello would aid Chile's intellectual development. Bello responded to the offer partly for monetary reasons, since he feared that he would have no inheritance to leave his children, and also by his fear of the anarchic conditions in Gran Colombia. The "climate and hopes for tranquillity" thus attracted the literate sage, Bello, friend of Jeremy Bentham and James Mill. From his arrival Bello warmly supported the Prieto government, which provided the order necessary for his intellectual pursuits. He worked diligently as editor of the government newspaper *El Araucano*, and also edited and wrote several official speeches and documents.[12]

Soon after the founding of the Colegio de Santiago, Bello moved the classes of Roman law and natural law to his own home, thus allowing the best students to meet and discuss their work. Lastarria recalled one of these sessions:

In 1834 Bello began to teach two courses in his home. . . . The classroom was his private library, and all consultation of his works were made with his aid. We often had lengthy debates on the fine points of the law and we discussed all the details one by one.
    The study of language was a complete course in philology which included general grammar and the history of the Spanish language. . . . The professor habitually

11. *El Semanario de Santiago*, July 14, 1842.
12. Silva Castro, *Andrés Bello*, 27; Guillermo Feliú Cruz, *Andrés Bello y la redacción de los documentos oficiales del gobierno de Chile* (Caracas, 1951), and *La carrera administrativa de Andrés Bello en Chile* (Santiago, 1966).

wrote his textbooks while he was teaching the course. His treatise on the conjugation of verbs and the most interesting chapters of his book on Spanish grammar were discussed in detail in friendly and often lengthy meetings with his students. [13]

Despite Bello's contribution to Chilean intellectual life, Lastarria was often very harsh in his evaluation of his former mentor. [14] In his memoirs he often underestimated Bello's accomplishments and emphasized his faults. One apparent flaw which irritated Lastarria from the first was Bello's rigid adherence to the rules governing artistic expression, and his firm insistence that his students do the same. Lastarria remarked that "Bello, unlike the majority of philosophers, was imprisoned by empirical rules without understanding that the fundamental strength of literature was its independence of spirit." Bello taught his courses with the aim that his students follow his method without question. "He was an exceedingly serious man and very set in his ways of teaching. He never allowed refutation of his statements; he alone talked, beginning with the exposition of a question in order to stimulate the students' thought." Apparently, Bello was quite successful in his goals: "His influence was incredible in that epoch; it was almost a domination. His disciples entered the classroom in order to spread his ideas and methods." [15] During the 1830s Lastarria appeared to be the only one critical of Bello's methods, and it was not until 1842 that Bello's ideals were seriously challenged.

The arrival of the Argentine émigrés fleeing from Rosas' tyrannical rule acted as a catalyst to the thought and organization of the young Chilean intellectuals. The Argentines entered Chilean intellectual life with unusual ease, becoming writers, editors, professors, and self-appointed critics of the young republic. Lastarria recalled meeting the young Domingo Faustino Sarmiento and admitted that he was greatly impressed by him: "He was an extraordinary man—his thirty-two years appeared seventy. The liveliness and frankness of that young-old man made him extremely amiable and interesting." [16] A few introductions later and an exciting article in *El Mercurio* about the Battle of Chacabuco led to an offer of thirty pesos for three or four edi-

---

13. Lastarria, *Recuerdos*, 70–71.
14. For Bello's contribution to Chilean culture, see Miguel Luis Amunátegui, *Biografías de Americanos* (Santiago, 1854).
15. Lastarria, *Recuerdos*, 70–72.
16. Armando Donoso, "Sarmiento y Lastarria," *Revista Chilena*, X (1920), 5–6.

torials a week for the young Argentine. Sarmiento's meteoric rise was not exceptional. Vicente Fidel López soon began writing for the Valparaíso-based *Gaceta del Comercio* and, shortly after, published the *Revista de Valparaíso*. Bartolomé Mitre arrived in Chile soon afterwards, and he too assumed an editorship.[17]

However, despite the initial ease and warmth of the friendship between the young Chileans and the Argentines, a rivalry soon developed as Sarmiento and his cohorts attacked the intellectual ascendancy of Andrés Bello, who never forgave the foreigners for their audacity. Even after many years, Bello harshly reprimanded his prize students, the Amunátegui brothers, when they suggested that the Argentines "awoke the interest in literature among the Chileans."[18] Sarmiento launched his attack in a review of Bello's latest poem, a hymn to the Church of the Compañía, which was destroyed by fire during the last century. This awesome building inspired generations of Chilean writers since its haunting spires housed a dangerous firetrap which would periodically ignite and kill countless people. Sarmiento reviewed the poem quite favorably, but then he realized that this work was one of the few poems written by a "Chilean" that he had read. He then asked: "Why are there so few honors to the poetic Muse? Does the climate smother the imagination? Or do the Chileans lack sufficient education? . . . On the contrary, I believe that our youth possesses a lack of resolution and a laziness of spirit."[19]

From this moment relations chilled between Chilean and Argentine intellectuals. The Chileans resented the attack on their intellectual tradition and tried to defend it, while the Argentines found Chilean culture in its swaddling clothes. *Niño* and the budding flower became the most common metaphors in Argentine discussions of Chilean thinkers.[20] The year 1842 saw two lengthy debates on Chilean culture between the followers of Sarmiento and those of Bello. While the ensuing bitterness caused the Argentines and

17. Silva Castro, *Prensa*, 185–90.

18. Universidad de Chile, *Memorias de los egresados, Actas de la Facultad de Filosofía y Humanidades* (Santiago, 1957), I, 206. See also Hermelo Arabena Williams, "Los emigrados argentinos en la cultura chilena," *Boletín de la Academia Chilena de Historia*, VI (1938), 110–29.

19. M. L. Amunátegui, "El Templo de la Compañía de Jesús en Santiago de Chile," *Revista de Santiago*, May 15, 1872, and Benjamín Vicuña Mackenna, *El incendio del Templo de la Compañía* (Buenos Aires, 1971); *El Mercurio*, July 15, 1841.

20. Vicente Fidel López, "Sociedad literaria," *Gaceta del comercio*, May 31, 1842: "The first statement of the Literary Society was like the first words from a baby's beautiful lips which place a smile of joy on the mother's face."

the Chileans to drift apart, it also caused the Chileans to unite for the first time in defense of their national traditions. Both debates, one concerning Spanish orthography, and the other, the importance of Romanticism for Chilean literature, considered the value of the adherence to rules and tradition.

Sarmiento began the debate. A short dictionary of words used improperly in Chile and their proper usage appeared in *El Mercurio* of April 27, 1842. Although the work was written by Pedro Fernández Garfias, a former professor of grammar at the National Institute, Chileans read Sarmiento's hearty praise of the enterprise and assumed that he himself had written the original study. Sarmiento's review presented two suggestions which attacked the ideals of proper grammar which Bello had so patiently instituted in Chile. First, Sarmiento claimed that the spelling of a word should conform to its local pronunciation, and then he added that the idea of a Chilean equivalent to the French or Spanish Academy to regulate proper word usage was an absurdity. He reasoned that "the sovereignty of the people should be most respected in the domain of language. The grammarians are like the Conservative Senate which resists popular pressures and conserves routine and tradition."[21]

Bello realized that the article was directed against him, since he had advocated the foundation of such an academy, and he responded as the pseudonymous "Un quídam." That the attack thoroughly angered him was without doubt, since his normal posture as years passed was to remain above the debate and allow his students to present his position for him. He then asserted that the Chilean youth must study the "admirable models of Spanish literature" so it would not come to pass that one would find words of French-Spanish dialect in the daily newspapers as occurs in a certain South American country." The dig was directed at the Argentines, and Sarmiento responded quickly and somewhat viciously. He argued the study of these "admirable models" was the bane of Chilean intellectual life. All of this study had left the Chilean incapacitated, unable to produce a single work of merit. He added: "It is the perverse nature of studies in Chile that the influence of the grammarians, the respect for *admirable models*, and the fear of breaking the rules have bound the imagination of the Chileans. . . . There is no spontaneity, there is just a jail whose door is guarded by inflexible guardians of

21. "Popular Exercises in the Spanish Language," *El Mercurio*, April 27, 1842.

taste."[22] Typically, as the debate reached this heated pitch, Bello withdrew and allowed one of his students, José María Núñez (Otro quídam), to continue. Less astute than his mentor, Núñez was fooled by a clever article by Sarmiento which paraphrased the ideas of Mariano José de Larra, a Spanish critic who supported Sarmiento's ideas. Sarmiento then exposed his purposeful plagiarism, noting that Núñez was not smart enough to discover it.[23]

The relations between Chileans and Argentines became even more strained during the second debate, since more persons participated than in the orthography question. This new argument concerned the importance of Romanticism for Chilean literature. Salvador Sanfuentes, a Literary Society member, lamented: "How do I dare attempt to define a word which everyone uses but so few understand?" Despite his pessimism, a precise notion of Romanticism was understood both by the Argentines and the Chileans. First, it was the French phenomena that interested them. The North American manifestation of Romanticism, as represented by Washington Irving and William Prescott, was dismissed, partially because of America's idealization of the Spain of the Golden Age.[24] It would have seemed absurd for the Argentines and Chileans to worship the mother country after years of bitter struggle for independence.

The turn to France was not surprising. The Argentines idolized the French philosophers and the Chileans were soon to follow suit. Typical of this sentiment was a speech in *Ernesto*, an 1842 play by Rafael Minvielle, a Literary Society member, wherein Ernesto's father suggests that he "go to France, the country which is the center of knowledge and civilization, where the light of philosophy and tolerance will make the happiness and well-being of your spirit live once again."[25] The Argentines argued that a particular aspect of French Romanticism could prove useful to the Chileans. First, they dismissed an early penchant of French Romanticism which tended to idealize the past and, in particular, the Middle Ages. Vicente Fidel López argued that this trend was moved by a reactionary spirit, desirous of re-creating the past,

22. *El Mercurio*, May 22, 1842.

23. J. Guillermo Guerra, *Sarmiento, su vida y sus obras* (Santiago, 1938), Ch. 4.

24. M. L. Amunátegui, "Anecdotas literarias," *La República*, January 6, 1872. (Sanfuentes made this statement on November 26, 1841): David Levin, *History as a Romantic Art* (Stanford, 1959); Guillermo Feliú Cruz, *El Imperio Español y los historiadores norteamericanos* (Santiago, 1960).

25. Pinilla, *La generación chilena de 1842*.

and unfavorable to revolutionary movements.[26] The past, and especially the Spanish past, was what both the Chileans and the Argentines had to change. Any worship of the past, similar to Chateaubriand's paean to the Middle Ages in *Génie du christianisme* (1802), could only be unfavorable to Chile's future development.

What then remained of French Romantic doctrine that would be useful to the Chileans? A second tendency of Romantic thought, which can be traced to Victor Hugo and Alphonse de Lamartine, concerned itself with the present and the future rather than with the past. The Romanticism of Chateaubriand's era, which had been ultra-Royalist and mystical, became liberal and democratic after the appearance of Hugo's *Cromwell* (1827), which denied all classical rules governing the drama.[27] Fidel López traced the change to the Revolution of 1830: "This political revolution substituted in the place of Romanticism a new literature which no longer searched for antecedents in the Middle Ages or antiquity, but, rather, in contemporary society. . . . This literature not only concerned itself with the past, but also with the present and future."[28]

The main criterion of this new literature was that "art should be the expression of a society and of an epoch."[29] Implicit in this notion was an attack on the classical school of literature which emphasized the importance of past models for literary production. Hugo fought the Classicists in France, as the Argentines were to attack Bello, the symbol of this school in Chile. The second rule, or non-rule, of this literature was that there were no rules. López again declared: "Romanticism has destroyed the despotism of grammatical and rhetorical rules. These rules aspire to infallibility and strict rigidity and, therefore, deny the ability of language and literature to progress. Additionally, these rules deny the progressive nature of human intelligence."[30]

Thus the abolition of rules or the "admirable models" professed by Bello would allow the Chilean youth to express themselves free of weight of past tradition. Also, this new literature would possess a second favorable attribute: it would be useful. Since it would be "an expression of the society," it

26. Fidel López, "Clasicismo y Romanticismo," *Revista de Valparaíso*, no. 4, May, 1842.
27. Matthew Josephson, *Victor Hugo* (New York, 1942), 122.
28. *Gaceta del comercio*, August 4, 1842.
29. *Ibid.*, August 2, 1842.
30. *Revista de Valparaíso*, May, 1842.

could become an "aid to the people and an instrument of progress."[31] Art had to become functional, and its goal was Chilean progress. Sarmiento explained that "writing in order to improve society was the duty of those who study the necessities of the era in which they live. Writing merely for the sake of writing was mere vanity and the attitude of those without principles or true patriotism." Thus the Argentines repudiated the doctrine of art for art's sake. It was this particular aspect of French thought, which Roger Picard has called "social Romanticism," or "art with a moral orientation," that the Argentines urged the Chileans to adopt.[32]

The Argentines believed, however, that there was a definite reason that "social Romanticism" was not being accepted in Chilean society. Fidel López argued that an innovation in literary thought which promoted ideals such as the freedom from rules and the responsibility to one's own people could eventually lead to a political revolution which a conservative government would be anxious to suppress. "All new ideas," he claimed, "provoke doubts, reflection, and revelations which are potential death blows to the continued domination of the *ancien régime*. This is the seed of revolution that all new literary ideals bear within them."[33]

The Chilean response to the Argentine challenge was half-hearted at best, as most students of Bello seemed confused as to the definition of Romanticism. The arguments of Salvador Sanfuentes, José Joaquín Vallejo (Jotabeche), and Antonio García Reyes in the pages of *El Semanario* often strayed from the issue at hand and descended to personal attacks on the Argentines.[34] Sarmiento confessed that he was deeply hurt by the charges that he was both "ignorant and a charlatan." As the attacks in the daily press became more virulent, Lastarria realized that the persistent name-calling could only hurt the attempt of the Chileans to assert their intellectual independence. He devised a hasty compromise with Sarmiento, and assured him that *El Semanario* would respect the "free actions of the Argentine writers who might, if they wished, aid the Chileans in their literary movement and

31. *Ibid.*

32. See Ricardo Donoso, "La labor educativa y literaria de Sarmiento en Chile," *Universidades* (Buenos Aires), I (April–June, 1961), 17; Roger Picard, *Le romantisme social* (New York, 1944).

33. *Revista de Valparaíso*, May, 1842.

34. *El Semanario de Santiago*, July 21, 28 and August 4, 1842; *El Mercurio*, July 23, 1842; *El Semanario de Santiago*, August 4, 1842.

help them propagate liberal ideals."[35] In this manner a bitter debate was drawn hastily to a close. However, the Chileans and the Argentines agreed on one issue, that there was a need for a new school of literature, "neither classic or romantic," but, as Fidel López suggested, "progressive."[36] Of all the young Chileans the one most responsive to the ideas of the Argentines and French "social Romanticism" was José Victorino Lastarria, who was to become the acknowledged leader of the intellectual movement of 1842.

The forum for the discussion of the new literary ideas became the Literary Society, which met eighty-six times in 1842 and 1843, thus displaying a permanence heretofore uncharacteristic of such gatherings. Several students and their friends met in March, 1842, and began soliciting contributions which could be used for the rental of a meeting hall. Shortly after, a private hall was donated to the youths for their meetings. After the initial sessions it was decided that new members might be proposed by a present member, and they had to receive a majority vote in order to enter the group. The meetings were held weekly, and members presented discourses on a variety of topics. The discussions ranged from Juan Bello's "History of Egypt" and Javier Rengifo on the freedom of the press, to Francisco Bilbao's tract on "the relationship of psychiatry to the sovereignty of the people" and a "Dissertation on the Aristocratic and Feudal Spirit in Chile" by Cristobál Valdés, who proposed that "all discourses be about the political state of Chile." Contests were often held to encourage new studies. For a prose or poetic study of the sixteenth of September, Chilean Independence Day, Juan Bello and Santiago Lindsay won copies of recently published books. All meetings, however, did not consider such lofty subjects. For three meetings the question of whether to allow smoking was debated. Similarly, the problem of members who refused to pay their weekly dues often occupied the attention of the Literary Society.[37]

Perhaps the most memorable work produced by the Literary Society was the inaugural address of its director, Lastarria. Although his speech followed the ideas of the Argentines closely, it must be remembered that Lastarria delivered his discourse just six days after Sarmiento's first article on orthogra-

35. Sarmiento to Lastarria, reprinted in Lastarria, *Recuerdos*, 144, 146.
36. *El Semanario de Santiago*, July 21, 1842; *Gaceta del comercio*, July 30, 1842.
37. "Actas de la Sociedad Literaria, 1842–1843," in Julio Durán Cerda (ed.), *El movimiento literario de 1842* (Santiago, 1957), I, 171–222.

phy. Thus Lastarria was not merely mimicking the ideas that appeared in the debates in the daily press. Rather, the timing of the speech would indicate that Lastarria reached his conclusions both personally and perhaps in discussions with his friend Sarmiento.[38]

Lastarria first discussed the necessity of a truly national literature. He noted that Chilean intellectuals had "an ardent desire, very common in new nations, to earn a place alongside older civilizations and hold their head up proudly before European philosophers. While "Chileans might take advantage of the discoveries of European thinkers," he asserted that "our literature must be exclusively our own, and it must be wholly national." This initial part of the speech was a response to a common habit among Chileans, that of borrowing elements of culture from Europe without considering how they might be modified in Chile. For example, one student read Simonde de Sismondi's *Recherches sur les constitutions des peuples libres* and commented: "In this work one may find all rules concerning the nature of good government. We need not be original, we need not tire ourselves out with the study of history . . . we may just take advantage of these proven laws of political science."[39]

Lastarria scorned this lazy tendency of Chilean youth. However, he argued that there was one nation that Chile could profitably imitate: France. France was chosen as a model because French writers have "led a literary rebellion, freeing their literature from the rigorous and petty rules that had been considered inviolate and sacred." The French have looked for truth "in human nature, which is the oracle to consult for all decisions," and this ideal must be imitated by the Chileans. The nascent Chilean literature had therefore to be based on "independence and the freedom of genius."

In addition to stressing the French Romantic tenet of freedom from rules, Lastarria also stressed aspects of "social Romanticism" when he listed the tasks facing Chilean intellectuals. He asserted that intellectuals could no longer be without a social conscience and claimed that "they should sacrifice themselves for the utility of their country." He then explained that he wished Chile to become a true democracy, an "exceedingly difficult task due to the ignorance of the Chilean people." The prime requisite of democracy, Lastarria reasoned, was the enlightenment of the citizenry, and he believed that the writings of the Literary Society members could serve this goal. He then

38. Donoso, "Sarmiento y Lastarria," 12.
39. *El Semanario de Santiago*, December 1, 1842.

urged his audience to "write for the people, enlighten them; combat their vices and encourage their virtues; remind them of heroic historical facts; accustom them to worship their God and their institutions. . . . Thus we will strengthen the ties that bind them and make them view their liberty and social existence as one and the same. This is the only way we should accomplish the great task of making our literature *national*, *useful*, and *progressive*."[40]

The goals seemed lofty, and perhaps inflated at the time. How could literature become "national, useful, and progressive" if very few Chileans could read? By 1843, only 10 percent of the Chilean people had attended primary school. The goals that Lastarria set for the Literary Society necessitated the presence of a literate audience, and more than a flourish of new writing was needed to accomplish these aims. Thus, in order to ensure the "enlightenment of the Chilean people," the members of the Literary Society also concerned themselves with the wider diffusion of their writings via new newspapers, textbooks, and the reform of the educational system as well as experimentation in literary techniques.

Sarmiento viewed the newspaper as the prime means of spreading knowledge and enlightenment throughout the country. Yet, he lamented the fact that Boston with only 80,000 people in 1834 offered forty-three daily papers, while the entire nation of Chile, with a population of one million, had only one daily newspaper. By 1841, when Sarmiento was writing, the nation's capital had no daily newspaper, since *El Mercurio* was printed in the coastal city of Valparaíso. In 1842 two political exiles attempted to start new newspapers in Chile and each failed miserably. *El Museo de ambas américas*, edited by Juan García del Río, a Columbian, was designed as a "useful newspaper which desired to interest, instruct, improve and please the people." However, a subscription list of 169 Santigueños, which included several Literary Society members as well as the nation's top political leaders, was unable to save the paper from an early demise.[41] Similarly, the *Revista de Valparaíso*, edited by Fidel López, had a miniscule circulation and expired after six issues.

The inability of private support to guarantee a newspaper's existence led

40. This speech is reprinted in Lastarria, *Recuerdos*, Part I, Ch. 15. Italics mine.
41. *El Mercurio*, July 4 and August 7, 1841; Lastarria, *Recuerdos*, 88. My figures from the subscription lists of *El Museo de Ambas Americas* in *Biblioteca Nacional* differ slightly from those in Encina, *Historia*, XII, 429.

the Vial Formas brothers, relatives of President Bulnes and Finance Minister Rengifo, to propose that the government finance the publication of a daily paper for Santiago, which Sarmiento would edit. A lengthy debate in the Chamber of Deputies revealed opposing ideas of the importance of the press to Chilean society. The minister of the interior, Ramón Luis Irarrázaval, asserted that this "necessary expense would stimulate the enlightenment of our country since the paper could not survive without the protection of the government." However, Deputy Palazuelos argued that "newspapers did not offer the least utility for Chile since the people did not know how to read, nor were they interested in the questions discussed in the press." He added that the best means of spreading civilization was by religious teachings. The Chamber, however, supported the former view by a considerable majority, and the Senate followed suit eight votes to three. The government then alloted 9,794 pesos for the first year's publication expenses.[42]

Members of the Literary Society conferred with Andrés Bello about the idea of starting a newspaper, and he suggested that "their first duty was to vindicate their national honor" to the Argentines and "demonstrate and affirm the intellectual progress of Chileans." The fruit of this discussion became *El Semanario de Santiago*, a literary weekly which the editors claimed would "present a true miscellany designed to unite the useful and the agreeable, and to urge all classes of people to fully realize their aspirations."[43] *El Crepúsculo* ("the dawn") followed soon after the closing of *El Semanario*, which had spent most of its time challenging the Argentine's Romantic credo. Interestingly, the succeeding journal eliminated all those who had earlier opposed the Argentines (Sanfuentes, Vallejo, and García Reyes) and left Lastarria loyalists as contributors.[44] The latter magazine assumed a more political stance than its predecessor, which in turn led to its quick demise, as the government closed the editorial offices after the publication of Francisco Bilbao's incendiary tract *La Sociabilidad Chilena* in 1844.[45]

Coupled with the attempt of the Literary Society members to encourage new newspapers and magazines was a desire to increase the audience for their writings by a reform of the educational system. Some participated in educa-

42. Diego Barros Arana, *Un decenio de la historia de Chile* (Santiago, 1913), I, 313–16.

43. Lastarria, *Recuerdos*, 130; *El Semanario de Santiago*, July 14, 1842.

44. For a list of members, see Roberto Vilches, "Las revistas literarias chilenas del siglo XIX," *Revista Chilena de Historia y Geografía*, XCI (1942), 339–40.

45. See Chapter 2 herein for a discussion of Bilbao.

tional planning directly as members of the Faculty of Philosophy and Humanities of the University of Chile. This new university was established in 1842 to replace the colonial University of San Felipe, abolished in 1839. The brainchild of Andrés Bello, this new scholarly institution was modeled after the French Institute, one of the most famous scientific institutions in Europe at that time. Both were divided into five academic divisions, which in Chile were philosophy and humanities, mathematical sciences and physics, medicine, law and political science, and theology. The university was designed as an academic and consultative institution, since the teaching of higher education itself remained in the National Institute.[46]

The Faculty of Philosophy and Humanities was placed in charge of primary education. Its tasks included the translation and publication of textbooks, the inspection of schools, and the presentation of statistical reports on the educational system. Of the first nineteen members chosen, eight were former Literary Society members or active participants in the intellectual activities of 1842.[47] The faculty faced an extremely difficult task since the educational system had been left in total disarray after the Independence era, when less than thirty public schools served the country. Portales, sensing the deficiency, required all convents to open primary schools. This decree was generally ignored, and by 1842 there were only fifty-six public schools in the provinces and none in Santiago. The capital had seventy-three private schools, which required payment for education. The level of education was considered mediocre, and the students only learned the three "R's"—reading, 'riting, and praying (*rezar*). Less than 10 percent of the school-age children had been able to attend school as late as 1848 (23,131 of 235,600).[48] Bello summarized the deplorable situation in a survey of primary educational facilities for the Faculty of Philosophy and Humanities:

There are few civilized countries in the world today in which it is so difficult to increase the number of schools. Chile, with its vast territory of such difficult terrain, with mountains and forests in one area, and valleys and deserts in others, makes the existence of large population centers impossible. . . . Also complicating our task is

46. Eugenio Orrego Vicuña, *Don Andrés Bello* (Santiago, 1935), 193.

47. Universidad de Chile (ed.), *La Facultad de Filosofía y la Humanidades: Conferencias comemorativas de su primer centenario, 1843–1943* (Santiago, 1944). A list of members is included in Guirao Massif, *Historia de la Facultad*, 12–15.

48. Galdames, *A History of Chile*, 277; Guirao Massif, *Historia de la Facultad*, 19; Jobet, *Doctrina y praxis de los educadores representativos chilenos*, 202.

the lack of money in our national treasury and the resistance of the people of the countryside to sending their children to school, whether because of lack of interest, the great distance from the schools, or because they need their children's help on the farm.[49]

However, the faculty was unable to offer much immediate aid to the beleaguered school system since its function was basically regulatory, and, as yet, no legislation decreeing the existence of a public primary school system had been passed by Congress. Lastarria led the fight for public education as the representative from Elqui and Parral in 1843.[50] Almost immediately, he drafted a bill which proclaimed that the "State had an obligation to maintain free schools for persons of both sexes who were unable to afford private education." His legislation also proposed means for increasing the number of teachers, and allowed the parents and teachers to participate jointly in educational planning for each district. Both the Congress and the daily press found Lastarria's proposals too general, so he withdrew the bill and submitted it to the Faculty of Philosophy and Humanities for possible suggestions and improvements.[51] Rafael Minvielle, Sarmiento, and García Reyes worked on the legislation for six years, and it was not until 1849 that the majority of the propositions were approved by the legislature.

The state achieved faster action to remedy yet another ill of the Chilean educational system—the lack of teachers. At this time the occupation of primary school teacher was singularly unremunerative and considered a vocation of low social status. Miguel Luis Amunátegui recalled the case of a thief who had been discovered stealing the candelabra of the Virgin in the Church of Merced. The court sentenced the scoundrel to three years hard labor as a school teacher in Copiapó.[52] Both Manuel Montt, minister of public instruction and a former director of the National Institute, and Sarmiento stressed the importance of a school for training teachers. Montt insisted that ten thousand pesos be allotted for the "Normal School for Teachers" which was established in 1842 with Sarmiento as director. Students were offered one-

49. Amanda Labarca H., *Historia de la enseñanza en Chile* (Santiago, 1939), 122.

50. For details of the election, see Alejandro Fuenzalida Grandón, *Lastarria i su tiempo* (Santiago, 1911), I, 9.

51. José Victorino Lastarria, *Obras completas* (Santiago, 1909), III, 12–32.

52. M. L. and Gregorio Víctor Amunátegui, *De la instrucción primaria en Chile, lo que es, lo que debería ser* (Santiago, 1856), 197.

hundred-peso scholarships and free room and board in order to tempt them to become teachers. An additional requirement stipulated that all scholarship students must teach for at least seven years after graduation. Twenty-eight students entered the first class, and seventeen had to be expelled for "behavior problems or lack of knowledge." Succeeding classes, however, improved considerably.[53]

Once the question of the audience had been tentatively resolved, and the opportunities for the diffusion of new literary works increased, the members of the Literary Society turned their attention to the question of genre. Lastarria suggested in the meeting of May 31, 1842, that the group should attempt to produce a work "that in its writing style and method was suitable for the masses' level of comprehension."[54] He asked whether there was a particular literary form that could successfully fulfill the goal of making Chile's literature "national, useful and progressive." As a result the society's members experimented with drama, the short story, and poetry in hopes of discovering a literary form which could best serve the Chilean people.

Sarmiento first acknowledged the importance of "the theater as an element of culture" to the young Chileans. He argued that "all classes and social hierarchies" would gather together for a common purpose in the theater audience. The theater would then function as a "school," since it would lead to the "regeneration of customs and ideas." This, for Sarmiento, was the "true glory of the theater."[55] The idea had antecedents in France as well as in Chile, for Voltaire viewed the theater as an important vehicle for the propagation of his ideas, as did Camilo Henríquez, a priest of the Independence era, who wrote *La Patriota de Sud América*, which argued that Chile must be freed from Spanish rule.[56]

Chileans welcomed with enthusiasm the first drama by a Literary Society member, but the Argentines found little to applaud in Carlos Bello's *The Loves of a Poet*. Sarmiento wondered why a Chilean writer would even bother to write a work about France: "Why neglect this land [Chile] which has so

53. Ministerio de Educación Pública, *Sarmiento, Director de la escuela normal* (Santiago, 1942); Labarca H., *Historia de la enseñanza*, 113–14; Fernando Campos Harriet, *Desarrollo educacional, 1810–1960* (Santiago, 1960), 18–21.

54. Donoso, "Sarmiento y Lastarria," 428.

55. *El Mercurio*, June 20, 1842.

56. M. L. Amunátegui, *Camilo Henríquez* (Santiago, 1888); Margaret V. Campbell, *The Development of the National Theatre in Chile to 1842* (Gainesville, 1958).

many beautiful flowers to be gathered?"[57] *Ernesto*, by Rafael Minvielle, was the first original work of the period to transfer the action to American soil during the Wars for Independence. Similarly, Lastarria translated a French play, *The Exile*, by Frederick Soulié, and moved the action from a farm in Grenoble in 1817 to Santiago in 1816 during the Spanish Reconquest. However, despite the change to a Chilean locale, drama was generally ignored as a vehicle for Literary Society members. Political and social interests were still foreign to the stage, and Manuel Talavera, drama critic of *El Semanario*, complained that *Ernesto* was "too talky and too political" and that "the plot should pay more attention to the love interest."[58]

Lastarria began experimenting with the short story as the medium of expression for his ideas and wrote *El Méndigo* ("The Beggar"), generally acknowledged to be the first Chilean short story. This romantic tale of the Spanish Reconquest, published in Lastarria's literary journal *El Crepúsculo*, glorified the efforts of the Chilean people in the fight for independence. The patriots were described as loyal and brave, and capable of triumphing against magnificent odds. Spanish and Peruvian society was depicted as decadent, the Spanish army as eager to enslave the Chileans, and the villain, naturally, was a Spanish spy. Alvaro, the hero, may have lost his true love and fortune by the story's end, but, as Lastarria argued, he would always have his nation and a common heritage which would unite him with his countrymen. Alvaro, reduced to begging, met the narrator on the road. One was rich; the other poor. Yet the narrator's father and Alvaro fought in the same trench at Rancagua. Although Alvaro had no money, he proclaimed to the gentleman: "I am finally in my native country—this is my consolation."[59] Unlike *Ernesto* or *The Exile*, this story made the Chilean terrain an integral part of the plot, as Lastarria argued that the nation and its culture gave man his sense of identity.

While Lastarria was responding to the task of developing a national literature, Salvador Sanfuentes was answering the criteria that literature be "use-

---

57. *El Semanario de Santiago*, September 12, 1842; *El Mercurio*, September 1, 1842.

58. Julio Durán Cerda, *Panorama del teatro chileno, 1842–1959* (Santiago, 1959), 20–21; Sarmiento in *El Mercurio*, February 15, 1842; M. L. Amunátegui, *Las primeras representaciones dramáticas en Chile* (Santiago, 1888), 293–94; *El Semanario de Santiago*, October 13, 1842.

59. Lastarria, "El Méndigo," in Silva Castro, *Antología de cuentistas chilenos*; Raúl Silva Castro, "Lastarria, nuestro primer cuentista," *Atenea*, XC (1948), 20–26.

ful and progressive," in his epic poem *El Campanario* ("The Belfry"). The work itself was designed as a challenge to the Argentines, an attempt to prove that creative genius did indeed exist in Chile, as well as to exhort Chilean youth to dedicate themselves to the writing of literature.[60] *El Campanario* is the tale of a rich marquis who has inherited everything he owns. He wishes his daughter to wed someone of title, but she rebels, vowing that she will marry no one. However, she falls in love with an army private of obscure lineage. Her irate father discovers the romance and has the soldier killed. The daughter enters a convent and soon after hangs herself from the belfry. This lengthy poem is considered to give the best idea of the domestic life of Chileans during the colonial period, and herein lies its tone of condemnation.[61] Sanfuentes depicted colonial life as overwhelmingly rigid, and all actions strictly governed by tradition. Leonor, the daughter, tried to break from the past, and in turn, died for her defiance. Leonor's suicidal act was glorified, as Sanfuentes argued that the individual should attempt to break the bonds of tradition if they threaten one's individuality and personal freedom. Leonor became a double symbol—that of Chile rebelling against her colonial heritage and a representation of the young intellectuals attempting to free themselves from the literary rules of the past.

Uniting all of these experiments in drama, story, and poetry was a common interest in Chile's past and how the decadent Spanish traditions, culture, and society might be changed to ensure Chile's future progress. This orientation toward history was characteristic of the Literary Society members from the first. A writer noted in *El Semanario* that "one of the principle objectives of the Society was the study of the philosophy of history." He argued that the study of history could be of utmost importance for the Chilean nation: "If one does not limit himself to the memorizing of a confusing chaos of isolated facts, but, on the contrary, studies history with a philosophical method, it can be one of the most important realms of knowledge for a lawyer or public official. History, the study of mankind, gathers the collective experiences of many centuries and of all the peoples of the world, and allows

60. "Pero sé también, chilenos
   que, si nunca comenzamos
   campo vastísimo damos
   a los dicterios ajenos."   The poem is reprinted in M. L. Amunátegui, *Don Salvador Sanfuentes* (Santiago, 1892), 143.
61. *Ibid.*, quoting Domingo Arteaga Alemparte, 155.

one to consider all of the events which might bring happiness or disaster to a nation."[62]

The exiles in Chile also recognized the importance of the study of history for a new nation. Juan García del Río published a list of books that he felt all Chileans should read. Of his sixty-three choices, twenty-seven were historical works.[63] Vicente Fidel López agreed strongly, and suggested to the Literary Society that it study the philosophy of history, "the prime philosophy for a new nation, since it explains the connection between what is and what will be," thus allowing men to predict and plan their future.[64]

The Literary Society apparently took these suggestions to heart, and by April, 1843, initiated weekly readings from historical works in their Friday night sessions. The first selection was from Johann Gottfried von Herder's works, "since they were the most readily available," and subsequent discussions considered "Segur on ancient peoples, Goldsmith on Greek and Roman history, Fleury on the Middle Ages and the Modern Era, and Robertson's History of America."[65] These weekly sessions and the comments of the Argentines widened Lastarria's concept of the utility of literature to include history, a notion he often discussed with members of the Literary Society.

Although both the Argentines and the members of the Literary Society acknowledged the importance of historical writing to Chile's cultural development, none had ventured to prepare a historical work. The gap between theory and practice appeared quite formidable in a nation that had paid virtually no attention to its historical record prior to 1842. Therefore, Lastarria's decision to write a historical study which fulfilled the ideals of the Literary Society excited his intellectual companions. Yet, the first flush of enthusiasm soon gave way to doubt and confusion as Literary Society members began to debate the extremely important question: How should the history of Chile be written?

62. *El Semanario de Santiago*, February 2, 1843.
63. Pinilla, *La generación*, Ch. "Juan García del Río."
64. Joaquín Rodríguez Bravo, *Don José Victorino Lastarria* (Santiago, 1892), 76–79.
65. "Actas de la Sociedad Literaria," April 4, 21, 28 and May 6, 12, 1842, in Durán Cerda (ed.), *El movimiento literaria de 1842*.

2

THE PHILOSOPHY OF HISTORY
IN CHILE

THE LASTARRIA—BELLO DEBATES

WITH THE BIRTH of a new nation the Chilean historian was faced with the task of defining his past and finding how to study it. There were problems of historical sources, methodology, and function. Were all documents of the colonial period to be given equal credence, or were certain chronicles or narratives more reputable than others? Were current European historians such as Guizot, Michelet, and Hegel to be chosen as models for their writings, or were the ancients such as Tacitus and Thucydides more suitable? Were American models necessary (such as Bernal Díaz del Castillo's chronicle) or should Chilean historians shun subservience to any models? The most important problem, however, was the question of the function of history: Was it to be a romantic form to entertain the masses or the province of a select few who collected large libraries for their own pleasure? Was history to maintain a scientific objectivity or was it to be used in political debates, as the basis for policy recommendations? The possibilities are varied when a new field of science or literature is developed. The Chilean experience saw all of these suggestions rigorously debated.

Before 1842, however, Chileans had few domestic models of historical writing to offer them aid. Since the Portalean era had begun, only one history of Chile had appeared, *El chileno instruído en la historia topográfica, civil, y política de su país* (1834), written by a Franciscan, José Javier de Guzmán.[1] Sponsored by the Prieto government, which published 5,000 copies of the work,

1. See Andrés Bello, *Obras completas* (Santiago, 1884), VII, 209–20.

this curious history offered little inspiration for future historians. Written in the form of a dialogue between an elderly man and his nephew, this moral history of Chile was designed to divert the attention of the youth from the "romantic, heretical, or scandalous novels" that they had been reading.[2]

The Society of Chilean History, formed by students of the National Institute in 1839, similarly produced little that future historians could examine or emulate. Antonio Varas, Manuel Montt, and Antonio García Reyes, future luminaries of Chilean political life, attended the organizational meeting and resolved "to gather all documents of importance to the history of Chile."[3] In the second meeting, each member presented plans for future studies, and in the third meeting, a month later, each member offered excuses for not having completed his work. The fourth meeting was similarly fruitless, and in the fifth meeting, García Reyes and Varas suggested the society be disbanded, since the members were so busy that they had no time to devote to their scholarly efforts. The session ended on an optimistic note, as Varas suggested that all members would be notified in the future should the meetings resume. Unfortunately, this never occurred.

The lethargy which characterized the beginnings of historical studies in the Republic of Chile was to be overcome only by government initiative, which unwittingly unleashed the debates on the proper method of writing history, which were to preoccupy Chilean historians for years to come. Mariano Egaña, minister of public instruction in 1839, engaged a young Frenchman, Claude Gay, who had lived in Chile since 1828, to prepare a political history of Chile.[4] Gay, although primarily a botanist, adapted his scientific skills with great ease to the writing of history. He diligently examined archives in Argentina, Peru, and Bolivia in search of documents of importance to Chile's past, and additionally interviewed many survivors of the Independence era. The resultant work, *La historia física i política de Chile*, appeared a resounding success to Andrés Bello, who appreciated the "exactitude and diligence" of the writer. Others, however, were less impressed with

2. José Francisco Javier de Guzmán, *El chileno instruído en la historia topográfica, civil, y política de su país* (Santiago, 1834), 34.

3. "Actas de la Sociedad Chilena de Historia, establecida en 1839," in Domingo Amunátegui Solar, *El Instituto Nacional bajo los rectorados de Don Manuel Montt, Don Francisco Puente, i Don Antonio Varas, 1835–1845* (Santiago, 1891), II, Ch. 9.

4. Diego Barros Arana, "Claudio Gay i su obra," *Revista Chilena*, II (1875), 492; Guillermo Feliú Cruz, *Conversaciones históricas de Don Claudio Gay* (Santiago, 1965).

Gay's study, objecting to his adherence to the narrative method of historical writing and his inability to discover the meaning of the facts he had uncovered. Sarmiento commented caustically, "In America we do not need mere collections of facts, but the philosophical explanation of causes and effects."[5] While Bello championed Gay's work, the younger writers found his methodology outmoded. Gay later wrote to his friend Manuel Montt, minister of public instruction during the Bulnes era:

A dear friend has told me that the daily papers are criticizing my work, claiming that I have written a chronicle rather than a true history because I do not understand the philosophy of this science well enough to write a good work on the subject. Without a doubt, I enjoy these brilliant theories discovered by the modern school very much, and, I, too, would like to learn of these seductive spiritual combinations. . . . But, before this can be done, the journalists should ask themselves if the study of the bibliography of American, and, especially, Chilean historical literature is advanced enough to supply the necessary data for a work of this nature.

He concluded his letter noting that "since history is the science of facts, it is more valuable to relate these facts as they occurred and leave the reader free to draw his own conclusions."[6]

Nevertheless, Gay's critics objected to the definition of history as a "science of facts," and found themselves attracted to another method of historical writing, the "philosophy of history." Ironically, the first work of this genre was also encouraged by government initiative. Article XXVIII of the university charter proclaimed that every year "the university would meet in full session, and at that time, a discourse would be read which discussed the most important facts of our national history." The proposal required that the history "rely on details from authentic documents, and be written with impartiality and truth."[7] Bello decided that his former student Lastarria should be entrusted with the task of preparing the discourse for the session celebrating the university's first anniversary. He walked into Lastarria's office one morning and suggested he prepare a study of any period of Chilean history that interested him.

Lastarria accepted his mentor's confidence and began writing *Investigaciones sobre la influencia social de la conquista i del sistema colonial de los españoles en*

5. Bello, *Obras*, VII, 60; *El Progreso*, August 20, 1844.
6. Guillermo Feliú Cruz and Stuardo Ortiz (eds.), *Correspondencia de Claudio Gay* (Santiago, 1962), 75, 76.
7. Guillermo Feliú Cruz, *Historiografía colonial de Chile* (Santiago, 1958), 336.

Chile, which he presented to the university faculty on September 22, 1844. That evening Lastarria advocated a new method of writing history. He argued that an historian interested only in facts would prepare studies that were useless to modern society. A philosopher of history, however, could see the importance of history to present and future generations. He viewed the facts merely as experimental data in the attempt to discover useful lessons for society or general laws of great value in the conduct óf business and political affairs. These lessons learned from the study of the past could then be used to promote the "happiness and perfection of the Chilean people."[8]

Thus Lastarria rejected the narrative method of writing history propounded by Gay and Bello in his attempt to discern the influence of the colonial past on Chilean society. Relying strongly on the *Noticias secretas* of Jorge Juan and Antonio de Ulloa, Lastarria presented a dismal portrait of Chilean society during the colonial period: "The Chileans were reduced to servile dependence under a tyrannical system of laws, awakening from their sedentary state only to repel frequent Indian attacks." He then claimed that the colonial system had hindered the development of Chilean industry and agriculture and had retarded Chilean political life by limiting all outlets for individual initiative and thus causing the citizen to rely on the government to supply all his needs. Lastarria then urged "the public officials who retain the fate of our nation in their hands," to learn from this shameful experience and attempt to eradicate all remnants of the colonial heritage from Chilean society.[9] This appeal to public officials was not a fruitless cry, since the audience for this important university affair usually included "the president of Chile, the ministers of the interior and of war, the supreme court justices, as well as the rector, the deans, and the secretaries of the faculties of the university.[10]

After Lastarria finished reading the introduction to his work to his scholarly audience, he realized his efforts were being greeted with a "glacial indifference." Bello found Lastarria's study too impassioned, and criticized his harsh treatment of Spanish civilization. He argued that Lastarria violated Article XXVIII of the university statutes which emphasized the study was to be based on facts and documents. He commented: "Lastarria is not interested in

8. José Victorino Lastarria, *Obras completas* (Santiago, 1909), VII, 28, 29.
9. *Ibid.*, 43–44, 141–42.
10. *El Progreso*, October 13, 1846.

the investigation of facts, but the various systems of writing history which are being disputed at this time." Only a year later, on the occasion of the second discourse presented to the faculty, would Lastarria receive official thanks from Bello for the work he had contributed in 1844.[11]

For members of the university, the debate between those who championed the philosophy of history and those who favored the narrative method was apparently settled in favor of the latter. Despite efforts to revive the issues considered in 1844, the discussions fell on deaf ears. Vicente Fidel López attempted to support Lastarria's activist view of history in his acceptance speech when elected to the Faculty of Philosophy and Humanities in 1845: "The goal of history is to teach men to live as good patriots of their nation; to learn the virtues of a citizen; to defend what is right on all occasions; and, to know the desires of the state and try to fulfill them as best they can."[12] He placed great faith in man's free will and pictured him as the author of his progress. History, he stated, had proved that mankind "had progressed toward its ultimate perfection," and the Chilean people were not an exception to this "famous axiom." His speech echoed Lastarria's thoughts in the 1842 speech to the Literary Society and in the *Investigaciones* and, likewise, received few favorable comments from the press or the university faculty members.

Lastarria's friend Alejandro Reyes attempted to raise the issue anew in a January, 1847, faculty meeting, when he proposed that the university adopt the texts of the French historian Jules Michelet for the study of modern history. The younger historians revered Michelet, who believed as they did that "history demonstrated the progressive triumph of liberty," while Bello saw him as the symbol of the youths' slavish adherence to foreign models of historical writing.[13] Vendel Heyl, a Frenchman who taught Latin, Greek, and philosophy in the National Institute, echoed Bello's position, and opposed adopting Michelet's works as textbooks. He believed it would be better to choose a text which clearly narrated the facts, since Michelet appeared to judge the facts himself rather than present them objectively. Lastarria argued that it was indeed necessary to present the facts in accordance with a certain

---

11. Lastarria, *Obras*, VII, 6; Feliú Cruz, *Barros Arana, historiador* (Santiago, 1959), IV, 84; Lastarria, *Obras*, VII, 6.

12. *Anales de la Universidad de Chile*, October 19, 1845.

13. Reprinted in Ana Guirao Massif, *Historia de la facultad de Filosofía y Humanidades* (Universidad de Chile 1957), 131; *El Progreso*, May 5, 1846.

theory in order to give a methodological arrangement and interest to the textbook. He also objected to the common practice of making students memorize facts without appreciating their development or causal relationship. He concluded his speech by noting: "If the doctrine of Michelet is not false or pernicious, I see no danger in teaching it to our youth." The faculty evidently thought otherwise, for, after a short discussion, the choice of a new text was referred to committee and not acted upon for two years.[14]

During these years the proponents of the philosophy of history remained in disrepute. Caustic jokes were often told about their activities. Diego Barros Arana related the following anecdote about a student who had come to visit his history professor:

The student recalled some facts about Chilean history but with some astounding errors. According to him, Freire won the Battle of Chacabuco with a cavalry charge, and Manuel Rodríguez assumed command at Maipó because San Martín was drunk. I told him that none of these facts were true. He answered me quite frankly, "I am not interested in studying facts; that doesn't lead to anything. I only know and want to know the philosophy of history."[15]

The faculty apparently wished to contain this passing vogue, and, perhaps in anticipation of Lastarria's 1847 *memoria*, passed a ruling which prohibited all discourses from the individual faculties from being published without the inclusion of the report of the faculty commission. Perhaps this exhibited some advanced knowledge of the unfavorable review Lastarria was going to receive from the commission chosen by Bello, who, as Lastarria later recalled, "rarely agreed with my ideas."[16]

Lastarria's *Bosquejo histórico de la constitución del gobierno de Chile durante el primer período de la revolución durante 1810–1814* reopened the debates on the proper method of writing history. At first, this work seemed to obviate one of Bello's criticisms of Lastarria's 1844 work. As a study of the history of the constitutions written during the chaotic early years of Chilean independence, the *Bosquejo* offered the complete documents to the reader. Ideally, the documents or "facts" were thus supplied, and the reader could draw his own con-

14. *Revista de Santiago*, I (1848), 279; Reprinted in Universidad de Chile, *Memorias de los egresados, Actas de la Facultad de Filosofía y Humanidades* (Santiago, 1957), 132.

15. Diego Barros Arana, *Un decenio de la historia de Chile* (Santiago, 1905–1906), II, 546. Lastarria commented: "They never wished to understand that I was in no way condemning a history based on facts." See his "Prólogo de la edición de 1868," *Obras*, VII, 9.

16. *Anales de la Universidad de Chile*, III (December 20, 1847); Lastarria, "Prólogo," 4.

clusions from the work. But, again Lastarria stressed the "usefulness" of his historical studies, and attempted to discover general laws that "would work for the advantage of the Chilean people."[17] He again condemned the Spanish heritage which engendered a colonial mentality based on "self-interest and antisocial instincts." This was the cause of the bitter early years of the Independence era, as Chilean fought against Chilean, instead of organizing themselves against future Spanish attempts at reconquest, which came to fruition in 1814. Yet, he cautioned that this period of Chilean life should not be totally scorned since the men of 1810 did have the courage to break away from the Spanish Empire. Had these men not been so limited in their vision, due to their flawed Spanish education, the Republic of Chile might have been founded twenty years earlier and been flourishing by mid-century.

The Commission of the Faculty published a review which praised Lastarria's zeal, but condemned his methods. They believed that before undertaking a historical work, it was necessary to "organize and verify the facts (*poner en claro los hechos*)," since "the theory that would explain them would come later, walking with a firm step on a familiar terrain."[18] The position of the Commission and Bello was that Chile was a new country. The first task in writing its history was to assemble relevant documents, then edit and verify them. Nothing must be accepted uncritically. A philosophical history could be written only if domestic and foreign archives had been thoroughly searched and the facts established.

The Commission's report merely added fuel to the controversy. Jacinto Chacón, a friend of Lastarria's from the National Institute and the author of the prologue to the *Bosquejo*, came to his defense in the pages of *El Progreso*. Chacón lauded Lastarria's methodology, and further argued: "[The Commission] should allow anyone who is so inclined to leave the beaten track of historical writing and allow him to discover the nature of political parties and the character of constitutions on his own. My prologue has no other object than to protest the illegitimate exercise of university authority in the realm of the writing of history. As zealous lovers of tolerance and liberty, we protest all acts of exclusive or intolerant opinion of any political or literary authority that may commit them."[19]

17. Lastarria, *Obras*, IX, 4.
18. *El Comercio*, January 1, 1848.
19. *El Progreso*, January 1, 11, 25, 28, 29, February 11, 28, 1848.

Bello, who had written only one historical work, a history of Venezuela, fifteen years earlier, responded vigorously in the pages of the government-supported newspaper, *El Araucano*, and defended the narrative method of writing history.[20] Bello's quarrel was with both Chacón and Lastarria, since he believed that each offered slightly differing interpretations of the philosophy of history, and that at times Chacón "exaggerated the ideas of the *Bosquejo* and falsified them."[21] As Chacón continued his attacks in the press, Bello concentrated his efforts on discrediting Chacón and almost forgot that Lastarria's work had given birth to the dispute.

Bello differed with the Chilean philosophers of history, not only with respect to their method, but also their interpretation of the Spanish past and their slavish adherence to European models. Bello argued that there were two distinct methods of writing history. He found the *ad narrandum* method, as represented by the work of Claude Gay, ideally suited to the state of historical knowledge in Chile at that time. He believed that "narrative method was obligatory when the history of a country exists only in incomplete documents that are few and far between." Agreeing with opinion of the Commission of the Faculty, Bello reiterated that the first task of the historian was to analyze the facts and ascertain their veracity.[22] Once this was accomplished, and only then, could the facts be assembled in a chronological sequence in order to produce a work of history.

Bello characterized his opponents, "the philosophers of history," as advocates of the *ad probandum* method of historical writing. He criticized "their desire to philosophize as prejudicial to the severity of history . . . since they see the past through a colored glass which gives a false tint to the object of their study."[23] This method proposed by Lastarria was merely a hasty ransacking of the annals of history in order to prove a theory or support a political stance. The philosopher of history was thus more a lawyer than a historian.

20. Bello, *Obras*, VII, 101–30. See Walter Hanisch Espindola, S. J., "Tres dimensiones del pensamiento de Bello: religión, filosofía, historia," *Historia*, IV (1965), 8–190; Ricardo Krebs, "La idea de nación en el pensamiento de Bello," *Revista de Historia de América* (Mexico City), LXVII–LXVIII (1969), 160–74.

21. Bello, "Constituciones," *Obras*, VII, 127–33.

22. Bello, "Modo de estudiar la historia," *Obras*, VII, 120; Bello, "Historia de la conquista del Peru," *Obras*, VII, 175–201.

23. *La Araucana*, September 6, 1844.

Bello also objected to Lastarria's portrayal of the colonial period of Chilean history. While Lastarria argued that the Chilean people were "reduced to such an abject condition that they lacked every social virtue," Bello insisted that the Spanish kings were not "fierce tyrants, since their political system was one of privation rather than of blood." [24] While they did little to encourage agriculture or the arts, they did contribute some positive traits to the Chilean people. After all, he reasoned: "A people thoroughly vilified, completely crushed, devoid of all virtuous sentiment, has never been able to execute the great deeds that glorified the battles of our patriots, the heroic acts of abnegation, and the sacrifices of all kinds by which Chile and the other American nations won their independence." [25] Thus Bello believed that some facets of the Spanish colonial system actually prepared Chileans for their fight for independence. [26]

Finally, Bello viewed the young historians' subservience to European historical writings with scorn. He believed that a philosophical history of Chile could not be written until Chilean historians "had climbed the road of historical writing," beginning first with the chronicle, and only at a later date writing a philosophy of history. Chacón had argued that it was unnecessary for Chile to walk the same "path of knowledge" as Europeans since their discoveries belonged to humanity. Chile did not have to begin as a niño in the study of history. The same was true of the railroad, in that the Chileans did not need to reinvent the wheel and then the wagon before the railroad might be brought to Chile. Bello responded: "A machine can easily be brought from abroad and produce the same effects in Chile as in Europe. But the philosophy of history of France, the explanation of the actions of the French people throughout their history, lacks meaning when applied to the Chilean people. The only aid to our work would be a study of Chilean facts." [27]

Thus, the generalizations of European historians were not necessarily valid in the Chilean context. Following these theories blindly and uncritically would "be as absurd as trying to draw a map of Chile by utilizing the

24. Bello, "Investigaciones sobre la influencia de la conquista i sistema colonial de los españoles en Chile," Obras, VII, 80.

25. See Leopoldo Zea, The Latin American Mind, trans. James H. Abbott and Lowell Dunham (Norman, Okla., 1962), 270–71.

26. This argument remains current today. See Jaime Ezyaguirre, Ideario y ruta de la independencia chilena (Santiago, 1972).

27. Bello, "Modo de escribir la historia," Obras, VII, 116.

theorems of Euclid." A complete study of "Chilean facts" had to be under-taken before any general laws applicable to Chile might be discovered. He concluded his final article, *Modo de estudiar la historia*, by noting that the best way to imitate European historians was to imitate their independence of thought rather than blindly following their theories: "Young Chileans! Learn to judge for yourselves; aspire to independence of thought. Investigate each civilization by its works; ask each historian for his sources. That is the first philosophy we ought to learn from Europe." [28]

However, the younger historians were not mindlessly adopting whatever was in fashion in Europe. The philosophy of history was not the only method of historical writing that Europe offered. Even Bello's school was well repre-sented by several European antecedents. A minor current of Enlightenment historical thought, initiated by Pierre Bayle, had succumbed to the scientific and investigative zeal of that era and viewed the fact as the "point towards which" (*terminus ad quem*) historical knowledge proceeded. Bayle's object was to reveal the false rather than the true via a careful analysis of available data. His search for errors in so-called factual knowledge led to a rupture with revealed religion and traditionally sanctioned myth. Furthermore, he be-lieved that the historian must adhere solely to the interests of truth and ig-nore the passions of patriotism, religion, or politics. [29]

What appeared only a minor effort in Enlightenment historical thought soon blossomed into a full-fledged school during the Romantic era in France. While Romanticism usually symbolized a lack of respect for binding rules, it also involved a reawakened interest in the past. [30] The narrative school of French historians followed this trend and sought to re-create the past, and especially the Middle Ages, exactly as it was. The effort of the historian was to present a vivid tableau, much as Chateaubriand had done in the *Génie du christianisme*. Adolphe Thiers reacted violently against the attempt to insert present-day passions into the study of the past or to falsify it in any manner whatsoever: "Mais l'histoire! Mentir dans le fond, mentir dans la couleur, c'est chose intolérable . . . l'histoire doit être vraie, simple, sobre." Au-

28. Bartolomé Mitre, "Revista de Santiago," *El Comercio de Valparaíso*, July 19, 1848; Bello, *Obras*, VII, 124–25.
   29. Ernst Cassirer, *The Philosophy of the Enlightenment* (Boston, 1966), Ch. 5.
   30. See A. O. Lovejoy, "The Meaning of Romanticism for the Historian of Ideas," *Jour-nal of the History of Ideas*, III (June, 1941), 258–78, and "On the Discrimination of Romanti-cisms," *Essays in the History of Ideas* (Baltimore, 1948), 166–82.

gustin Thierry wished to write a history of France "uninterrupted by any philosophical reflections or any modern additions whatsoever." And, like Bello, he reacted strongly against "that method coming from Germany, which sees in every fact the sign of an idea and in human events a continual mad development."[31]

Thus the youth could have turned to Europe, and France in particular, and adopted a method of writing history similar to that of Bello. Yet, they opposed this narrative school of historical writing and deliberately chose the philosophy of history for quite specific reasons. Jacinto Chacón, during a competition for a teaching position at the National Institute, explained the importance of the philosophy of history to Chile's future.[32] He argued that Chile need no longer march aimlessly toward the future because European historians had already discovered the laws which governed man's progress and revealed his destiny. Chileans could borrow these teachings in much the same manner as they had advantageously used the discoveries of chemistry, botany, and other sciences. Thus far only the Europeans had been able "to decode the book of history," and, for this reason, "Chile must pay attention to her lessons." Thus the philosophy of history was useful to Chile, while the narrative method was not. The concept of *utilidad*, emphasized by the Literary Society members in 1842, seemed to govern the young historians' choice of foreign models.

The philosophy of history attracted Lastarria, Chacón, and others for a variety of reasons, but, primarily, their hope for Chile's future determined their decision. This method of writing history turned Bayle's concept of the fact upside-down. For Montesquieu, Voltaire, and other *philosophes*, the fact became the "point from which" (*terminus a quo*) historical knowledge proceeded. These historians viewed the facts as tools to achieve their goal: the discovery of a series of laws comparable in rigor and certainty to the laws governing nature discovered by Newton. This is not to dismiss these men as dilettante historians, since all recognized the importance of archival research. Rather, they believed that these facts should be synthesized in such a manner as to achieve scientific utility for human society.

It was this precise notion of the philosophy of history as developed by the

31. Roger Picard, *Le romantisme social* (New York, 1944), 264, 270–72.
32. Jacinto Chacón, "Discurso redactado con motivo de la oposición a las cátedras de istoria i literatura del Instituto Nacional," *El Progreso*, May 21, 23, 27, 1846.

French *philosophes* that most attracted Chilean youth. Earlier conceptions of the philosophy of history, such as those of Bishop Jacques Bénigne Bossuet and Giambattista Vico, had to be rejected, as they presented man's free will as limited. Consequently, they blighted any hope for Chile's future, since they argued that man's activities were governed by rigid laws which could never be mastered or escaped. Bossuet's providential scheme of historical progress and Vico's cyclical theory of growth and decline of civilizations offered little hope for man's control of his environment. Lastarria thus commented in his memoirs: "We read Vico's *Ciencia nueva* in 1840 and rebelled against it, for in these philosophical conceptions of history the liberty of man and his progress disappears."[33] The *philosophes*, in contrast, denied any limitations on man's free will. The concept of original sin was denied, and man, for the first time, was viewed as having the potentiality of attaining perfection, as the Marquis de Condorcet had claimed in his *Esquisse d'un tableau historique des progrès de l'esprit humain*.

Although French intellectuals may have eliminated Divine Providence as the prime controller of man's destiny, such an uncompromising view appeared difficult for Chileans to follow. It was agreed that the acceptance of providential schemes of historical development would imply a denial of man's freedom, thus making Lastarria's dreams of progress futile. It would give history, and consequently life, a sense of fatality which would counteract any desire for human improvement. Nevertheless, the opposite extreme was untenable for more politic reasons. Francisco Bilbao, a friend and student of Lastarria, had denied God and the Catholic Church in his article *La sociabilidad chilena*[34] in June of 1844, and the results were catastrophic.

Bilbao's tract denied the Catholic religion on grounds that it had no rational base, that it denied free will and progress, and imprisoned man in his past. His work also attacked the Spanish colonial system and presented a rationale for revolution against despotic regimes. Such views coming from a student of the National Institute were seen as outrageous. Both the government and the Catholic press attacked Bilbao's ideas. The new *Revista Católica* printed a special edition which argued that "Bilbao claimed the New Testament was a web of contradictions" and that he "discussed the Catholic religion with contempt and scorn."[35] He was quickly accused of "blasphemy,

33. Lastarria, *Obras*, X, 266–69.
34. Francisco Bilbao, *Obras completas* (Santiago, 1897–1898), I.
35. *Revista Católica*, July 1, 1844.

immorality, and sedition," and tried on June 13, 1844. Although the state prosecutor dropped the sedition charge, the Church had enough power to insist on the conviction of Bilbao for blasphemy and immorality. As punishment, all copies of *La sociabilidad chilena* were burned in the Plaza de Armas, and Bilbao was forced to resign from the National Institute. Soon afterward, he left for Europe. Many others were affected by the prosecution of Bilbao. Doctor Guillermo Blest, who had aided Bilbao when he fainted after the trial, mysteriously lost his position on the faculty of medicine of the university soon after the incident. He received no explanation. Lastarria, whose newspaper *El Crepúsculo* was closed because it published Bilbao's work, found it necessary to resign a ministry post as a result of the furor.[36]

The recent memory of this incident, showing the influence of the Catholic Church, was fresh in Lastarria's mind as he wrote his history, which led to a curious ambivalence in his treatment of the Church's role in Chilean history and the concept of providential schemes of history. Unlike Bilbao, Lastarria exercised the prudence which was to mark his political activity until the end of his days. He emphasized "the stupid fanaticism [supported by the Church] and the blind intolerance against everything new, which is needed by these powers [the Church and the state] to maintain the people stationary, ignorant, and always submissive to their will." Yet, he immediately followed this sharp comment with a prudent retreat: "I do not deny that the Christian religion has a most powerful influence on the morality of the societies that fortunately profess it, nor do I mean that people do not benefit from it in their character and habits."[37] Thus, by a cautious distinction between the Church and the religion it professed, Lastarria avoided the uncompromising view of Bilbao.

But what of the question of providential schemes of history? How was Lastarria to resolve his dilemma? Was he to deny man's freedom and his ability to plan his destiny and dampen his generation's dreams for Chile's future, or was he to strictly follow French Enlightenment thought and perhaps incur the same fate as Bilbao? His 1844 study conveniently avoided this quandary, and, as inspiration Lastarria credited Herder, "the wisest and most profound philosopher of the eighteenth century."[38] Why did Lastarria turn to Herder,

36. Barros Arana, *Un decenio*, I, 523–28; Pedro Pablo Figueroa, *Historia de Francisco Bilbao* (Santiago, 1894).

37. Lastarria, *Obras*, VII, 121, 122.

38. *Ibid.*, 20.

a German philosopher, at this time when French thinkers formed the preponderant influence on his historical thought?

Lastarria first read Herder's *Ideen zur Philosophie der Menscheit* in Edgar Quinet's French translation *Idées sur la philosophie de l'humanité* (1827) with its ample introduction by the translator. Quinet and Lastarria interpreted the original work somewhat differently, as each chose to resolve a tension in Herder's thought in his own manner. In the original work there seemed to be a question of the limits of man's freedom. In one sense, Herder reacted against current Enlightenment thought and returned to a providential scheme of man's history. He noted that a "wise Goodness disposes the Fate of Mankind [and] therefore there is no nobler Merit, no purer and more durable Happiness than to cooperate in its designs."[39] In this scheme, in which God revealed himself in the laws of nature, "man is but a small part of the whole." Thus a sense of fatality pervaded part of Herder's work. Indeed, Andrés Bello, Lastarria's adversary, confessed that Herder had given history all its dignity by discovering the designs of Providence.[40]

Yet, as others observed, Herder gave man a great freedom in this world created by God. He noted: "Man is placed in it [his environment] as a sovereign of the Earth, to alter it by art. . . . We may consider mankind, therefore, as a band of bold though diminutive giants, gradually descending from the mountains, to subjugate the earth, and change climates with their feeble arms," and, "God made man a deity upon Earth; he implanted in him the principle of self-activity, and set this principle in motion from the beginning, by means of the internal and external wants of nature."[41] Thus a second perspective can demonstrate an image of God as a beneficent ruler who set the machine moving and stepped back and allowed it to take its course. The only limits imposed upon man in this system were the effects of time, place, and his own capabilities.

Quinet, in the introduction to Herder's work, assumed the first view. He found Herder's framework too restrictive, limiting man's free will. Quinet commented: "History, indeed from beginning to end, is the drama of liberty,

39. Johann Gottfried von Herder, *Reflections on the Philosophy of History of Mankind*, trans. T. O. Churchill (Chicago, 1968), 112. For a discussion of Herder's philosophy, see F. M. Barnard, *Herder's Social and Political Thought* (Oxford, 1965); Robert T. Clark, *Herder—His Life and Thought* (Los Angeles, 1955); A. Gillies, *Herder* (Oxford, 1965); and George G. Iggers, *The German Conception of History* (Middletown, Conn., 1968).

40. José Victorino Lastarria, *Recuerdos literarios* (Santiago, 1968), 266.

41. Herder, *Reflections*, 19, 94.

the protest of the human race against the world which enchains it, the triumph of the infinite over the finite, the freedom of the spirit, the reign of the soul. The moment liberty failed on earth, history would cease to exist."[42] Quinet wondered how man could accept the law which Herder established. If humanity could never be anything but in conformity with the accidents of time and place and could only be "ce qu'elle pouvait être et rien que ce qu'elle pouvait être," man's free will was destroyed. Yet Lastarria, while familiar with Quinet's opinion, chose to emphasize the appreciable degree of man's freedom in Herder's thought. He quoted Herder directly, noting that "God has established man as a divinity on this planet," and, "God has placed no other limits on man's capabilities than those that depend on time, place, and his own faculties."[43]

Thus, Lastarria, faced with the task of both preserving his political ideals and also remaining within the realm of thought considered safe by Church and state, deliberately duplicated the ambiguity inherent in Herder's work. He defined the action of God in two universes. The first was *el universo físico*. This was the natural world of trees, rocks, and magnets, where God's rules were invariable and perpetual. Magnets would always attract iron, and the sun would always rise and set. The other world was *el universo moral*, the world of men and ideas, where God imposed few limits on man's activities with the sole exception of time, place, and given physical and mental capabilities. Lastarria added to Herder's basic model the principle of *la espontaneidad*, which gave man the power to control his future progress within these specified limitations set by God.[44] In essence, Lastarria claimed that man was free to do as he pleased within a specific physical and temporal context, and, therefore, a Chilean in 1844 possessed almost total freedom over his own destiny and that of his nation. This was in a rather cautious way an implicit denial of God's influence over the progress of man. God could easily be substituted by Nature, which was, indeed, what occurred during the Enlightenment era.

While Lastarria's first statement of man's freedom was indeed cautious,[45]

42. Edgar Quinet, "Introduction to the Philosophy of History of Mankind," in Richard Heath, *Edgar Quinet, His Life and Early Writings* (Boston, 1881), 76.

43. Richard H. Powers, *Edgar Quinet: A Study in French Patriotism* (Dallas, 1957) 45–46; Lastarria, *Recuerdos*, 267.

44. Lastarria, *Obras*, VII, 23–24.

45. Raúl A. Orgáz, *Vicente Fidel López y la filosofía de la historia* (Córdoba, Argentina, 1938).

it allowed him to counter what he considered another flaw of the narrative school of historians: the inability to judge the past. In this view, the past had to be as it was, and it could not have been changed in any way. Lastarria dubbed the proponents of this school "historical fatalists." This led historians to sanction whatever atrocities occurred in the past. For example, Bello argued that "injustice and perfidy were not only characteristic of the Spaniards, but all races from time immemorial."[46] Thus, they could no longer be criticized for any excesses committed during the colonial period. The entire editorial staff of *El Mercurio* disagreed with Lastarria on this distinction. Miguel Piñero, in the first review of the *Investigaciones*, commented: "We cannot blame the conquistadors for deeds committed that were common to their era, nor can we blame the Mother Country."[47] This sentence so impressed Lastarria that he underlined it, retained the clipping, and used it in his memoirs thirty-four years later.[48]

Lastarria even attacked Gay, who had exercised such care to eliminate personal opinions from his work, for a similar interpretation: "Mr. Gay has demonstrated that he was a "historical fatalist" in his *Historia física i política de Chile*, a rather strange trait for such a distinguished man. Noting the iniquity of the means employed by Pedro de Valdivia to conquer the Indians, Gay added these words: "But the spirit of the epoch absolves them of any excesses those daring conquistadors committed." Gay thus excused the fact that the conquistadors "killed almost two thousand Indians and cut off the hands and noses of their prisoners." Lastarria then commented that the historian ought to "expose the facts truthfully and judge them in the light of justice." Such barbarous acts could not be excused merely because they occurred centuries earlier. He added that "the historian must remain impartial, but his is not the impartiality of a mirror which only reflects what occurs. Rather, the historian is a judge who listens and passes judgment."[49]

Also implicit in Lastarria's argument was the fact that history could be used to judge the present. The vices of Chilean society in the colonial period

46. Bello, *Obras*, VII, 77.

47. *El Mercurio*, September 30, 1844. See also Demetrio Rodríguez Peña, "Investigaciones," *ibid.*, October 7, 1844, and José Santos Tornero, *Reminiscencias de un viejo editor* (Santiago, 1889), 51–64.

48. *Fondos varios*, T. 315.

49. Lastarria, "Memoria sobre servicio personal de los indígenas i su abolición de José Hipólito Salas," *Revista de Santiago*, II (1848), 230–31; Lastarria, "Prólogo," 9.

that Lastarria described in the *Investigaciones* and the *Bosquejo* differed little from the habits common to the 1840s. Centralized authority which abused power, a Church that encouraged superstitious beliefs among the masses, and an egoistic aura of self-interest which motivated the actions of every citizen plagued the Republic of Chile as they had the kingdom of Chile years earlier.[50] Thus a discussion of the past could also be a thinly veiled critique of the present, and, as the Bilbao incident demonstrated, was quite the safer way of criticizing Chilean society.

Here, too, Lastarria looked to France for support for his contention that history could serve such a political function. France seemed a more important model than ever for Lastarria, since he noticed several similarities between French and Chilean society. He found that both Chile and France exemplified countries where revolutions for liberty and independence had failed. Both societies, in their attempt to break with the past, had unwittingly prepared for its revival. Despite its constitutional basis, the monarchy had returned to France by 1814 with Louis XVIII, and in Chile the authoritarian Portales had usurped the Liberal government of 1828. Like Chile, France was plagued by the undue influence of the Church (especially Villèle's clerical policy from 1822 to 1827), rigid press censorship, and liberal purges (Guizot, Cousin, Michelet, and Quinet lost their teaching positions at the university). The Bourbon Restoration and the July Monarchy revived the days of Louis XVI, thus nullifying the Revolution of 1789. While the French political system seemed as retrograde as that of Chile, the reviving state of the arts brought hope to Lastarria, who noted that "the first years of the Bulnes administration, like the first years of Louis Philippe's rule, were favorable to the arts."[51]

As Lastarria again looked to France for inspiration, he found that Michelet, Cousin, Guizot, and others had reacted similarly against the narrative and documentary approach to history represented by the early works of Thiers, Mignet, and Thierry, as history became the language and medium of political criticism during the Restoration.[52] The French Restoration marked the climax of the reaction of the Revolution of 1789, as the monarch, Louis

50. José Victorino Lastarria, *El manuscrito del diablo* (Lima, 1850).
51. Lastarria, "Prólogo," 2–3.
52. Jacques Barzun, "Romantic Historiography as a Political Force in France," *Journal of the History of Ideas*, II (June, 1941), 318–29; Shirley M. Gruner, "Political Historiography in Restoration France," *History and Theory*, VII (1966), 346–65.

XVIII, returned, accompanied by the aristocratic émigrés and a resurgent clergy. The Liberals soon saw revolutionary gains lost as the Ultras gained control in the Chamber of Deputies. A frontal assault by the Liberals was impossible—it was difficult, almost treasonable, to proclaim the political principles of the Revolution in an era which owed its existence to the defeat of those principles. Also, since the Conservatives used involvement in the Revolution as a yardstick for denying participation in political life, one of the most pressing tasks facing the Liberals became to persuade the men of the Restoration to accept the men of the Revolution; failing this, they would forfeit any chance for political power. Thus many Liberals, desirous of defending their political position, and eager to educate a younger generation in the glories of the Revolution, turned to history during the Restoration and produced more than forty million pages in 1825.[53]

The attempt of the Liberal historians was to prove, as Mme. de Staël noted, that "liberty was ancient." The Revolution was not an historical aberration, but an integral part of the French and European past. The French Revolution followed in the footsteps of the English Revolution of 1642 and was thus inevitable. Violence was not foreign to this universal struggle for liberty, as the image of the placid French past was shattered by the historical resurrection of the persecutions of Philip the Fair and the St. Bartholomew's Day Massacre. These images did not just grace historical works, for history, used as a political weapon, pervaded even the debates in the Chamber. It was not surprising to hear debates on the freedom of the press refer to the censorship policy of Francis I, nor to have the debates on the independence of Saint Domingue couched in terms of the colonial policies of Louis XI. With the politicization of history, it came as no surprise to note the presence of historians such as Guizot, Mignet, and Thiers on the staffs of daily newspapers or in the halls of Congress.[54]

Lastarria intended his historical works to function similarly to those in France. However, while French Conservatives challenged the Liberal interpretation of history consistently, no one in Chile bothered to present an opposing interpretation of the national past during the 1840s. As his essays

53. Stanley Mellon, *The Political Uses of History* (Stanford, 1958), 6. Three million pages were written in 1811.

54. *Ibid.*, 2. See aslo C. H. Pouthas, *Guizot pendant la restauration* (Paris, 1923), and Douglas Johnson, *Guizot: Aspects of French History* (London, 1963).

became the focus of a series of methodological debates, the political message of the *Investigaciones* and the *Bosquejo* was seemingly buried. One possible cause of this turn in affairs may have been the formalistic and apolitical concerns of Andrés Bello. There was no doubt that Bello staunchly supported the current political regime, as he had done since his arrival in Chile.[55] As long as a government maintained peace, order, and prosperity, and an intellectual climate suitable for work, then Bello was satisfied. He wrote to his friend Manuel Ancízar: "The youth of today rarely have any tolerance toward my ideas . . . especially in the political sphere. I profess no political philosophy but scepticism . . . I demand the credentials of experience and the guarantees of *social order*. This means to me *security, peace, reciprocal tolerance*, and *material well-being*, with a moderate dose of *liberty*." His apolitical stance also caused him to advise Marcial Martínez not to write a *memoria* concerning the Portales era, since he found the subject both too controversial and too political.[56] Bello's choice to discuss the methodological aspects of Lastarria's works may have therefore been a clever attempt to divert attention from the potentially incendiary nature of the *Investigaciones*, by defining the terms of the argument in an apolitical arena.[57]

Also inherent in Bello's dislike of Lastarria's attempt to define a new method of historical writing was, perhaps, the implicit challenge to his position of authority in the university and the intellectual standards he had patiently institutionalized. His critique of Lastarria seemed to have been undertaken with a vengeance. Lastarria later claimed that "the report of the Commission was in my judgment a result of the predominant antiquated opinion of the Rector."[58] The fact that Bello chose Antonio García Reyes as head of the Commission would seem to lend credence to Lastarria's belief. Although they were friends during the early 1840s, their relationship became tense as the years progressed, culminating in García Reyes' attempt to deny Lastarria his salary for a geography textbook he had written. García Reyes discovered a little-used statute which prohibited a professor in one discipline (Lastarria was a law professor) from receiving a fee for a textbook writ-

55. Raúl Silva Castro, *Don Andrés Bello* (Santiago, 1965), 22–23.

56. *Revista Chilena de Historia y Geografía*, CXV (1950), 422; *El Mercurio*, November 2, 1864.

57. E. E. Schattsneider, *The Semi-Sovereign People* (New York, 1960), Chs. 1 and 2.

58. Lastarria, *Recuerdos*, 258.

ten in another field (geography). Lastarria needed the money desperately at this time, and never forgot this slight. A few days later, García Reyes became minister of finance, and the textbook incident may have partially explained Lastarria's lack of sympathy for the new cabinet.[59]

Thus Lastarria and the philosophy of history seemed in disrepute by the end of 1840s. Lastarria himself lamented in his memoirs that "no one had advanced our system [of historical thought] in the three years following the first discourse."[60] Barros Arana noted that no one responded to an 1847 competition sponsored by the Faculty of Philosophy and the Humanities for the study of the proper method of writing history. The offer was repeated in 1848 and 1849, and still no one submitted an entry. For Barros Arana this was conclusive proof that Bello's articles had sufficiently answered the question of how history should be written. By 1852, he added that Lastarria's ideas about history were "completely dead."[61] Nevertheless, an analysis of the first university *memorias* reveals that reports of the death of Lastarria's ideas may have been a trifle premature. As practicing historians attempted to reconcile the theories of Lastarria and Bello, the dominance of either paradigm remained in question.

59. M. L. Amunátegui Reyes, *Don Antonio García Reyes i algunos de sus antepasados en la luz de documentos inéditos* (Santiago, 1930), IV, 194–95. See also Lastarria, *Diario político, 1849–1852* (Santiago, 1968).
60. Lastarria, *Recuerdos*, 257.
61. Barros Arana, *Un decenio*, II, 448, 546.

3

THEORY AND PRACTICE

THE FIRST HISTORICAL WRITINGS

(1845–1851)

THE FUNERAL WREATHS for Chile's fledgling philosophy of history have arrived continually since Barros Arana proclaimed its demise in the past century. Recent historians have followed this interpretation and have considered Lastarria's proposals as the extravagant fancies of a credulous youth. Guillermo Feliú Cruz found this episode entirely lacking in importance for the future of Chilean historiography. He commented that "the opinions of Bello ruled without challenge and forged the destiny of our historical writing."[1] However, a careful analysis of the first university *memorias* reveals that Bello's conquest was far from complete. While Bello undertook a concerted effort to institutionalize the *ad narrandum* method of historical writing within the University of Chile, his students and fellow professors remained curiously half-hearted in their allegiance to his system. Despite the supposed devotion to the importance of the facts and original documents, the early historians exhibited a marked ambivalence, as though torn between the two opposing methods of historical writing.

Bello tried continually to eliminate this vacillation. He constantly reiterated his position in the recent debates in both his literary critiques and reviews of the yearly *memorias*. When the Spanish edition of William Prescott's *The History of the Conquest of Peru* arrived in Santiago in 1848, Bello heartily praised the work as though Prescott had been an active participant in the

1. Guillermo Feliú Cruz, "Andrés Bello y la historiografía chilena," *Mapocho* IV (1965), 260. For a similar opinion, see also Francisco A. Encina, *La literatura histórica chilena y el concepto actual de la historia* (Santiago, 1935).

Chilean debates. "Prescott fulfills the duties of the historian with religious scrupulosity," Bello commented favorably. These duties implied the extensive use of footnotes, "copious quotations from primary sources," and a critical analysis of the documents.[2] Thus Bello sought eminent foreign historians to lend credence to his position, much as Chilean youth had sought inspiration from Herder and Sismondi.

Unlike Lastarria and his cohorts, however, Bello was not limited to informal means of persuasion, merely by the publication of articles intended to convince others of his views. He also possessed strict control of more substantive means which could force others to comply with his ideals. As rector of the university, Bello could choose the writer of the yearly *memoria*. Therefore, anyone disagreeing with his method of writing history might never have an opportunity to present a work to the University Council. Once the work had been completed, Bello could then select the committee that would judge its merits. If the work should ultimately be published, the university required that the author include the committee's report in the initial pages. An unfavorable review would certainly limit future sales, as well as damage the reputation of the historian.

The faculty committee that judged the new historical studies followed Bello's philosophy without question. Often the judges used the same words that Bello had written in his study *Modo de escribir la historia*. A composite image of the committee's report indicated that history must be "impartial" and "a faithful mirror-image of the time being described." Works were often faulted for "lack of facts, interesting incidents, and details." Miguel Luís and Gregorio Víctor Amunátegui found themselves criticized for "presenting the results of their investigation" and not "the details and documents which allowed them to formulate their ideas." The authors felt no shame in this attempt to "present and clarify the events of the past" and ignored all efforts at generalization. As two other historians individually commented: "If I have merely written a chronicle, others will write a history."[3]

Antonio García Reyes became the only continuing member of the faculty committee, and he was considered indispensable for the task of judging the

2. Andrés Bello, *Obras completas* (Santiago, 1884), VIII, 175–200.

3. *La Tribuna*, December 9, 1850; Diego Barros Arana, *Estudios históricos sobre Vicente Benavides i las campañas del Sur, 1818–1822* (Santiago, 1850), "Advertencia"; Manuel Antonio Tocornal, *El primer gobierno nacional*, in Benjamín Vicuña Mackenna (ed.), *Historia general de la República de Chile* (Santiago, 1866–1882), I, 122.

new *memorias*. When he left his position as the secretary of the Faculty of Philosophy and Humanities in order to work for the newly installed Montt regime, the faculty decided to wait until he returned before any decision could be made on the works presented in 1851. The faculty planned to wait only two weeks, but his absence extended almost two months. However, the delay was considered worthwhile, since García Reyes had "made a special study of Chilean history."[4] His views on the writing of history rigidly followed those of Bello. Since 1839, when he attempted to form a historical society among the students of the National Institute, he had been interested in the collection and critical editing of original documents. By 1848, as secretary of the faculty, he urged his fellow members to preserve "the treasure of rare manuscripts in the National Library" from the ravages of time. He also suggested that the government reprint these documents "in order that they may be read by all those interested in Chilean history."[5] Bello heartily supported this idea, and in his yearly report to the faculty, he noted that the university was currently collecting manuscripts, saving them from destruction "due to the passing of time and negligence." Additionally, he expressed his intention to "transcribe, complete, and analyze these documents, and encourage the publication of those of interest of those that are about to disappear for eternity."[6]

As for the philosophy of history, García Reyes headed the commission which lambasted Lastarria's 1848 historical work. His individual opinion can be discerned from his prologue to Barros Arana's study of Vicente Benavides: "The author of this study has done a great service for our history. Without pretension to a philosophy which is often vain and artificial, he has contented himself with presenting the solid base on which a philosophy may be formulated sometime in the future."[7] In this matter, the choice of García Reyes and other commission members could reasonably assure a review favorable to Bello's pretensions.

Seemingly, Bello maintained strict control over an apparatus which would ensure that all future historians would follow in his footsteps. However, Bello's battle to win adherents to his philosophy was not as effortless as many historians have claimed, as his continual insistence on the matter re-

4. M. L. Amunátegui Reyes, *Don Antonio García Reyes* (Santiago, 1930), IV, 171–74.
5. Guillermo Feliú Cruz, *Historiografía colonial de Chile* (Santiago, 1958), 310.
6. Bello, *Obras*, 381.
7. Barros Arana, *Vicente Benavides*, "Prólogo."

vealed. An analysis of these first historical writings suggests the historian's bewildering quandary, whether to comply with the ideals that were actively being forced on him, or remain true to his own beliefs. As a result of this dilemma, the early *memorias* retain a curious hybrid nature, as though the authors were wholly conscious of the debates concerning the writing of history, but were unable to decide which paradigm to choose. This ambivalence partly explained Lastarria's despair when he claimed that "no one advanced his system in the three years following his first *memoria*."[8] Yet, Bello also manifested a similar malaise, as revealed by his eight-year attempt to impose the *ad narrandum* method on the university faculty and the younger writers. While Encina and Feliú Cruz assumed the complete conquest of Bello's ideals, it actually appears that no one was satisfied, as the new historical writings followed either both, one, or none of the methods advocated by Lastarria or Bello. The interim result was more confusion than conquest by 1851.

Bello, eager to forget the extravagances of Lastarria's 1844 work, chose Diego José Benavente to present the succeeding year's memoria. Benavente and Lastarria differed in almost every respect. Benavente at fifty-six was twice as old as Lastarria. By the time Lastarria was born, Benavente had already distinguished himself in the Wars for Independence. Similarly, following the *Reconquista*, the venerable Benavente aided the new governments both as counselor and minister of state, and, by the 1840s, had become a distinguished senator. Lastarria, however, came to despise Benavente, calling him an "egotist" and chiding him for his eagerness "to serve any government," even if its "power were unconstitutional."[9] Bello, however, admired Benavente's patriotism, and found much to praise in his earlier work, *Opúsculos sobre la Hacienda Pública en Chile* (1841–1842). Bello especially appreciated the historical focus of this study of the Chilean economy: "In this work we find a historical sketch of the public economy of Chile, a fact which should recommend this work to Chilean and American readers who are interested in the economies of new states. Readers will find here an accumulation of data that cannot be found elsewhere. It would be shameful if anyone were unaware of these statistics."[10] Thus Bello might have reasonably expected a work quite different in tone and style from Lastarria's *Investigaciones*.

Bello promptly wrote to Benavente and encouraged him to prepare the

8. José Victorino Lastarria, *Recuerdos literarios* (Santiago, 1885), 257.
9. José Victorino Lastarria, *Diario político, 1849–1852* (Santiago, 1968), 35, 53.
10. Bello, *Obras*, VII, 443.

1845 *memoria*. He also suggested that he discuss the events of the Independence period in which he was intimately involved, since he had the "advantage of possessing documents pertaining to that era." Bello apologized for urging Benavente to write about the Independence era, since Article XXVIII of the university charter stipulated that "the writer may choose any period of Chilean history." But, after all, continued Bello, "your discourse would possess both authenticity and individuality" if you chose to write about Chilean independence.[11] Bello's subtle hints thus shifted the focus of the future *memoria* from the still controversial colonial period that Lastarria had sharply denounced, to the struggle for Chilean independence, which, as Bello thought, might have fewer possibilities for conflicting interpretations.

Benavente was extremely flattered when he read Bello's letter, and responded immediately. He explained humbly that he did not believe himself capable of the task, but would accept the challenge in order to "stimulate the youth to undertake similar ventures." Agreeing with Bello, he noted that he would have the advantage of having witnessed the "glorious battles of the first campaigns of our independence." Other participants, he commented, were dying off rapidly. Thus it seemed his patriotic duty to commit his memoirs to paper for the benefit of future generations. Oh yes, Benavente recalled, it seemed that he also possessed "the disadvantage of having been very close to the people who participated in these great events." He thus proclaimed that he would "attempt to rid himself of all passions, since he realized that he would be harshly criticized by those who always desire to exalt their friends and scorn their enemies" at the expense of the truth.[12] Apparently this "disadvantage" seemed minor to Bello, and plans for the 1845 *memoria*, *Primeras campañas en la guerra de la Independencia de Chile* proceeded apace.

The audience of university scholars, which also included President Bulnes, responded warmly to Benavente's reading of the prologue, despite some speculation that Bello had extensively revised the final work. Naturally, Bello greatly appreciated Benavente's venture, which maintained a firm respect for the study of primary sources. Benavente stressed that "in the fulfillment of his task he had attempted to follow scrupulously the original documents which he possessed even at the risk of breaking the unity of the narrative." The rationale for this method, claimed Benavente, was that "fu-

11. Mario Benavente Boizard, *Diego José Benavente* (Santiago, 1943), 457.
12. *Ibid.*, 458.

ture historians would have need of trustworthy facts, not political and moral reflections."[13]

Despite Benavente's high regard for the documents, his *memoria* did not wholly satisfy those who claimed to follow Bello's ideals of historical writing. Although the *Primeras campañas* assumed the form of an objective work based on original documents, the content belied this intention, since Benavente presented an impassioned defense of José Miguel Carrera, the revolutionary hero and Benavente's faithful ally. Two factors led to the extreme bias in Benavente's work. Naturally, Benavente possessed those documents that the *Carreriños* had written. Foremost among these papers was Carrera's personal diary, which presented the political struggles of the *Patria vieja* from his personal viewpoint.[14] Thus, the documents which Benavente utilized were heavily biased in favor of the political position of Carrera's followers. Exacerbating this initial predisposition in favor of Carrera was Benavente's desire to free Carrera from the dismal reputation he had earned for his activity during the wars of independence. In this manner, both the selection of documents and the wish to vindicate an old friend shaped Benavente's view of the past in his *memoria*.

Carrera had been a controversial figure since the day he returned from the peninsular wars and landed on Chilean soil in 1811. Within months of his arrival, he had succeeded in a purge of deputies in the new congress, and, two months later, led a coup d'état, overthrowing the provisional junta and congress and assuming personal control of the government. This brash young man of twenty-six promptly quelled provincial rebellions and attempted to regain the impetus of the Chilean revolution. Carrera's brazen new moves unfortunately led to deteriorating relations with Royalist Peru. Viceroy José Fernando de Abascal y Sousa sent a small force under Admiral Pareja to quell this incipient revolution. While Carrera battled with Royalist forces outside of Santiago, a new junta, dissatisfied with his conduct of the war, proclaimed Bernardo O'Higgins the new commander-in-chief of the patriot forces.[15]

13. Diego Barros Arana, *Historia general de Chile* (Santiago, 1884–1902), IX, 648–51; Bello, *Obras*, IX; Benavente Boizard, *Benavente*, 366.

14. Diego José Benavente, *Primeras campañas de la guerra de la independencia de Chile*, in Vicuña Mackenna, *Historia general*, II, 28. For a discussion of the Carrera diary as a historical document, see M. L. Amunátegui, "Memoria de los hechos más notables occuridos en la revolución de la República de Chile," *Revista de Santiago*, II (1848), 108–20.

15. See Vicuña Mackenna's early article: "El sitio de Chillán en 1813," *La Tribuna*, June 9, 1849.

From this date, relations between Carrera and O'Higgins, former allies, deteriorated to such an extent that a civil war seemed imminent. Carrera returned to Santiago and quickly overthrew the supreme director, Francisco de la Lastra, and O'Higgins disavowed all support for the new ruler. Although O'Higgins and Carrera attempted to reconcile their differences in the face of a third Spanish invading force, persistant rivalry and distrust led to a patriot defeat at Rancagua and the eclipse of the *Patria vieja*. Carrera went into exile, and, after years of intrigues aimed at regaining power, he found himself before a firing squad in 1821.[16]

Benavente had been a staunch supporter of Carrera's pretensions, and had gone into exile with him in Argentina in 1814. He maintained no affection for O'Higgins, who had him arrested during the campaigns against Carrera, and his *memoria* clearly displayed this attitude. Such a passionate defense of Carrera shocked Barros Arana, who noted that Benavente's "partiality for Carrera and his dislike for O'Higgins was manifested by the suppression of certain facts on some occasions, and the frank use of insinuations in order to censure or praise." Vicuña Mackenna found that Benavente's dependence on the diary of General Carrera "destroyed the impartiality of the study," and the work became a "polemic."[17]

These charges appear justified, as Benavente used every possible opportunity to exalt Carrera and denigrate O'Higgins. Following the recently published opinions of Thomas Carlyle in *On Heroes, Hero-Worship, and the Heroic in History* (1840), Benavente proclaimed Carrera one of the "great men" of history, defined by Carlyle as the "modellers, patterns, and in a wide sense creators of whatsoever the general mass of men contrived to do or attain." For Benavente, Carrera was "a man of genius who did not execute others' orders, but gave them; nor did he follow other men, because he was a leader. He was a hero comparable only to the immortal Washington." O'Higgins' men, however, were only of "middling caliber."[18]

In order to support his charges, Benavente was reduced to printing unfounded gossip, by claiming that O'Higgins accepted Royalist aid in his at-

16. Simon Collier, *Ideas and Politics of Chilean Independence, 1808–1833* (Cambridge, 1967), 92–102. See also Julio Robles Alemparte, *Carrera y Freire, fundadores de la República*, (Santiago, 1963), and Pedro Lira Urquieta, *José Miguel Carrera* (Santiago, 1967).

17. Barros Arana, *Historia general*, IX, 648–51; Vicuña Mackenna, *Historia general*, I, 10–11. See also *El Progreso*, October 3, 1845.

18. Thomas Carlyle, *On Heroes, Hero-Worship, and the Heroic in History* (Oxford, 1968), 1; Benavente, *Primeras campañas*, 21.

tempt to rid Chile of Carrera, and that O'Higgins himself was responsible for Carrera's death.[19] When Benjamín Vicuña Mackenna eventuallly edited the *memoria* for his collection, the *Historia general de Chile desde su independencia hasta nuestros dias*, he felt compelled to insert countless footnotes containing documentary evidence vindicating O'Higgins from these scandalous claims. Thus, Benavente's *memoria* actually exacerbated the debates on historical method, as several critics claimed that it approached the *ad probandum* method of historical writing despite the fact that it remained *ad narrandum* in form.

Once again, it was thought that the following year's *memoria* might once and for all quiet this debate. The choice of the writer seemed auspicious, as Bello selected Antonio García Reyes, the young lawyer and congressman, who had professed an interest in the collection and preservation of historical documents since his days in the National Institute. García Reyes prepared a study of *La primera escuadra nacional*, and its role in the emancipation of the New World. Again, the work assumed the format of a chronicle of the fleet from its formation until 1825. Ample statistical data was supplied, which detailed the tonnage, manufacturers, captains, nationality of crew, and the number of cannons. Bello responded favorably to the work, noting that it was "an excellent historical work . . . in the narrative style." He only chided the author for his tendency to lapse into words of French derivation, thereby "setting a bad example for the youth."[20]

Despite Bello's praise of the form of the work, the content appeared discordant with his ideals of historical writing. Even the daily *El Progreso* commented that García Reyes attempted "a philosophic consideration of the nature of our naval force, by analyzing what it had been and what it might be." The goal of the *memoria* became a direct plea for government support for the construction of new vessels for the Chilean navy. It must be remembered that García Reyes' assertions were not vain cries in the wilderness, passive suggestions to an academic audience, but active policy statements to a group which included President Bulnes and the ministers of the interior and war.[21] Even the first sentences of the preface were addressed directly to Bulnes: "It had not been in vain that Divine Providence has placed the country which you

19. Benavente, *Primeras campañas*, 136.
20. Vicuña Mackenna, *Historia general*, IV, 19; Bello, *Obras*, VII, 89, 97–98.
21. *El Progreso*, October 13, 1846.

rule at the base of mountains which lie near the ocean." García Reyes then mentioned that Congress had threatened to suspend further financial aid from the navy. For this reason, he "decided to refresh His Excellency's memory of the events of years past, and in this manner offer service to the public cause."[22]

Although García Reyes admitted that "a historical work was not the place to present projects for the organization of a new navy," the content of his study suggested the contrary. For example, he noted the dangers of a naval fleet staffed entirely by foreigners, who maintained no allegiance to the Chilean government. During the Independence period, all the captains and subordinates spoke only English, and all official correspondence was in English as well. This system led to conflicting loyalties, especially in the affair of San Martín and Lord Cochrane, when the British chief of the Chilean naval fleet refused to obey orders and attempted to control the course of American emancipation on his own.[23] García Reyes presented statistical tables which documented the low participation of Chileans in the naval aspect of the War for Independence. The inference was evident: Chile must begin the construction of her own fleet and train Chileans for all positions of command. He concluded his preface by noting that Chileans "must study our own history in order to deduce the future from what has passed,"[24] words similar to those of Lastarria and López. Like Benavente's work of the proceeding year, García Reyes' study managed to follow the *ad narrandum* method in form, but the *ad probandum* method in content.

Manuel Antonio Tocornal's study of the *Primer gobierno nacional* (1847) must have seemed a welcome relief to Bello. Here at last was a work that unabashedly followed Bello's ideals of historical writing. Tocornal, a young lawyer and former student of Bello, confessed that he "may have written a chronicle, but, if so, others will write a history." His discussion of the day-to-day events which led to the creation of a national junta even assumed the form of a chronicle. Within each chapter, Tocornal selected important dates, and discussed the events of the preceding week in precise chronological

22. Antonio García Reyes, *Primera escuadra nacional*, in Vicuña Mackenna, *Historia general*, IV, 20.

23. *Ibid.* 20, 21–24. See also Vicuña Mackenna, *El General Don José de San Martín* (Buenos Aires, 1971), 77.

24. García Reyes, *Primera escuadra nacional*, 24. See also Donald E. Worcester, *Sea Power and Chilean Independence* (Gainesville, 1962).

order. He thus successfully accomplished his intent, which "was primarily limited to the narration of the events which led to the installation of the junta." Bello, eminently satisfied, praised Tocornal for "sound judgment" in his first historical work.[25]

Bello's pleasure was short-lived, however, for succeeding *memorias* did not follow his example as unswervingly as Tocornal. Almost at the same time that Tocornal was completing his essay, the Faculty of Philosophy and the Humanities was attempting to decide which work would receive the prize for "a composition in prose or verse concerning Chilean history."[26] This competition marked the beginning of a series of faculty *memorias* concerning history. Unlike the university *memorias*, provided for in Article XXVIII, these new essays would be presented to the individual faculty. Each of the five faculties would receive 200 pesos yearly to be awarded to the work of greatest merit. The competition was open to all, and the works were submitted anonymously with the author's name in a sealed envelope. The faculty had offered previous competitions in 1844, 1845, and 1846, which asked for dissertations on "the goal of education in Chilean society," "primary education in Chile," and "the origins, progress, and tendencies of literary taste in Chile," but none of the entries was deemed worthy of an award.[27] Lastarria won the 1847 competition for his *Bosquejo histórico de la constitución de Chile*, which attempted to further the arguments on historical method which he had proposed in 1844. The opportunity to submit a work anonymously allowed Lastarria to give his methodology another hearing before the Faculty of Philosophy and the Humanities, since it had become obvious that Bello had no desire to give him a second chance to write a university *memoria*.

While Lastarria's *Bosquejo* reopened the debates on the proper method of writing history, the authors of the succeeding university *memorias* followed the pattern set by Benavente and García Reyes. Each historian, recognizing that his work would be judged by Bello and those who followed his ideals, claimed great respect for the objectivity of the narrative method of writing history, but then proceeded to prepare his final work exactly as he had wished. José Hipólito Salas, a cleric who presented the 1848 *memoria*, which concerned the abolition of slavery in Chile, professed his sincerity in a man-

25. Tocornal, *Primer gobierno nacional*, 122, 228; Bello, *Obras*, VII, 136.

26. *Anales de la Universidad de Chile*, III, 47.

27. Ana Guirao Massif, *Historia de la Facultad de Filosofía y Humanidades* (Santiago, 1957), 74.

ner that reflected his consciousness of the debates raging around him: "I am limiting myself to the pure exposition of the facts (which can be found in irrefutable documents) and abandoning all philosophical judgments to the impartial judgment of the reader." Despite these lofty goals, Salas left no mystery as to where his sympathies lay: "The poor Indian, sad victim of that system of greed and ambition! Rented, bought, sold, separated from his home, destroyed by a war of extermination, persecuted everywhere, and in the middle of a Catholic people, in the shadow of the tree of death, his condition is like that of the pariah in India."[28]

Similarly, Ramón Briseño's 1849 study also asserted impartiality, but offered a firm support for the current political regime. The periodization of the *Memoria histórico-crítica del derecho público chileno desde 1810 hasta nuestros días* demonstrated this bias, as Briseño depicted the era from 1810 to 1830 as "the period of attempts at political organization," while 1830 to 1849 became the "period of peace and consolidation."[29] Few opponents of the Portalean system and the Constitution of 1833 would agree with this assertion, but Bello found Briseño's essay to his liking for this precise reason. He commented, "I do not know whether the similarity of my ideas with those of the author influence my judgment, but I still recall the great emotion I felt as I read the introduction." Bello thus staunchly supported Briseño's contention that the Chilean Constitution of 1833 was "the wisest in South America," being the "sole cause of the twenty years of peace which have conserved the plenitude of Chile's political and social order." Bello claimed that the work was "of great usefulness and undeniable importance," and Claude Gay, after reading Briseño's study in Paris, felt compelled to name a new species of plant (the *Brisignoa*) after the author. Gay, who was primarily a botanist, often honored a "work of great intelligence or an act of patriotism" in this fashion.[30]

Briseño's work appealed to Bello for yet another reason, since it supported his views in the continuing debates with Lastarria. Both authors considered the history of constitutions, Lastarria from 1810 to 1814 and Briseño from 1810 to 1833, but they approached the constitution as a historical doc-

28. José Hipólito Salas, *Memoria sobre servicio personal de los indíjenas i su abolición* (Santiago, 1848), 46, 49. For a discussion of Salas, see Chapter 5 herein.

29. Guillermo Feliú Cruz, *Historia de las fuentes de la bibliografía chilena* (Santiago, 1966), II, 71–72.

30. Bello, *Obras*, VII, 166–67; Feliú Cruz, *Historia de las fuentes*, II, 76.

ument differently. Lastarria believed that a study of succeeding constitutions might be revealing in an analysis of the "changing political ideas of the leaders of the *Patria Vieja*." Bello actually agreed with this opinion, but he found an assertion by Jacinto Chacón in the prologue to the *Bosquejo* somewhat less defensible. Chacón claimed that the study of constitutions was the best way to understand "the heart of a society," that is "the political, religious, moral, literary, and economic factors" which governed man's actions.[31] Chacón, with one eye pointed toward France, noted that "constitutions were the results of social movements" and thus expressed the will of the whole society.[32] Bello found this opinion overstated, believing that it grotesquely exaggerated the ideas of Lastarria's *Bosquejo*, which never expressed such a concept of the relationship between the constitution and the society. Bello countered by arguing that "written constitutions were often dictated by special-interest groups, or even by one man, who did not necessarily represent a political party, but possessed his own political notions, philosophic speculations, personal interests, and utopian ideals." Bello's conception of the nature of the constitution paid more respect to Chilean history, by alluding to the Constitution of 1823, written almost single-handedly by Juan Egaña, and the Constitution of 1833, written by a small group of men in order to institutionalize the Portalean system and ensure Conservative domination of the political system.[33]

Briseño thus entered an on-going debate and presented a work which both reconsidered the period of the *Patria Vieja*, which Lastarria had discussed, and, presented a brief which soundly refuted the propositions of Chacón. He believed that constitutions were usually "imposed on a people" and that they influenced the society rather than vice-versa.[34] Therefore, Bello's pleasure with Briseño's study reflected both similar political beliefs as well as a reaffirmation of the principles espoused in the debates with Lastarria and Chacón.

Thus a debate which had originally been seen as a defeat for Lastarria, and an unquestioned victory for Bello, still raged on inconclusively. As the decade began the Faculty of Philosophy and Humanities saw the debut of two men, Miguel Luis Amunátegui and Diego Barros Arana, who would

31. Lastarria, *Obras*, IX, 60, 38–39.
32. *El Progreso*, January 28, 1848.
33. Bello, "Constituciones," *Obras*, VII, 127–33; Collier, *Ideas and Politics*, 260–63.
34. Feliú Cruz, *Historia de las fuentes*, II, 73.

rank among the greatest of the nineteenth-century historians. It was hoped that they would bring a decisive end to the unresolved Lastarria–Bello debates. Their first works seemed a victory for Bello's methodology, but the authors maintained an ambiguity in their position which might someday lead them closer to Lastarria.

Miguel Luis and Gregorio Víctor Amunátegui responded promptly to the request from the Faculty of Philosophy for a study of "national history from 1814 to 1817 or from the Battle of Rancagua to the Battle of Chacabuco."[35] Their *memoria* on *La Reconquista Española* pleased the faculty committee of García Reyes and Miguel de la Barra, deacon of the faculty, and the youths received the 200-peso prize. The work fully vindicated Bello's methodology, and the committee praised it for "impartiality" and "being a faithful mirror of the times it described. However, despite the fact that the work followed Bello's suggestions, the youths dedicated their study to Lastarria: "It was you, señor, who first encouraged us to write; by right our first work should be dedicated to you. Whatever its merit, receive it as a proof of our affection." Similarly, in a letter to Lastarria, Miguel Luis noted: "We are gathering data in order to write a history of 1813 and 1814. Perhaps we have tackled a job that is too great for our combined forces; but we are Basques in origin and in will. . . . We will manage to complete it, and you will not be ashamed to call us your disciples."[36]

This profession of support for Lastarria seemed doubly surprising. First, all of the youths' early historical works owed a profound debt to Bello's methodology. Secondly, while Lastarria may have been the Amunáteguis' professor, it was Bello who took them under his wing and saved them from certain poverty after their father died. Bello noticed Miguel Luis during the Latin examinations at the National Institute and was pleasantly surprised by his profound knowledge of Horace and Virgil. As a result, he recommended Miguel for a professorship at the institute, despite the fact that he was two years below the minimum-age specification. Similarly, he encouraged both youths to visit his home frequently, and use his library as often as they wished. Thus, the dedication of their work to Lastarria demonstrated a cer-

35. Guirao Massif, *Historia de la Facultad*, 74. For a discussion of each brother's contribution to Chilean historiography, see Amunátegui Reyes, "Intimidades," in Raúl Silva Castro, *Miguel Luis Amunátegui Reyes* (Santiago, 1951), 263–313.
36. *La Tribuna*, December 9, 1850; Vicuña Mackenna, *Historia general*, II, 219; *Revista Chilena*, IX (1919), 45–46.

tain sympathy for his views and deeds, although the work itself followed Bello's methodology unquestioningly.[37]

As the Amunáteguis submitted their first complete work to the faculty, the first writings of Diego Barros Arana made their appearance in the daily press. Soon thereafter, he also responded to the faculty's request for "a study of national history during 1811 and 1812." The Amunáteguis also entered a study in the competition, *Los primeros tres años de la revolución de Chile*, which ultimately won the prize because it considered one year more than Barros Arana's work, and also because it was written "more pleasingly and correctly."[38]

Barros Arana's early works followed Bello's suggestions implicitly. In a study of Vicente Benavides, he found occasion to repeat Manuel Antonio Tocornal's remark: "If I have written a chronicle, others will write a history." Similarly, his study of General Freire professed the same goal, that of "expressing the facts with clarity and simplicity with the exactitude of a chronicler." Barros Arana's "limited goals" so dismayed Vicuña Mackenna that he stated "the facts in his works come before the ideas, and the inflexible exacitude of the dates come before enlightening thoughts."[39]

Yet, if circumstances dictated, Barros Arana might easily abandon the strict objectivity and narrative approach which he habitually followed. His fifth historical study, in 1851, a lengthy review of the new *Historia eclesiástica, política, y literaria de Chile* by José Ignacio Víctor Eyzaguirre, a young priest, lacked the sense of control that had marked his earlier studies. Eyzaguirre, like Barros Arana, maintained close ties with the higher echelons of Santiago society, and his ancestors included several leaders of the independence movement. But Eyzaguirre, unlike the great majority of the aristocracy and clergy, shifted his support from the dominant *pelucón* party, the supporters of the Portalean system and the Constitution of 1833, to the newly formed Liberal party. In 1848 he was elected to the Chamber of Deputies and soon became vice-president of the Chamber. Diego Antonio Barros, Barros Arana's father, remained a staunch Conservative and supporter of Manuel Montt for the 1851 presidential candidacy, and as a result he soon became a

37. Barros Arana, "Don Miguel Luis Amunátegui," in C. Morla Vicuña (ed.), *Don Miguel Luis Amunátegui* (Paris, 1889), 4–22.

38. Amunátegui Reyes, *Don Antonio García Reyes*, 173.

39. Diego Barros Arana, *El General Freire* (Santiago, 1852), 117; Vicuña Mackenna, *Historia general*, I, xiv–xv.

target for critical barbs from the Liberal dailies, *La Barra* and *El Progreso*. The elder Barros solicited aid from Eyzaguirre, asking him to quiet these constant attacks, but he coldly refused. From this day, young Diego believed that the intransigent priest had betrayed his father and the honor of the Santiago aristocracy, and his review of Eyzaguirre's historical work in *Sud-América* reeked of animosity.[40]

The harsh tone of the critique forced Juan María Gutiérrez to write to his friend Barros Arana and reprimand him for his intemperance: "I well understand your determination to criticize the *History* of Eyzaguirre. However, you should not do it with a hostile mind or for political vengeance. At your age it is necessary to cultivate generosity and an elevated viewpoint. . . . [Your review can] only bring great harm to your reputation as a historian."[41]

As the regime of General Bulnes came to an end, and Montt ascended to the presidency, the yearly regularity of the university and faculty *memorias* slowed somewhat, as affairs of state diverted the young historians from their scholarly tasks. Vicuña Mackenna lamented this when he examined these early historical works, proclaiming them either "chronicles or polemics" and noting that an "impartial history" of Chile had yet to be written.[42]

Despite the diversity of these early historical works, they had two themes in common. First, no one managed to praise Spain for her activity during the colonial period. Whether it was the predominance of the "Black Legend" or the acceptance of Lastarria's interpretation in his 1844 work, Bello's moderate view of the Spanish past was totally rejected. Chile, unlike Mexico, would never have a Lucás Alamán to defend the colonial heritage.[43]

Secondly, almost all of the works maintained a curious ambivalence between the methods of historical writing presented by Bello and Lastarria. Part of the blame for this confusion must lie with Bello himself. He rarely listened to the views of Lastarria and his supporters, and when he dubbed them proponents of the *ad probandum* method he committed a grievous error. The term itself implied that Lastarria's method was subjective, and consequently of dubious scientific and scholarly merit. Yet Bello failed to recog-

40. For a discussion of Eyzaguirre, see Chapter 5 herein.
41. This episode is fully discussed in Guillermo Feliú Cruz, *Barros Arana, historiador* (Santiago, 1959), V, 130–48.
42. Vicuña Mackenna, *Historia general*, I, xx.
43. See Moisés González Navarro, *El pensamiento político de Lucas Alamán* (Mexico City, 1948).

nize that the *ad narrandum* method might be just as subjective. While attributing a scientific honesty to the analysis of the documents, Bello ignored the fact that the historian's bias could affect his work at any time. The past presents an infinity of facts or small events which could never be presented in their totality by the historian. He must decide which facts are important to his study. Which should he choose? Was the Chilean historian to interest himself mainly in military events or political affairs? Did he concern himself with the social and economic life of the people? Did he follow Carlyle and study only the "great men" of history, or should he study in the activities of the Araucanian Indians, *inquilinos*, or black slaves? After this decision was made, a myriad of past events were eliminated from the historian's vision.

Once the selection process was completed, the historian faced the problem of emphasis. Was one fact necessarily more important than another? For example, it was widely known that O'Higgins had opposed a clause in the Chilean Declaration of Independence which proclaimed Catholicism as the exclusive state religion. Yet, it was also known that the clause appeared in the final document, that O'Higgins attended mass regularly, and that he protected the Catholic religion during his rule. These contrary facts perplexed Chilean historians in their attempt to determine whether or not O'Higgins was or was not a good Catholic. Which event was to predominate in the analysis of O'Higgins' personality?[44]

Many facts, those deemed unimportant by the historian, are thus eliminated in the final work, producing only a partial vision of the past. Although each fact may have been independently verified, it did not follow that the completed work was of the same order of veracity. As the historian compiles and selects the building blocks of his trade, the same bias that Bello attributed only to his opponents may also enter into the final work.

Thus young historians desirous of following Bello's definitions saw no incompatibility between the *ad narrandum* method and a subjective approach to writing history. For this reason, Benavente could defend Carrera, García Reyes could urge the construction of a new naval fleet, and Briseño could counter Chacón's ideals, as long as a narrative method was followed. Form thus became as important as content and interpretation.

This initial experience revealed a curious irony, as history eventually became functional, as Lastarria had suggested in his 1842 speech, with no ap-

44. Jaime Eyzaguirre, "Una controversia sobre la religiosidad de O'Higgins," *Boletín de la Academia Chilena de Historia*, II (1942), 75–80.

parent incongruity with Bello's ideals. Documents might be analyzed and edited as before, but in the preparation of the final historical work, *utilidad* could be of paramount importance. While Lastarria urged that literature be "national, useful, and progressive," these early writings revealed that other, more personal goals might also motivate a historical work.

As a result, a functional approach to history was accepted alongside an adherence to Bello's views. This double allegiance led to a predictable pattern in the second half of the nineteenth century. The historians continually asserted their objectivity in the initial pages of their works. Barros Arana began his *Historia general de la independencia en Chile* in this manner: "In my pages there is no flattery nor grudges—I narrate the facts as I conceive them in the light of the documents." The image was that of a judge. He added that "the historian must write without fear, be incorruptible, frank, and a friend of liberty and truth." Vicuña Mackenna carried the metaphor still further. Who was more honorable and incorruptible than a judge? "A priest," he answered.[45]

Nevertheless, despite the assertions of Encina and Feliú Cruz, these protestations of impartiality rarely inhibited the historian from using his works for a specific purpose. The second part of this study examines the uses of history which evolved in the second half of the nineteenth century, as historians blended the ideas of Lastarria and Bello. Four distinct functions of historical writing can be discerned:

First, it was discovered that history might be used as a political weapon, providing thinly disguised critiques of current problems, as well as concrete policy proposals. This was particularly evident in the campaigns against Manuel Montt (Chapter IV), the debates on the secularization of Chilean society (Chapter V), and the discussions of foreign policy (Chapter VI).

On a less exalted level, history also became used as a means of defending family honor and bolstering personal reputations (Chapter VII).

Thirdly, the importance of history was recognized as a means to educate Chilean youth to become moral and patriotic citizens. The emulation of appropriate heroes and the knowledge of the lessons of the past could thus be used to aid Chilean progress (Chapter VIII).

Finally, history was also considered the storehouse of human knowledge

45. Carlos Orrego Barros, *Diego Barros Arana* (Santiago, 1952), 56–57; Benjamin Vicuña Mackenna, "Mi defensa ante el jurado de Valparaíso," *Revista Chilema de Historia y Geografía*, LXX (1931), 90.

which might reveal the existence of general laws governing human conduct. Once these laws were understood, the future of Chilean society might be efficiently planned (Chapter IX).

These patterns in nineteenth-century Chilean historiography evolved during the 1850s, as young historians passed from an initial methodological confusion toward a belief in a functional approach to history which blended the ideas of both Lastarria and Bello. The rise of this hybrid school of historical writing coincided with the presidency of Manuel Montt. The relationship was hardly coincidental, since the individual historians' contacts with the new regime strongly influenced their ultimate commitment to the *utilidad* of historical writing.

Part II

THE FUNCTIONS OF HISTORY IN NINETEENTH-CENTURY CHILE (1851–1900)

4

FROM AMBIGUITY TO ACTION

HISTORY BECOMES A POLITICAL WEAPON

CHILE'S MAJOR HISTORIANS of the nineteenth century began to write as their nation underwent a transformation from a former backwater of the Spanish Empire to a major power of the continent. Benjamín Vicuña Mackenna, Miguel Luis Amunátegui, and Diego Barros Arana were swept into Chile's political life during the end of the Bulnes presidency and the first term of Manuel Montt. This passage from the academic to the political arena slowly changed their attitudes concerning the importance and relevance of their work. During the Montt era these young historians managed to reconcile the ideas of Lastarria and Bello, and give a new direction to Chilean historiography.

Lastarria was the first of Chile's historians to lend his talents to politics. While serving as a moderate deputy from Rancagua, he envisioned a new political force which might challenge the omnipotent Conservative party, which had exercised a virtual stranglehold on Chilean political life.[1] Lastarria explained the desires of a new "Progressive" party in *Bases de la reforma*, a manifesto issued in late 1850, and cosigned by a young deputy, Federico Errázuriz. These proposals amounted to a complete repudiation of the Constitution of 1833. Lastarria argued that a new charter had to be promulgated which recognized the "political power or sovereignty resided in the nation

1. See José Miguel Yrarrázaval Larraín, *El Presidente Balmaceda* (Santiago, 1940), Chs. 2–4, and Diego Barros Arana, *Un decenio de la historia de Chile* (Santiago, 1913), II, 103.

. . . not in the hands of an individual, a family, or a privileged class."[2] As a result, the suffrage had to be broadened, and free education guaranteed to all citizens. The remaining suggestions reversed the intentions of the Constitution of 1833, by strictly limiting the powers of the chief executive. The president could no longer be re-elected after his first five-year term, nor could he proclaim a state of siege, which had previously allowed "unhindered personal dictatorships." A new legislature, directly elected and unicameral in form, would be established, thus eliminating the president's firm control over the choice of the senators. Additionally, Lastarria urged that municipalities be given considerable self-government.

Although the tone of the *Bases* recalled the defunct Constitution of 1828, the prime purpose of this program was the reversal of the political factors which had made possible Conservative domination since 1830. This new "Progressive" party would eventually assume the name "Liberal," both in tribute to the men of the 1828 constitution as well as those who respected "liberal principles." Lastarria used the term *liberal* as synonymous with *republican*, and in sharp contrast to the "restrictive politics" of the *pelucón* government.[3]

The leaders of the new Progressive party decided to choose Ramón Errázuriz for the 1851 presidential nomination. The Conservative majority had not foreseen any opposition in the coming elections and were taken aback by this display of audacity. Nevertheless, the candidate himself excited little fear in the hearts of Conservatives, since the elderly Errázuriz could just as easily have been a Conservative candidate. A representative of one of the oldest families in Santiago, he was selected for his role primarily "for his political antecedents, his education, and his character."[4] He also appealed to the Progressives because he had been one of the leaders of a moderate opposition to Portales (the *filopólitas*) in the 1830s. As the year progressed, this extremely quiet man emerged primarily as a figurehead, allowing the Liberal deputies to take full charge of his campaign and all policy decisions.

Despite the recent and brazen appearance of a new opposition party in the Chamber of Deputies, the young Liberals offered no serious threat to the Conservatives, who had yet to choose a presidential nominee. Far more im-

2. J. V. Lastarria, *Obras completas* (Santiago, 1909), 502–503.
3. J. V. Lastarria, *Diario político, 1849–1852* (Santiago, 1968), 30.
4. *Ibid.*, 45.

portant for the Conservatives was the news of the French Revolution of 1848. The workers there had overthrown a king, and Conservatives wondered whether a similar event might occur in Chile.

The arrival of two young Chileans, recently returned from France, soon made these fears a reality. The first was the unrepentant Francisco Bilbao. The Conservatives had thought that they had been well rid of this obstreperous youth who had caused so much commotion with his *La sociabilidad chilena* in 1844, but Bilbao returned as uncompromising as ever. Soon after his arrival, Bilbao published *Boletines del espíritu*, a work which attempted to display the recent knowledge he had acquired in France. At best, this panegyric to Michelet, Quinet, Lammenais, and the Araucanian Indians has been described as "unintelligible" and "incomprehensible" by Bilbao's supporters. Nevertheless, a few clear ideas showed through the morass of words with intense fury. Bilbao's harsh attack on the Catholic religion and its doctrine caused Archbishop Valdivieso to excommunicate him and all those who subscribed to the ideas in his works.[5]

During this affair Santiaguinos also noticed the presence of yet another young radical, Santiago Arcos, who had been a friend of Bilbao in France. Arcos' radicalism appeared surprising to all. His father had been a rich Spanish merchant, and the youth had been raised in the home of the Bishop of Santiago. After the fall of O'Higgins, the Arcos family emigrated to France, where the father prospered as both a merchant and a banker. His son, however, had read and applauded the writings of the social reformers and utopians, especially Robert Owen and François Fourier, and actively participated in the workers' demonstrations of 1848.[6] In 1849, Arcos' father returned to Chile with the intention of establishing a bank. His son had other ideas.

Shortly after his arrival, Arcos and Bilbao formed a new political association, the *Sociedad de la Igualdad*, which attempted to organize the working classes of Santiago.[7] The club sponsored educational lectures as well as classes in music, arithmetic, political economy, and even English, taught by a Jamaican cook who had jumped ship. The workers who attended the political

5. Benjamín Vicuña Mackenna, *Historia de la jornada del 20 de abril de 1851* (Santiago, 1878), 17; Barros Arana, *Un decenio*, II, 476.

6. See Domingo Miliani, "Utopian Socialism, Transitional Thread from Romanticism to Positivism in Spanish America," *Journal of the History of Ideas*, XXIV (1963), 523–38.

7. José Zapiola, *La Sociedad de Igualdad y sus enemigos* (Santiago, 1902), 8.

meetings, many of whom were skilled artisans, often appeared more radical than their aristocratic leaders. When the chairmen of the society decided to expel Bilbao after his excommunication, the workers supported him whole-heartedly. Workers also participated in the club's decision-making process. In Santiago, both a tailor and a carpenter sat on the club's first directorial board.[8]

The goal of this society was primarily political and openly revolutionary. The first issue of the group's newspaper, *El Amigo del Pueblo* (named after Marat's journal), expressed the desire to become the "echo of the revolution" and to "rehabilitate the people after twenty years of darkness." The members also demanded the dismissal of Manuel Montt, whom they viewed as "fatal to liberty, fatal to education, and fatal to the Republic." Unfortunately, the more the group insisted that Montt not be a presidential candidate in 1851, the more likely a candidate he seemed to Bulnes and the Conservative party. As Vicuña Mackenna noted: "It was not Bulnes or the Conservative party which imposed the candidacy of Montt against the wishes of all interested parties. Rather, two men, Francisco Bilbao and Santiago Arcos and the *Sociedad de la Igualdad*, unaware of their role in this decision, insured the choice of Montt.[9] As the workers became more vocal, Conservatives overcame their initial resistance to the Montt candidacy. While they feared Montt's uncompromising attitude, they also feared the workers and possible disturbances of order even more. Sarmiento voiced the ambiguity of the Conservatives in the title of his election pamphlet: "Whom do they fear and deny? Montt./ Whom do they support and desire? Montt./ Then who is the candidate? Montt."[10]

It has often been said of Bulnes that during times of peace he moved to the left of the Conservative party, and during domestic strife he moved to the right. As the current ministry was being challenged on every move in Congress, and the workers began to voice their demands, Bulnes ended his hesitation and moved to insure the Montt candidacy.[11]

Why Montt? Montt's reputation as a savior for the Conservatives and an

8. Vicuña Mackenna, *20 de abril*, Ch. 3.
9. *Ibid.*, 71, 95.
10. Barros Arana, *Un decenio*, II, 477.
11. Alberto Edwards, *El gobierno de Don Manuel Montt, 1851–1861* (Santiago, 1932), 47; Luis Barros Borgoño, *Proemio para la obra de Don Alberto Edwards, "El gobierno de Don Manuel Montt"* (Santiago, 1933), 47.

anathema to the Liberals and the members of the *Sociedad de la Igualdad* stemmed from his controversial role as minister of the interior in 1845 and 1846. As the opposition press increased its attack on his ministry and began searching for a possible opponent for Bulnes, Montt encouraged Bulnes to request a state of siege in response to Santiago Ramos, editor of a minor newspaper, *El Pueblo*, who called the people to revolt against the government. The pretense was feeble, but it allowed the government to arrest several opponents of the Bulnes regime. Many were exiled to Peru, or imprisoned in Valparaíso or distant Chiloé. With potential opposition leaders removed from scene, an overwhelming triumph for the government in the 1846 midterm elections was assured. From that day forward Montt lost whatever prestige he had gained with the moderate opposition from his earlier attempts to improve the educational system, and incurred their enduring disdain. [12]

Thus far, the fear of a revolution in Chile was based more on imagination than fact. Despite the Liberal opposition in the Chamber and the workers' participation in the *Sociedad de la Igualdad*, the calm that had reigned in Chile during most of Bulnes' administration continued. However, by late 1850, the aura of tranquillity began to fade as a series of regional revolts challenged the government's authority. In San Felipe, a branch of the *Sociedad* arose to protest the Intendant's ruling that it had desecrated the Chilean flag by adding the motto, "Respect for the law—Valor in the face of arbitrary authority." [13] As government forces attempted to remove the offending banner and arrest those involved, the leaders of the *Sociedad* called for armed revolt by the workers, and swiftly deposed the government authorities and formed a revolutionary junta.

Although government troops soon regained control of the province, Bulnes and Montt responded with unusual severity by declaring a state of siege not only in Aconcagua, the scene of the revolt, but in Santiago as well. In order to quell any rebellion in the capital, the government did not differentiate between the Liberals in Congress and the radicals of the *Sociedad de la Igualdad*. The government dissolved the *Sociedad*, arrested its leaders as well as the prominent members of the Liberal party, and closed all opposition

12. Barros Arana, *Un decenio*, 97; Domingo Amunátegui Solar, *El Instituto Nacional bajo los rectorados de Don Manuel Montt, Don Francisco Puente, i Don Antonio Varas, 1835–1845* (Santiago, 1891), II, Parts 1 & 3.

13. Vicuña Mackenna, *20 de abril*, 255.

newspapers.[14] Santiago remained quiet for the one-month state of siege, but as soon as the controls were lifted, dangerous portents for the future began emanating from Concepción, where a *cabildo abierto* proclaimed General José María de la Cruz its presidential candidate.

Concepción had already given the republic four leaders, and the province apparently wished 1851 to be no exception. Cruz, a staunch member of the Conservative party and a nephew of Prieto and a cousin of Bulnes, actually differed little with the philosophy of Montt. Yet, with unparalleled swiftness, the Liberals dumped Errázuriz as their candidate and proclaimed for Cruz, who agreed with none of their ideals. Nevertheless, Cruz maintained control of the army in Concepción, and Liberals, confident that they could never win by legal means at the polls, decided that Montt's candidacy could only be defeated by armed rebellion.[15]

Since Cruz believed in the validity of the electoral process, he refused all attempts to persuade him to move against Montt before the election of June 25. However, some of his supporters did not feel themselves bound by similar ideals, and on April 20, 1851, Colonel Urriola led the Valdivia regiment against the presidential palace. In the meantime, Bilbao and his allies attempted to raise barricades on the Alameda in Santiago and incite the masses to revolt. All remaining troops stayed loyal to the government, and they swiftly quelled the rebellion. More than 200 died during this brief battle.[16]

Any disorder automatically improved Montt's chances in the coming election. After a repetition of the arrests of the preceding December, Santiago remained quiet until the election, which, unsurprisingly, Montt won with 132 electoral votes against 29 for Cruz. As Montt delivered the presidential oath, a fusillade of cannon fire celebrated his victory. Lastarria, at his home some two miles away, could only shudder as he heard the barrage: "This means," he remarked, "that Montt, imposed on Chile by the most disgraceful of her citizens (that is, Varas, Mújica, the political speculators, and the imbecilic *pelucones* who support him out of fear) is president!"[17]

The cannon fire augured more than the advent of a new presidency, as

14. René León Echaiz, *Evolución histórica de los partidos políticos chilenos* (Santiago, 1939), 2.

15. Vicuña Mackenna, "Diario desde el 28 de octubre de 1850 hasta el 15 de abril de 1851," *Revista Chilena de Historia y Geografía*, I (1911), March 24, 1851.

16. Vicuña Mackenna, *Historia de los diez años de la administración Montt* (Santiago, 1862), III, 53–54; Agustín Edwards, *Cuatro presidentes de Chile* (Santiago, 1932), I, 47–48.

17. Lastarria, *Diario político*, 119.

regional revolts again erupted throughout the country. The *Sociedad de la Igualdad* in La Serena overthrew the elected officials, and, after Cruz returned to Concepción, he also led an attack against government forces. Again the revolts were suppressed quickly but not without considerable bloodshed, as more than 2,000 died at the decisive battle at the Loncomilla River. With all armed resistance definitively crushed, and most of the opposition in exile, Montt began his first term with a state of siege in effect. He assured his supporters of the "dominion of liberty and order in the public government, with neither liberty lacking order, nor order lacking liberty, but just harmony of these two saving principles of the Republic." [18]

The order fostered by the Montt regime brought unprecedented economic prosperity to Chile as private entrepreneurs and the government cooperated in the construction of new railroads and interurban telegraph lines and the foundation of savings and mortgage-loan banks. British capitalists viewed the improved economic situation so optimistically that Chile was able to negotiate a sizable loan under the most favorable terms since the coming of independence. [19] Unfortunately, opposition leaders were unable to participate in the benefits of the new regime since most remained in exile at the beginning of the decade. The historians, who had distinguished themselves in the university and the opposition campaigns of 1849–1851, fared particularly poorly during Montt's government. Exiled, persecuted, fired from positions of importance, the young historians vehemently opposed Montt, and, as a result, they used all means at hand to challenge the legitimacy of his rule and prevent the continuation of *pelucón* domination of politics by the nomination of Montt's favorite, Antonio Varas, in the 1861 election. Any resistance which Lastarria, Amunátegui, Vicuña Mackenna, or Barros Arana may have had to the use of history for political motives faded by the end of the decade, as the repressive Montt regime impelled them to such action.

Lastarria was the first to feel the wrath of the Montt government. He had hardly returned from Lima after the first state of siege of the presidential campaign, when he again found himself threatened with arrest after the up-

18. Ricardo Donoso, *Las ideas políticas en Chile* (Mexico City, 1967), 294; Donoso, *Desarrollo político y social de Chile desde la Constitución de 1833* (Santiago, 1942), 51; Januario Espinosa, *Don Manuel Montt, uno de los más grandes estadístas de América* (Santiago, 1944), 178–79.

19. Daniel Martner, *Estudio de política comercial chilena e historia económica nacional* (Santiago, 1923), I, 278–79.

rising of April 20, 1851. A Conservative commission recommended the cancellation of his congressional privilege and urged his immediate arrest, claiming that he had participated with sword in hand in the futile rebellion.[20] Lastarria, a cautious man by nature, and fervently opposed to violence, had learned of the rebellion by dawn and proposed to observe rather than take part. He had been seen huddled in a doorway opposite the Church of San Francisco, and therefore quite distant from the center of the battle. Judged as a "suspected revolutionary," he found himself forced to return quickly to Peru.

Adding to Lastarria's humiliation and anger was the loss of his professorship of constitutional law just four days after the attempted coup. Since he had "participated in public acts of subversive tendencies," the government decided to remove him from his position "lest he attempt to inculcate similar ideas among the students under his direction." Lastarria commented that he was fired because "the government feared that the teaching of political science was a school for revolutionaries." Yet, not only the political scientists were singled out, as other opposition members in the National Institute—Manuel Recabarren, professor of political economy, and Juan Bello, who had translated Michelet's *History of France* as a textbook—also lost their positions. Lastarria eventually returned to Chile in late 1852, but settled safely and quietly in the northern city of Copiapó and participated in a local mining concern, until he established his own law firm. He avoided all politics during the first half of Montt's period of rule.[21]

Benjamín Vicuña Mackenna, a fledgling historian who had contributed a few historical essays to *La Tribuna* and Jacinto Chacón's 1849 Literary Society competition, joined the fighting of April 20 in a more active fashion than Lastarria.[22] Younger, and with less to lose than his esteemed mentor, he galloped fervently into battle, sighing romantically that he "hoped that some man would summon those who truly loved liberty." If this man called, Benjamín intended to rush to "his side, and if they fell, riddled with bullets, they might have the name of their native country lingering on their dying

20. Alejandro Fuenzalida Grandón, *Lastarria i su tiempo* (Santiago, 1911), I, 215.
21. *Ibid.*, 217.
22. For early unpublished works of Vicuña Mackenna, see *Archivo Benjamín Vicuña Mackenna*, T. 144, 157ff. On the literary society, see *El Progreso*, August 30, 1849; *La Tribuna*, September 26, 1849. For *Introducción histórica a la revolución de Chile*, see *Archivo Benjamín Vicuña Mackenna*, T. 156, 161.

lips." Benjamín rode through the streets of Santiago as a special emissary for the leaders of the rebellion, until disarmed and arrested by troops "ordered to shoot him if he attempted to flee." Condemned to death by the Council of War, he was later pardoned and sent to jail, where he wrote his first critique of Montt, the *Tablas de sangre de la candidatura Montt*. He escaped from his cell on July 4 dressed as a woman, and promptly joined his former co-conspirators, who suggested that they participate in the rebellion in the North. Vicuña Mackenna joined in the overthrow of the regional administration in La Serena, but, soon after, as government forces approached, he went into hiding for the first ten months of 1852, until he left Chile for a lengthy voyage. After a hasty escape, Vicuña Mackenna remained in self-imposed exile in Europe and America for three years.[23]

Miguel Luis Amunátegui fared somewhat better than his fellow historians. Although he had assisted the Liberals in the Congress, he had not participated in the events of April, and was thus allowed to continue teaching in the institute. For this reason, Lastarria once called him a "moderate liberal," meaning "one who is afraid to go to jail for his principles."[24] Amunátegui disapproved of Montt's tactics, but appeared unwilling to attack them openly, for fear of losing his position, since he needed to support his family after his father died. He freely aided the government in its foreign policy endeavors by preparing two historical studies which defended Chile's territorial claims to Patagonia.[25] Yet, he was unable to condone Montt's domestic policy, and, for this reason, refused the opportunity to edit the government newspaper, *El Araucano*, despite the fact that he was offered a healthy annual salary of 2,000 pesos.[26]

Thus, Amunátegui walked a thin line during the early years of the Montt regime. Only once did he challenge Montt's principles of government, but in an extremely cautious manner, hiding his criticism in a historical work, *La dictadura de O'Higgins*. This 1853 faculty *memoria* marked a definite departure for Amunátegui for yet another reason, as the young historian formally em-

23. Ricardo Donoso, *Don Benjamín Vicuña Mackenna: Su vida, sus escritos, y su tiempo* (Santiago, 1925), 31, 41. See Augusto Iglesias, "Benjamín Vicuña Mackenna, aprendiz de revolucionario," *Anales de la Universidad de Chile* (1943), 75–204.

24. Lastarria, *Diario político*, 110.

25. See Ch. 6 herein.

26. Diego Barros Arana, "Don Miguel Luis Amunátegui," in C. Morla Vicuña (ed.), *Don Miguel Luis Amunátegui* (Paris, 1889), 36.

braced the *ad probandum* method of writing history. He attempted to establish that "the republic was the form of government which best corresponded to the spirit of the century, and, that every new state that appears must necessarily be republican." In order to prove his thesis, he discussed the "fruitless attempts of Bernardo O'Higgins to establish a dictatorship in Chile. He concluded noting that "it was impossible to implant a dictatorship in any of the New World nations."[27]

The work, although supposedly a critique of O'Higgins' administration, actually attacked Montt's philosophy of government. Diego Barros Arana recalled the audience reaction to Amunátegui's reading of the study, noting that no one was fooled for a minute by the supposed historical intent of the work:

One must understand that Amunátegui read his work before the highest officials of the state. Many condemned this work as blasphemous, since it challenged the authoritarian doctrines of the Constitution of 1833. Only those who lived in this era can understand how audacious the doctrines that Amunátegui sustained in his book appeared to the audience. . . . The work caused a true sensation, and nothing proves it better than the fact that the numerous copies printed by the university were sold within a few weeks.[28]

If Amunátegui offered only temperate criticism of the Montt regime, Barros Arana offered none. A member of a foremost *pelucón* family, Barros Arana appeared extremely satisfied with Montt's leadership and his suppression of the Revolution of 1851. Just a year after the elections, he wrote to his friend Juan María Gutiérrez: "Chile advances with the speed of wind. The telegraph cable joins Valparaíso and Santiago, and the construction of the railroad begins in September at several intermediary locations in order to hasten its completion. Copiapó becomes richer as time passes, and the commerce improves. . . . Montt, animated by a spirit of conciliation, works hard and with great success for his country."[29]

Barros Arana continued his historical writing and amassed a library of over eight hundred volumes during Montt's first five-year term. Untouched

27. *Ibid.*, 44; M. L. Amunátegui, *La dictadura de O'Higgins* (Santiago, 1914), 5, 9.
28. Barros Arana, "Amunátegui," 43–45. See Lastarria, *Recuerdos literarios* (Santiago, 1967), 286.
29. Barros Arana, "Veintiuna cartas," *Revista Chilena de Historia y Geografía*, LXXXVI (1939), July 9, 10, 1852.

by Montt's repression of the opposition, Barros Arana was able to speak of a "spirit of conciliation," despite the fact that Montt stubbornly refused to grant an amnesty for those who participated in the 1851 revolt. Although only twelve opposition leaders remained in exile by mid-decade, Montt's hesitance to enact appropriate legislation limited opposition participation in government, since they feared reprisals might be taken at any time.

Yet, even Barros Arana became disenchanted with the Montt regime, as he noticed that he himself was not exempt from the persecution that Montt had at first limited to the opposition. He first noted public disapproval of the administration early in Montt's second term:

In spite of all this (the economic prosperity), the country is not satisfied with the present administration. The government has done a great deal, but the country demands more activity. Few sympathize with the Varas ministry, which has attempted to direct everything in the nation, by putting relatives and discredited men in positions of great authority. Now this does not mean there is a possibility of revolution or even formal opposition. Everyone just grumbles, but does not concern himself with affairs of government, since people are too preoccupied with their own affairs.[30]

Soon thereafter, Barros Arana began the publication of a newspaper, *El País*, which offered an outlet for his historical writings as well as a "program of prudent and cautious reform."[31] This cautious criticism advocated the replacement of Varas as minister of the interior by Jerónimo Urmeneta, a moderate and a relative of Barros by marriage. After a congressional threat to delay passage of the budget forced Montt to appoint Urmeneta, *El País* suspended publication. Soon afterwards, however, Montt switched subsidiary cabinet members to men more pliant to his will and caused severe difficulties for Urmeneta. These actions angered Barros Arana, and he soon joined with Ramón Sotomayor Valdés, a Conservative, in founding a newspaper, *La Actualidad*, with a goal of "terminating the severe and terrible politics of Montt." The newspaper and a *Manifesto of the Opposition of Santiago to the Republic*, written by Barros Arana and Sotomayor, claimed that the "Constitution of the republic was dead, as the president had become the supreme arbiter of the life, death, and liberty of the citizens of Chile." Thus, "personal liberty had been substituted for the rule of law," and, in the process, "the

30. *Ibid.*, March 28, 1856.
31. Ricardo Donoso, *Diego Barros Arana* (Mexico City, 1967), 26.

Liberal party has become a race of pariahs." Additionally, the two collaborators used every possible opportunity to expose numerous cases of fraud in the
recent elections.[32]

Montt's forces responded promptly and in a typical fashion. At 6:30 A.M.
Barros Arana was awakened by four policemen who ordered him to jail. The
arresting officers searched the house and discovered Barros Arana's old friend,
Robert Souper, an active participant in the Revolution of 1851, asleep on the
couch in the next room. Souper, whom Barras Arana had met accidentally on
the street the day before, had suddenly complained of a headache, and Barros
Arana offered him lodgings. The surprised Souper was quickly frisked and
the police discovered a small handgun. Souper claimed that he was delivering
a large sum of money to an area frequented by thieves, and therefore needed
the gun. The patrolmen, however, thought otherwise, and promptly led him
to jail. The case was dismissed the next day because of lack of evidence, but
this event confirmed Barros Arana's hatred of the Montt regime. Soon thereafter, he wrote to Gutiérrez that he could not "enumerate in a book the
countless outrages (theft of money from the public treasury, persecution of
the opposition, the spirit of exclusivism, the death of municipal power, the
lack of progress of education) that the government had committed."[33]

Vicuña Mackenna's return to the political scene soon presented more
problems for Barros Arana. After an unsuccessful attempt to be elected as
deputy from La Ligua, Vicuña Mackenna brought his campaign against
Montt to the pages of a new newspaper, *La Asamblea Constituyente*, which
advocated the reform of the Constitution of 1833, in tones far more lurid
than those considered by Barros Arana. Vicuña Mackenna claimed that the
present constitution "removed all the powers that the Constitution of 1828
had granted to the people. Our basic liberties were plundered and our rights
were surrendered to the centralist capital and an all-powerful executive. The
nation was annulled and the president of the republic assumed all power."[34]

Several contributing writers and congressional deputies decided to form a
Club de la Unión, which might be the center of a new opposition party. The

32. Barros Arana and Ramón Sotomayor Valdés, *Manifiesto de la oposición de Santiago a la República* (Santiago, 1858), 18.
33. *La Actualidad*, October 15, 1858; Barros Arana, "Veintiuna cartas," December 15, 1858.
34. Vicuña Mackenna, "Portales i Montt—parangón político," *Miscelanea* (Santiago, 1872), II, 107–22; "La Constitución de 1833 juzgada por la práctica," *La Asamblea Constituyente*, no. 4 (1858), 33–34.

leaders chose December 11, 1858, for a mass meeting, and, in the pages of *La Asamblea Constituyente*, presented a manifesto which called for the reform of the Constitution. Although the Intendant of Santiago prohibited the meeting, a few hundred people gathered. More than 150 of these were promptly arrested. Although most were freed after payment of a small fine, Vicuña Mackenna, seen as a perennial troublemaker, was sent to jail for two months.[35] In February of the following year, he was placed aboard a ship bound for a destination unknown to him. Captain William Lesley was given 3,000 pesos to deposit him in Liverpool. In the meantime, the government closed the presses of *El Correo Literario*, which published *La Asamblea Constituyente* and *La Actualidad*, and Barros Arana found it politic to begin a European voyage to avoid further reprisals.

The Montt regime ended as it began. A revolutionary junta in Santiago, composed of opposition leaders, attempted to coordinate a full-scale uprising, even larger than in 1851, to protest government intervention in the recent congressional elections. The strategists envisioned a series of local revolts in key cities throughout the republic, thus dividing the government forces. Despite initial rebel successes in the North and in Talca, near Santiago, the South remained hesitant, thus allowing the government forces to bring the rebels into submission within a few months. Montt, weakened by the second "revolution" against his rule, at last attempted to compromise with the opposition. The ultimate result of Montt's diminished authority was the inability to impose Antonio Varas as the next presidential candidate. Varas, realizing the intense opposition, declined to run, and Montt was forced to seek a compromise candidate, José Joaquín Pérez, who became president in 1861.[36]

The *Cuadro histórico de la administración Montt* reached Santiago bookshops just as Pérez took the presidential oath. The anonymously written, clandestinely published work appeared as if out of nowhere, but immediately captivated Santiago society, causing the first edition to be promptly sold out.[37] The authors, who included Lastarria and Barros Arana, dedicated this curious history of the Montt regime to the new president, so he might see

35. Vicuña Mackenna, "Mi diario de prisión. De 12 de diciembre de 1858 a 23 de febrero de 1859," *Revista Chilena de Historia y Geografía*, XVIII (1928), 153.
36. Agustín Edwards, *Cuatro presidentes*, I, Ch. 14.
37. Víctor M. Chiappa, *Bibliografía de Don Diego Barros Arana* (Temuco, Chile, 1907), 20.

"how low the prestige of the government had fallen" during the previous decade. Explaining that this era "of degeneration and egotism" nullified all the desires of the Chilean people, the authors hoped that Pérez would choose a markedly different course of action during his presidency.[38]

This new history represented a major departure from previous historical works. Formerly, historians had considered the colonial and independence eras as the only periods worthy of study. Until 1861, no one had written a history of the years following 1830. Suddenly, after Montt's regime, a new "contemporary history" came into fashion. Unlike the histories of past generations, the new contemporary history could be written by "those witnesses and actors who had actually participated in the events," and thus, according to Barros Arana, attain a higher level of veracity than a work based on the analysis of ancient documents.[39] Once the new study had been published, "public opinion" could then judge the truthfulness of the assertions, and debate could become possible, as the reading audience had also witnessed the important events of recent years.

While Barros Arana especially hoped that contemporary history would eventually allow a true vision of the past, the reverse often occurred. As historians chose topics nearer to the present day, the writers' passions became hopelessly involved. Exiles or political prisoners of the 1850s would hardly be expected to present an unbiased view of the Montt period, in much the same way that Antonio Varas might be expected to produce a panegyric to the former ruler. The closer the period of history to be studied approached the present, the objectivity that Andrés Bello had attempted to instill became more difficult to attain. By 1862, after a flurry of historical studies of the Montt regime, Martín Palma, writing for *El Ferrocarril*, proposed to study the past decade "in the light of justice," and not write a "stinging diatribe." Yet, he confided that this ideal would earn the "disgust of all," for the goal of impartiality had become offensive.[40]

38. Lastarria, Barros Arana, Santa María, *et al.*, *Cuadro histórico de la administración Montt (escrito según sus propios documentos)* (Valparaíso, 1861), dedication. Such historical critiques of presidential administrations became quite common. See also Isidoro Errázuriz, *Historia de la administración Errázuriz* (Valparaíso, 1877), and Carlos Walker Martínez, *Historia de la administración Santa María* (Santiago, 1889).

39. Lastarria, *et al.*, *Cuadro histórico*, 587; Barros Arana in *El Correo del Domingo*, May 18, 1862; Vicuña Mackenna, *El Mercurio*, March 18, 1861.

40. Martín Palma, *Reseña histórica—filosófica del gobierno de Manuel Montt* (Santiago, 1862).

The conversion to this new approach to history was not easy for all to accept. Barros Arana had always insisted on strict objectivity when writing history. Just a few years previously, he confided to a friend: "I write what is good and what is bad about everyone—I write without nationalistic passions or the hatred engendered by party disputes." As a matter of fact, he added, on occasion he even "praised the Spaniards, the enemies of our country, for I have never criticized them if their conduct deserved praise." But, in the face of what he called a "formal dictatorship," Barros Arana also participated in the preparation of the "extremely biased" *Cuadro histórico*, so that the "Montt regime might be damned by contemporary readers and by history."[41]

Yet, despite Barros Arana's desire to condemn the Montt regime so that all eternity might know its crimes, he still maintained an initial ambivalence toward using history in such a vindictive fashion. Rather than depicting Montt as the enemy of the Chilean people, Barros Arana characterized him as the enemy of the historian. Montt's paramount crime became the attempt to ensure his role as a great statesman in the eyes of history by nefarious means. To accomplish his goal, Montt proceeded to falsify documents and misrepresent the facts. For example, Montt supported only those newspapers which favored his administration. A well-spent 63,331 pesos ensured continual praise in all the newspapers of the period, for any periodical critical of Montt found it difficult to survive without such sponsorship. Thus, while hundreds of rebels in the Revolution of 1851 were executed without trial, the newspapers talked only of the "great material progress, such as the railroad in Copiapó (which was actually begun under the previous administration) or the new electric telegraph." Similarly, Barros Arana accused Montt of hiding or destroying documents after he attempted to find references to the capture of the Chilean ship *Arauco* by the British: "In vain I searched for a document, a sentence, a word, an allusion of any sort to that horrible scandal. Montt wished to save himself from the judgment of history, and therefore he hid all documents which might be useful to the historian."[42]

While Barros Arana displayed a cautious stance in the committment to use history as a political weapon, his fellow collaborators felt no similar hesitation. Lastarria, who had often proclaimed the usefulness of history, attacked Montt directly on what had often been considered his strongest point,

41. Barros Arana, "Veintiuna cartas," July 14, 1857, March 28, 1859, February 28, 1862. See also *El Ferrocarril*, September 23, 1861.
42. Lastarria, *et al.*, *Cuadro histórico*, 43–61, 36.

his support for public education. While Barros Arana wrote as an anonymous historian, Lastarria referred to his personal experiences, thus venting his bitter resentment for the man who had him fired from the National Institute. Thus, he recalled how Montt "had surpressed the course on Constitutional Law because the government feared that the students would understand the true nature of Chilean society and its political institutions."[43] Similarly, he blamed Montt for the failure of his congressional projects on educational reform.

Perhaps the most revealing aspect of the *Cuadro histórico* was the collaboration of Barros Arana and Lastarria, former opponents in the Lastarria–Bello debates. Barros Arana, a former student of Bello, had firmly believed in the importance of objectivity in historical writing, an ideal seemingly violated in his critique of the Montt administration. Actually, Barros Arana had not repudiated Bello. Rather, he accepted his methodology and combined it with Lastarria's sense of purpose. Thus Barros Arana found that he could reconcile two seemingly disparate approaches to historical study. He shared Bello's respect for historical documentation, but he also learned to assemble his facts for a purpose, as Amunátegui and Vicuña Mackenna had done years earlier.

Thus, by 1861 the Lastarria–Bello debate had virtually ended. Two seemingly irreconcilable paradigms had blended into one as historians combined Bello's respect for historical methodology with Lastarria's notion of the "utility" of all literature. Ideas which had seemed in conflict merged as a result of political pressure during the Montt regime which had been absent in the initial university debates.

Bello, therefore, gave Chilean historiography the methodological respectability which has been praised by Feliú Cruz and Encina, while Lastarria gave it a sense of political purpose. The only remaining tension between the two paradigms hinged on the fact that historians often used Bello's cloak of respectability to mask an underlying political purpose. As the historian was drawn further ino Chilean political life during the period from 1861 to 1900, history became an able and forceful ally in the debates concerning the future of the young republic. Constitutional reform, with regard to the status of the Catholic Church, became one of the first subjects of concern for Chile's foremost historians.

43. *Ibid.*, 359.

5

THE CATHOLIC HISTORIAN IN NINETEENTH-CENTURY CHILE

THE RELIANCE ON HISTORY as a political weapon expanded in direct proportion to its use. As proponents of a certain issue manipulated past events to further current political goals, their opponents found it necessary to borrow similar rhetorical tools in order to validate their arguments. The evolution of Catholic historiography, which defended the prerogatives of the Church in a secular age, was fostered by the critiques of anticlerical historians. A historical response soon became the only reply to a historical attack.

Until mid-century few challenged the role of the Church in Chilean society. Church and state maintained an alliance which was codified in the Constitution of 1833.[1] The charter declared Catholicism the state religion and included "the duty to preserve and protect the Catholic religion" in the presidential oath of office. While the Catholic religion was to maintain a privileged position in Chile, the Church itself was not. The president retained the *patronato*, the right to nominate archbishops, bishops, canons, and sacristans, and the right to control diplomatic relations with the Vatican.[2] Despite these limitations, internal Church affairs remained relatively undisturbed during the first twenty-three years of the Constitution's rule, until President Montt challenged the independence of the Church.

1. Francisco Encina, *Historia de Chile desde la prehistoria hasta 1891* (Santiago, 1942–1952), X, 558–59.
2. J. Lloyd Mecham, *Church and State in Latin America* (Chapel Hill, 1934), 252–53. See also Frederick Pike, "Church and State in Chile and Peru," *American Historical Review*, LXXIII (1967–1968), 30–50.

The relative calm in Church-state relations which marked the first years of the republic came to an abrupt halt over what seemed at first a fairly minor incident, "the affair of the sacristan," in 1856. A sacristan, feeling he had been unjustly expelled from the service, brought a complaint before the ecclesiastical council. Two canons, dissenting from the majority, agreed with the sacristan's protestations of innocence. Their position, interpreted by Archbishop Rafael Valentín Valdivieso as a sign of disrespect for their superiors, resulted in their suspension from their duties. The canons then appealed the case to the Chilean Supreme Court, which revoked the decision of the ecclesiastical tribunal. Valdivieso responded that a civil court could have no jurisdiction over administrative matters within the Church, and asked President Montt to intervene in defense of the Church. Montt declined, noting that the Constitution prohibited interference with Supreme Court decisions. The archbishop was then given the choice of exile or restoring the sacristan and the canons to their positions.

This must have been a difficult decision for Montt. He had already alienated ultra-Catholic supporters by his suppression of the tithe and his refusal to appoint a cleric as the head of the National Institute. The "affair of the sacristan" proved the final straw and ultimately fractured the coalition that had brought Montt to power. The far right joined with Liberal opponents of the Montt regime, forming the "Liberal-Conservative Fusion." Brought together by their hatred of Montt, these former enemies had few common goals. Their campaign slogans were thus often limited to calls for "administrative reform," which alienated no one in this diverse coalition. Those who supported Montt and the doctrine of presidential dominance formed the "National party" or "Montt-Varista party," which lacked the power of the previous coalition that had brought Montt to the presidency. Montt became so weakened as a result of this party split that he was unable to choose his successor, a common practice in Chilean politics to this date.

Although a hasty compromise was arranged in the sacristan affair, the interference of the state in an internal affair of the Church opened the door for further discussion of the Church's role in Chile's future.[3] Was the Church to retain an equal status to that of the state or was Chile to be secularized? Nineteenth-century legislation dictated the latter part, as the Church's priv-

    3. Luis Galdames, *A History of Chile*, trans. I. J. Cox (New York, 1941), 294–95. See also Ricardo Donoso, *Las ideas políticas en Chile* (Santiago, 1967), 182.

ileged position slowly crumbled before the laws decreeing the civil registration of births and deaths, the abolition of the ecclesiastical law courts, the
strengthening of the *patronato*, and the alteration of Article 5 of the Constitution, which sanctioned Catholicism as the official state religion.

To add insult to injury, the clerics found that while their future role was
being threatened, their past was also being called into question. Often the
same men who passed laws limiting the powers of the Church began ransacking the annals of history for any event which could bring disfavor to the
Church, and thus support the rationale of the secular legislation. Every
supposed act of hypocrisy or greed on the part of the Church was revealed,
every act of complicity with the Spaniards during the bloody Conquest was
emphasized.

This anticlerical reinterpretation of the Chilean past capitalized on the
belief that the Conquest and colonial period had been detrimental to Chilean
progress, and depicted the Church as the willing partner of Spain in this
somber period of history. The Conquest became more than just a search for
wealth in the New World. Barros Arana claimed: "The battle between the
Indians (who defended their land and liberty) and the Conquistadors (who
against all reason and justice came to confiscate their property and reduce
them to slavery) became a Holy War in the minds of the Spaniards." Thus
the religious goals rationalized the Conquest into a pacification. Miguel Luis
Amunátegui insisted that this ruse was deliberate, as the Spanish monarch
used the Church and the Catholic religion to buttress his power in the New
World and keep the colonial territories submissive.[4]

Once the Church and the state joined forces, they did everything within
their power to forestall thoughts of independence. The Inquisition became
the prime villain. There was no doubt, contended Barros Arana, "that the
Inquisition and the Catholic religion were the causes of the literary and scientific decadence of Spain at the end of the seventeenth century. . . . Spain
believed that the diffusion of knowledge involved a danger to the conserva-
tion of the Catholic faith and the stability of the monarchy."[5]

During this gloomy era, not one churchman worthy of note or emulation
could be found. The Jesuits were depicted as deceptive hucksters interested

4. Diego Barros Arana, *Historia general de Chile* (Santiago, 1884–1902), I, 274; M. L.
Amunátegui, *Los precursores de la independencia de Chile* (Santiago, 1870–1872).
5. Barros Arana, *Historia general*, II, 231.

only in obtaining gold and property. The sly Bishop Rodríguez Zorilla was revealed as the man who almost betrayed Chile's independence. Even the Pope himself, Leo XII, was depicted as a partner in this conspiracy with his Bull of September 24, 1824, which exhorted the bishops of America to praise the Spaniards as the true defenders of the Catholic faith.[6] Similarly, heroes of the Independence period who had always been revered as good Catholics became subject to reanalysis as the anticlerical historians insisted that these patriarchs were followers of Voltaire.

Unfortunately for the Church, these charges were not isolated in the pages of history books. Benjamín Vicuña Mackenna condemned the Inquisition in speeches to the University Council as well as in the pages of *El Mercurio* while he was editor. Both he and Amunátegui used the floor of the Chamber of Deputies as a forum for their ideas, and Amunátegui's pamphlet on the Papal Encyclical of 1824 was merely a copy of his speech to Congress. Domingo Santa María and the *Revista Católica* argued for weeks whether José Miguel Infante, a hero of the Revolution, confessed as a Catholic before he died.[7]

However, the incident that most offended the clerics was a debate that erupted as the remains of Bernardo O'Higgins were being laid to rest. A crowd of men, women, and children filled the Plaza de Armas in Santiago to honor the hero of Chilean independence. The priests praised O'Higgins' faithfulness to the Catholic religion. Salvador Donoso eulogized: "In the six years of his government, O'Higgins was always a good Catholic, fulfilling all the precepts of the Church. . . . Moreover, O'Higgins showed himself worthy of the mission which he exercised by the will of God who allowed him to govern this Catholic nation."[8] Barros Arana, however, shocked everyone present as he delivered his eulogy. He emphasized that O'Higgins had disagreed with a phrase in the Declaration of Independence which argued that Chile should "protect the Catholic faith and exclude all other religions."

6. Barros Arana, "Las riquezas de los antiguos jesuítas de Chile," *Obras completas* (Santiago, 1905–1906), X, 43–135; M. L. Amunátegui, "El Templo de la Compañía de Jesús en Santiago de Chile," *Revista de Santiago*, May 15, 1872; Domingo Santa María, *Vida de Don José Miguel Infante* (Santiago, 1856); M. L. Amunátegui, *La encíclica del Papa León XII contra la independencia de América* (Santiago, 1874).

7. Benjamín Vicuña Mackenna, *Francisco Moyen o lo que fué la Inquisición en América* (Valparaíso, 1868); *El Museo* (1853), nos. 23 & 28; *Revista Católica*, November 20, December 10, 24, 1853.

8. *La República*, January 14, 1869.

He then quoted O'Higgins' remark to his advisers: "This prohibition will merely hinder the emigration of talented people and hard-working laborers from Europe. I cannot discover any reason which obliges us to advocate the defense of the Catholic religion in the Declaration of Independence." This comment infuriated the Catholic press. Crescente Errázuriz responded in the *Revista Católica*: "Anyone who proposes to present a eulogy should not paint a hero as a hypocrite to the eyes of the Catholics. The historian may believe whatever he desires, but he falsifies history if he depicts men as he wishes and credits them with beliefs that were not their own."[9]

In order to answer these critiques, a new breed of historian developed: the Catholic historian. This was not a new occupation for Chilean clerics, since the best chronicles of the colonial period had been written by men of the cloth: Alonso de Ovalle, Miguel de Olivares, Ignacio Molina, and Diego de Rosales.[10] However, these men wrote in an era that accepted the Catholic faith without question. Their works of the seventeenth and eighteenth centuries emphasized the participation of saints, angels, and even the devil in the Conquest of Chile. Such examples of divine interpretation appeared absurd to the secular historians of the nineteenth century. For the Catholic historian to insist on seeing history as the concrete demonstration of God's will could only weaken his argument.[11] Thus, Divine Providence was pushed to the sideline as a causal force in man's progress. God was indeed always present, but more as an interested observer than as an active participant.

Once this step had been made, the Catholic historians could face the anticlerical historians on their own terms. And, like the anticlerical historians, they faced the classic dilemma: Should they reveal the truth as they discovered it or should they devote their allegiance to the needs of the Church? Crescente Errázuriz, author of *Los oríjenes de la iglesia chilena*, expressed the duties of the Catholic historian as follows: "Certain historians use only those facts that add stature to the person they are discussing, and, at the same time, keep silent about any facts that can harm his image. Whoever

9. Jaime Eyzaguirre, "Una controversia sobre la religiosidad de O'Higgins," *Boletín de la Academia Chilena de Historia* II (1942), 75–80; *Revista Católica*, February 1, 1869.

10. Crescente Errázuriz in *El Estandarte Católico*, March 10, 1877; Juan Ignacio Molina, *The Geographical, Natural, and Civil History of Chile* (London, 1808); and Alonso de Ovalle, *Histórica relación del reino de Chile* (Santiago, 1969).

11. For the Catholic philosophy of history, see Mariano Casanova, "Filosofía de la historia bajo el punto de vista católico," *Anales de la Universidad de Chile* (1860), 332–53, and the speech of Francisco Vargas Fontecilla on July 12, 1852, reprinted *ibid.*

does this lacks the prime qualities of the Catholic writer. Not being impartial and completely truthful will not aid the Church, but, on the contrary, give arms to its enemies." Yet, at the same time, he noted that the Catholic historian would find "immense advantages [in the writing of history] enabling him to defend religion against its numerous and expert critics." [12] Thus the double criteria of an allegiance to the search for truth in the writing of history as well as to its use as a political weapon presented itself to the Catholic historian and his opponents, and both discovered that these divergent banners were not mutually exclusive. One could proclaim his objectivity, but at the same time use his research to serve a political function. A contradiction was never apparent.

José Hipólito Salas first attempted to undermine the anticlerical historians' interpretation of the harmful influence of the Church on Chilean progress by proclaiming a novel idea in his *Memoria sobre servicio personal de los indíjenas i su abolición*, which he delivered to the full session of the University Council in 1848. Formerly, José Victorino Lastarria and others had argued that the years before 1810 were years of *tinieblas*, years of darkness. The revolution of 1810 was the work of a few strong-willed men who were able to break the bonds that the colonial system had imposed upon them. Salas, a young cleric and a professor of theology at the National Institute, argued differently. [13] He believed that 1810 was preceded by a two-century struggle by the missionaries for the liberty of the enslaved Indians, and this "triumph of social liberty was the precursor of the political liberty of 1810." [14] Andrés Bello found this a "novel idea," and certainly a profound change from the writings of Bilbao and Lastarria, which saw the Church and its missionaries as the prime bulwark of the colonial system. While Bello expressed surprise, others were less kind in their analysis of this new interpretation of Chilean history. *El Progreso* commented: "It seems that the cause is quite distant from the effect. Why not argue that the *Conquest* was the *cause* of the revolution of independence?" Miguel Luis Amunátegui, later one of the historians most often at odds with the Church, argued further: "In many passages of this *Memoria*, [Salas] cites laws and royal decrees which denounced the mistreat-

---

12. *El Estandarte Católico*, March 10, 1877.

13. J. V. Lastarria, *Obras completas* (Santiago, 1909), VII, 151–55; Domingo B. Cruz, *El Illmo. Sr. Don José Hipólito Salas* (Santiago, 1921), Ch. 7.

14. Andrés Bello, *Obras completas* (Santiago, 1884), VII, 151–55; *El Progreso*, November 30, 1848.

ment of the Indians and tried to remedy it, yet, it is certain that these laws were not always carried out and at times their effect was cancelled out by other decrees." Additionally, Salas never stated that many clerics sided with the *encomenderos* in the debates on *servicio personal*.[15]

Despite these unfavorable comments, Salas offered a new interpretation which all future Catholic historians adopted. Salas presented a picture of the Church operating alone during the colonial period struggling for the "sacred rights of man" against the Spaniards. The Spaniards claimed they were committing Indians to slavery as a means of "propaganda of the sword," which was merely a hasty rationalization of the greedy Spaniards' desire for gold. Since the Church had no power to influence Spanish policy, it operated as best it could in hopes of ameliorating the plight of the Indians, who were "rented, bought, sold, separated from their homes and destroyed by a war of extermination."[16]

As the standard-bearer of the Church that fought for the "rights of man," Salas resurrected the image of a young Jesuit of the seventeenth century, Luis de Valdivia, as the true representative of Church policy.[17] Valdivia rebelled against crown policy since he believed the current practice of subjugating the Araucanians by force of arms was fruitless, and the proposal to exterminate the Indians similarly absurd, since it merely hardened their desire to fight. Rather, Valdivia proposed a policy of "defensive warfare" to Philip III. The plan included cessation of all offensive operations against the rebels, establishment of the Bio-Bio River as the dividing line between Araucanians and whites, fortification of this line with military garrisons and towns, and the use of missionaries to convert the rebels and persuade them to live in peace with the Spaniards. The scheme was not wholly visionary, since Valdivia spoke the Araucanian language fluently and had personally discussed these plans with tribal heads. Philip III and a special *junta de guerra* appointed by the Council of the Indies were favorably impressed by the idea and gave Valdivia sufficient power to put his plan into effect.

Valdivia's attempts to convince Philip III of his plan's feasibility were not

15. *Revista de Santiago*, II (1848); Eugene H. Korth, S.J., *Spanish Policy in Colonial Chile* (Stanford, 1968), 122.

16. José Hipólito Salas, *Memoria sobre servicio personal de los indíjenas i su abolición* (Santiago, 1848), Ch. I, 19, 43–46.

17. For a brief summary of the life of Luis de Valdivia, see Antonio de Egaña, S.J., *Historia de la iglesia en la América Española* (Madrid, 1966), II, 231–35.

easy, nor, once his project was put into practice, were the results clear-cut. A massacre of three Jesuit missionaries at Elicura in 1612 convinced local *encomenderos* that peaceful coexistence was impossible. Despite these problems, Salas painted Valdivia as a veritable super-hero in his attempt to save the image of the Church and the Jesuits, which had been so sullied by the anticlerical historians. Salas noted that, "despite the fact that all opinion in the Spanish court was against him . . . his discourse, sustained by the fire of inspiration, caused Philip III to reverse an order he had just signed." Actually the deliberations lasted from January 2 to December 9, 1610. Similarly, Salas claimed that the king wished to honor the "disinterested apostle with the position of Bishop of Concepción, but, with his regrets, Valdivia accepted only the position of visitor general."[18] The king realized that a recalcitrant bishop might thwart Valdivia's attempts, and offered Valdivia the position despite the fact that Jesuits were forbidden to accept episcopal honors unless commanded to do so by the Pope. Salas painted Valdivia as disinterested, but, actually, his superiors prohibited the acceptance of the position while Valdivia urged the *junta de guerra* to find a way to circumvent the restrictions. By no means did Valdivia refuse the offer immediately as Salas suggested.[19]

But Salas' claims of the success of the project of "defensive warfare" seemed the most exaggerated: "Among them, without any arms but a crucifix, with a happy and serene countenance, Valdivia penetrated the Indian tribes, and his sweet words of peace and charity were listened to as messages from the great God of heavens. By this means, he gained the sympathy of all, fulfilling his promise to pacify the most bellicose nation of the universe without firing a shot."[20] The account ended somewhat abruptly, praising the success of defensive warfare, and noting that *servicio personal* was abolished in 1633 and slaves were to be given their freedom in 1662, two laws which had almost no practical effects.

Despite the critiques of Amunátegui and the daily press, Salas' interpretation of the Chilean past went basically unchallenged within the Church, and his argument was followed by all future ecclesiastical historians. All attempted to separate Spain's corrupt and greedy activities during the Con-

18. Salas, *Memoria*, 91, 92.
19. Korth, *Spanish Policy*, 123–37.
20. Salas, *Memoria*, 94.

quest and colonial period from the noble deeds of the Church. Similarly, they tried to emphasize the heroic activity of various bishops, clerics, and missionaries. While members of the Faculty of Philosophy and Humanities criticized Salas' work, the Faculty of Theology warmly accepted José Ignacio Víctor Eyzaguirre's *memoria*. The Faculty of Theology approved the work for publication in 1849 and lauded Eyzaguirre for the manner in which he praised the Church, as well as for his use of documents.[21]

Eyzaguirre had been working for several years on the *Historia eclesiástica, política y literaria de Chile*. A member of one of the most influential families in Chile and a nephew of Portales, Eyzaguirre possessed a large archive of papers dealing with the colonial and independence periods. He began his investigations in 1837 and started writing in 1842. In addition, he spent over 6,000 pesos in the acquisition of new documents. He attempted at first to write only an ecclesiastical history of Chile, but realized after reading Abbot Ducreux that "the history of nations is so intimately interwoven with the history of the Church, that to separate them in the narrative is to present an imperfect image of the past."[22]

Eyzaguirre followed Salas' argument by noting that two contradictory forces operated during the Conquest: the Church, which carried the olive branch of peace, and the conquistador, who carried the sword. This led to a problem with a conversion of the Indians, since, while the conquistador professed the Christian faith, he broke all of its rules. The Indians were thus unable to differentiate between those who did and did not obey the Catholic faith, and a scorn for Christian values developed. After explaining the different motives of Spain and the Church during the Conquest, he selected several heroic bishops and missionaries and praised them for their deeds. But the most heroic was again Valdivia: "We would be committing an injustice if we did not name the most illustrious of all the famous men, not only in Chile but in the whole continent of America; a man who possessed the gift of directing souls along the road to heaven; and a man who freed more than one

21. José Ignacio Víctor Eyzaguirre, *Historia eclesiástica, política, i literaria de Chile* (Valparaíso, 1850), Ch. "Antecedentes."

22. Guillermo Feliú Cruz, *Barros Arana, historiador* (Santiago, 1859), V, 133; Carlos Silva Cotapos, "Eyzaguirre," *Anales de la Universidad de Chile*, CXLII (1918), 316; Bartolomé Mitre, "Introducción," in Eyzaguirre, *Historia*, xxv; Cotapos, "Eyzaguirre," 317. Francois Ducreux was a French Jesuit historian. See Firmin Didot Fréres (eds.), *Nouvelle Biographie Général* (Paris, 1856).

thousand persons from the horrors of slavery." He then compared his hero to Bartolomé de las Casas, but, unlike Salas, Eyzaguirre recounted the horrors of Elicura and noted that Valdivia died before all his work could be completed.[23] Barros Arana, however, found the glorification of members of the Church in Eyzaguirre's study rather exaggerated, and commented caustically: "The bishop in the church, the nun in the convent, the friar in the monastery, the missionary among the Indians: all are equally great and virtuous. I have searched in vain for an outstanding figure in the work of Sr. Eyzaguirre, but all I find is a row of giants, all the same stature and moral standing, so it is therefore an impossible choice."[24] Except for Barros Arana, who had personal reasons for disliking Eyzaguirre, the work was warmly accepted. Bartolomé Mitre, exiled from his Argentine homeland, wrote the introduction to the work published in 1851, and found it "a rich source for study in which future historians will find copies of many documents."[25]

The *Historia eclesiástica, política i literaria de Chile* essentially followed the arguments presented by Salas, except for a few minor details. These slight deviations eventually brought Eyzaguirre into disrepute among the Chilean clergy and irreparably damaged his relations with Archbishop Valdivieso. The debates between Valdivieso and Eyzaguirre were quite revealing in the analysis of limits placed upon the Catholic historian in his search for historical truth.

Valdivieso had known young Eyzaguirre from infancy and had fondly watched him accept the priesthood in 1840 at the youngest age possible, twenty-three. Eyzaguirre's rise was meteoric. After a short period as secretary to the archbishop-elect, his uncle José Alejo Eyzaguirre, in 1845, he was elected a member of the Faculty of Theology of the University of Chile, and soon after became dean (1847–1851). During this period, Valdivieso offered fatherly advice, and even claimed to have encouraged Eyzaguirre in his historical studies: "For my part, I have encouraged the Faculty of Theology to concern itself with the ecclesiastical history of Chile, until now unstudied, and I am flattered to have contributed to the publication of *Servicio personal de los indígenas* by Salas and to have stimulated José Ignacio Víctor Eyzaguirre to write his ecclesiastical history."[26]

23. Eyzaguirre, *Historia*, 32 and Ch. 4.
24. *La Tribuna*, April 19, 22, 1851.
25. Feliú Cruz, *Barros Arana, historiador*, V, 130, 134.
26. Guillermo Feliú Cruz, *Historiografía colonial de Chile* (Santiago, 1958), I, 114.

Soon, however, Eyzaguirre became alienated from Valdivieso as a result of his election as deputy from Putaendo in 1849 and his apparent concern for secular affairs. Although elected on a ticket supporting the government, swift changes in the ministries in 1849 soon found Eyzaguirre aligned with the opposition against the future presidential candidacy of Manuel Montt, who had played a major role in the forced resignation of his uncle, José Alejo Eyzaguirre, from the archbishopric. Despite the fact that he fought continually for the rights of an independent Church in the Congress, his association with the Liberals apparently offended the clergy. His voyage to Peru during the state of siege before the 1851 election only confirmed the clergy's suspicion that he was allied with the revolutionaries in the abortive revolt against Montt.

These charges surfaced soon after when Eyzaguirre wrote to Valdivieso requesting letters of introduction for his upcoming trip to Europe. Since Eyzaguirre held no political or clerical position at that time, and, possessing an ample fortune, he decided it was an ideal opportunity for his long-delayed trip. Valdivieso sent the letters but included the phrase *ob adjuncta rerum Republicae exeuntem*, which meant that he was leaving Chile because of the political situation, thus implying that Eyzaguirre was a revolutionary in exile. He requested that the phrase be removed, and Valdivieso responded with a lengthy letter explaining the reason for the charges. He accused Eyzaguirre of association with revolutionaries, "men of evil ideas," and mentioned that he had received reports from Lima that Eyzaguirre had been espousing "liberal ideals." Even more strange, Valdivieso claimed to have noticed some uncharacteristic passages in the *Historia eclesiástica, política y literaria*, which previously he proudly claimed to have fathered: "By the same token, others who had read your history from cover to cover have noted propositions which are not theologically sound, especially those facts relating to the religious orders."[27] Eyzaguirre defended himself from these charges claiming they were untrue. He reemphasized his loyalty to the Church, and Valdivieso, apparently satisfied, rewrote the letters of introduction without the questionable phrase. Eyzaguirre promptly left for Europe, but the wounds were apparently unhealed.

Nine years after this episode, Eyzaguirre wrote to Valdivieso asking for his observations and suggestions for revisions of the second edition of the

27. Cotapos, "Eyzaguirre," 338–41.

Historia eclesiástica, política y literaria de Chile.[28] Between 1851, when the history was published, and 1863, when the revision was planned, more had changed than the relationship between Eyzaguirre and Valdivieso. Valdivieso himself had been faced with exile as a result of the "sacristan affair," and the once secure position of the Church in Chilean society seemed threatened. For this reason Valdivieso's letter of reply sharply criticized Eyzaguirre's work and an attached forty-six-page document noted every instance where he had strayed from accepted Church dogma.[29]

Valdivieso now criticized Eyzaguirre's methodology, which had been praised so highly in 1849: "When one examines the facts that you present, one finds that you do not provide the proof necessary to generalize about the vices and defects which you claim were characteristic of the colonial era. . . . In order to make your observations more concrete, perhaps you should heed the example of Gay, who adopted a different method of writing history."[30] All opponents of Claude Gay, author of the *Historia física y política de Chile,* were "philosophers of history," a standard epithet for historians who paid no attention to the facts. Valdivieso's remaining critiques were few. However, the most offensive error in Eyzaguirre's thought was the occasional sanction of the imposition of the state's power in the internal affairs of the Church. For example, Eyzaguirre noted that "the Cabildo of Santiago demonstrated very advanced thinking when they prohibited monasteries of the ascetic life." Valdivieso countered: "If people have the urge to be called to the contemplative life they have a perfect right to join a monastery. What would become of human liberty and the rights of man if the political authority could control the destiny of each member of the society? Could there be a system more oppressive?"[31] Once state incursions on the power of the Church could be historically sanctioned, Valdivieso reasoned, the Church could have no remaining defense.

The attached document, *Reparos a la "Historia eclesiástica, política, y literaria de Chile,"* furthered this interpretation. Ironically, the cleric who presented the corrections to Valdivieso used a work by Amunátegui[32] which was

28. Rafael Valentín Valdivieso, *Obras científicas i literarias* (Santiago, 1902), II, 351.
29. *Fondos Varios,* T. 254, pz. 33a.
30. Eyzaguirre, *Historia,* Ch. "Antecedentes," article by Ramón Valentín García; Reprinted in Feliú Cruz, *Historiografía colonial,* 62.
31. Valdivieso, *Obras,* II, 353.
32. M. L. Amunátegui, *Descubrimiento i conquista de Chile* (Santiago, 1856).

critical of the Church's role in Chilean history as his source. After criticizing Eyzaguirre for some factual errors, the anonymous critic scorned his irreverent attitude toward the Church. He was most piqued by Eyzaguirre's scorn for the Jesuits, who were belittled for their interest in making money instead of religion, and castigated him for not presenting a more severe censure of the expulsion order of Charles III. Like Valdivieso, the cleric dismissed all examples of state interference in the affairs of the Church. Eyzaguirre had criticized the tendency for minors to enter religious orders, which "inspired them with exaggerated ideas about the dangers of contact with society." The critic rebuked Eyzaguirre and noted that the exaggerated ideas were *his*, not those of the religious orders. This comment was no doubt related to a recent law which prohibited those under age twenty-one from entering a monastery.

Valdivieso thus made it clear that he would accept no criticism of Church policy and emphasized more strongly than ever that the Church and state had acted independently since the time of the Conquest. However, the rationale for this assertion had changed slightly since 1848. At first, Catholic historians were interested in separating the Church from the bloody deeds committed by Spain during the Conquest in order to counter the argument of the anticlerical historians. As the nineteenth century progressed, the Church's independence in the past was stressed for another reason, in a search for precedents to quell the rapidly growing instances of state incursions in the internal affairs of the Church. This was a lesson not soon forgotten by another Valdivieso protégé, his nephew Crescente Errázuriz.[33]

When Crescente Errázuriz' father died, Valdivieso assumed responsibility for the care of the six-year-old boy. He guided him through his studies at the Seminario de Santiago, the Church-run alternative to the public National Institute, and saw him take his vows in 1864, as well as study law at the University of Chile in 1857. Valdivieso persuaded his nephew to edit the *Revista Católica* from 1864 to 1874. This Catholic periodical, which had shone so brightly in its defense of the rights of the Church during the Bilbao affair in 1843, was slowly becoming irrelevant. Most detrimental was its biweekly publication schedule which made it unable to answer the daily

33. For biographical studies, see Crescente Errázuriz, *Algo de lo que he visto* (Santiago, 1934); Fidel Araneda Bravo, *El Arzobispo Errázuriz y la evolución política y social de Chile* (Santiago, 1956); Luis Galdames, "Crescente Errázuriz como historiador," *Revista Chilena de Historia y Geografía*, LXXII (1932), 22.

charges of the liberal press. The second crisis facing the *Revista Católica* during these years was one of personnel. Young Conservatives who had supported the ideals of the spiritual independence of the Church found the reluctance of the magazine to get involved in political affairs annoying. They contributed less and less to the *Revista Católica* once they founded the Conservative daily, *El Independiente*, in 1864, which concerned itself primarily with politics. To alleviate the malaise of the *Revista Católica*, Errázuriz and two friends, Ramón Astorga and Rafael Fernández Concha, decided to publish "a daily newspaper which openly supported ecclesiastical authority." Errázuriz commented about the new *El Estandarte Católico*, which was to publish many of his historical writings: "I assumed the editorship of this newspaper to please the desires of Valdivieso. The aim of this paper was to defend the interests of religion, and become involved in politics only when it concerned ecclesiastical matters."[34]

Valdivieso also guided Errázuriz toward historical studies. One evening the archbishop lamented that there was no ecclesiastical history of Chile, apparently forgetting the work of Eyzaguirre, which he had sponsored in its early stages, and urged that such a work be written. Mariano Casanova was in the room and Errázuriz suggested that he undertake the project. Valdivieso interrupted: "No, my friend, it is for you."[35] Valdivieso gave him new documents that he had acquired on his recent European trip, and Errázuriz began writing *Los oríjenes de la iglesia chilena, 1540–1603* due to his "uncle's insistence." Published in 1873, Errázuriz' work, while continuing the standard interpretation of the Church and Spain's independent action during the colonial period, offered the same change of emphasis that Valdivieso had suggested to Eyzaguirre. Errázuriz argued that the independence of the Church was not easily achieved in the face of the "exaggerated regalism of the state which hindered the beneficent action of the Church at every turn." The heroes of this new study were not only those who fought for the welfare of the Indian, but also those who resisted "the oppressive laws of the state which became more demanding each day."[36]

The prime cause of this strict assertion of the Church's independence was the damning charges in Miguel Luis Amunátegui's recent work, *Los precur-*

34. *Revista Católica* (1874), 587; *El Progreso*, April 28, 1945; Araneda Bravo, *Errázuriz*, 50; See also C. Errázuriz, "El periódico católico," *Revista Católica*, August 31, 1872.
35. Araneda Bravo, *Errázuriz*, 94–95.
36. Crescente Errázuriz, *Los oríjenes de la iglesia chilena* (Santiago, 1873), 16–17.

sores de la independencia de Chile (1870–1872), which argued that the Spanish crown used the Church as a tool in its attempt to keep the people of the New World in abject subjugation. The wily advisers to the king had noticed that the gullible conquistadors and early settlers claimed that God and his agents had aided them in the fight against the Araucanians. If the colonists could show the same reverence to the king as to God, there would be no problems in governing that distant land. Thus the king used the Church and its missionaries to spread his image as the legitimate representative of God on earth, and the clergy aided his efforts without question. Errázuriz noted in response that his study of the origins of the Chilean Church was both an objective historical investigation to determine whether "the Church defended the unfortunate Indian or allowed the *encomendero* to exploit him," as well as a critique of Amunátegui's study. "The publication of *Los precursores de la independencia de Chile* has forced me to print a refutation of a work that is so harmful to religion," claimed Errázuriz.[37]

Errázuriz fondly recalled his debates with Amunátegui several years later: "I will always remember this polemic as a model of serenity . . . not a harsh word was spoken; one might also say that it was as cordial as a discussion among friends in spite of the fact that we disagreed on many points."[38] Age apparently dimmed his memory, for these so-called discussions spanned six years and fostered two major historical works and more than twenty major newspaper articles. Exacerbating the tone of these articles was the fact that the Church had passed from a secure foothold in Chilean society when Amunátegui issued his challenge in 1871, to a threatened institution when Errázuriz began his replies in 1873.

With the election of Federico Errázuriz as president in 1871, the Church's position once again appeared safe. Conservatives dominated the cabinet and the minister of justice, religion, and public instruction, Abdón Cifuentes, had decreed the "liberty of education" which freed Catholic schools from the "state monopoly of educational institutions." The scandals ensuing from this decree thrust the Conservative ministry from power. Thus, many of the bills which threatened the prerogatives of the Church, including civil registration of births and deaths, marriage of dissidents, and immigration of non-Catholics soon were revived in the Congress. The tide seemed to have turned

37. Amunátegui, *Los precursores*; Errázuriz, *Oríjenes*, 13, 24.
38. Armando Donoso, *Recuerdos de cincuenta años* (Santiago, 1948), 237.

completely as the editorial board of the *Estandarte Católico* faced the specter of a non-believer for president in 1876.

Crescente Errázuriz himself became frightened as he saw the tentative alliance between Liberals and Conservatives splinter as a result of the attempted changes in the educational system, and promptly wrote to his cousin, the president, Federico Errázuriz. He noted that if he "separated from the Conservatives, he would be surrounded by men hostile to religion." Soon, despite the fact Federico was a good Catholic, he would "become an enemy of the Catholic cause due to events more powerful than his own will." Additionally, he reminded Federico how much he owed the Church and the Conservatives, who almost "singlehandedly supported him in his bid for the presidency." Federico Errázuriz replied to the letter the same day, and dismissing Crescente's charges as "inexact, erroneous, and injurious," he stopped writing to his cousin for several years.[39] Any hopes the Conservatives might have had seemed dashed, and Errázuriz thus faced Amunátegui's challenge with an uncompromising tenacity.

Amunátegui began his study claiming that he was only investigating the facts: "The historian is obliged to support his assertions with proof and documents if he does not want to be called an inventor instead of a narrative historian. I have had at my disposition a great number of documents, almost all unedited, which I have compiled with great labor and patience." Errázuriz responded that Amunátegui's reverence for facts and documents seemed empty. He noted that Amunátegui professed "a historical system which was detrimental to the study of history." Amunátegui worked backwards: "He established certain propositions and searched for the proof of his theories in past events. It was not the work of a historian, rather that of a lawyer."[40] This clear appraisal by Errázuriz revealed a prime characteristic of the nineteenth-century Chilean historian: the concern for facts, veracity, and objectivity could exist alongside an impassioned defense of an ideal, a person, or a political position without any sense of incongruity. Yet, why was it so easy to admit that another historian acted like a lawyer, merely using the concern for truth as an aura of respectability, but so difficult to see the same

39. Errázuriz articles in *El Estandarte Católico*, December 27, 1875, June 24, 1876.
40. M. L. Amunátegui, "Los oríjenes de la iglesia chilena, *Sud-América* (1873), Article I; Errázuriz, *Oríjenes*, 21, See also Gaspar Toro, "Los precursores de la independencia de Chile," *Revista de Santiago* (1872), 198–99. He suggested that Amunátegui was the "abogado de la historia."

pattern of activity in oneself? Errázuriz apparently faced the same criticism, since Amunátegui claimed that he also professed a historical system, that of the Catholic Church.[41]

Errázuriz was deeply offended by the charge: "In his reply, Sr. Amunátegui denies my work the only merit which I believe I have the right to claim: the complete impartiality in the exposition of facts and faithfulness to the sources that support my narrative."[42] Yet, unwittingly, Errázuriz seemed to profess that he also followed a system, that of the Catholic religion, which "was a secure guide and a firm support for his judgments." Thus certain bishops and priests became subject to criticism, namely, those "who supported the civil authority and sought its favors or protection, and those who did not give their superiors in the Church their most humble obedience."[43] The criteria for judgment became the dogma of the Catholic Church. Errázuriz' allegiance to this creed would produce a supreme irony, for soon after he would be forced to defend the heroes of the Independence period, sons of the Enlightenment, as good Catholics, and, at the same time, criticize the heroic Luis de Valdivia as a man who betrayed the teachings of his religion.

Amunátegui's next work, *La crónica de 1810*, professed to be a chronicle of the first days of the independence movement, and, ideally, as a chronicle, a purely objective narrative of the events. But, Errázuriz discovered a subtle argument in this work, as Amunátegui omitted any beneficent action of the Church and the clergy, and depicted everyone who favored independence as an "admirer of Voltaire, an enemy of the clergy," and all those who opposed independence as "good Catholics."[44] To successfully refute such arguments, Errázuriz was forced to argue that "the Catholic Church did not absolutely condemn revolutions," and that these followers of Voltaire were also faithful Catholics. The latter appeared difficult to prove, and in the face of a myriad of documents presented by Amunátegui, Errázuriz argued that the personal letters of José Antonio de Rojas to his son which claimed he was a non-believer were not necessarily proof of the man's opinions. After all, he could

41. M. L. Amunátegui, "Los oríjenes," Article I.

42. Errázuriz, "Los oríjenes de la iglesia chilena i el Sr. Amunátegui," *La Estrella de Chile*, July 27, 1873. See also August 10, 31, 1873, April 5, 1874.

43. *Ibid.*, August 10, 1873.

44. M. L. Amunátegui, *La crónica de 1810* (Santiago, 1876). The Errázuriz articles are reprinted in *Revista Chilena de Historia y Geografía*, I (1911), 372, 559; II (1912), 101, 361; III (1912), 34; IV (1912), 45; V (1913), 20; VI (1913), 5; VII (1913), 121.

have been lying to his son. Though he had responded to earlier Errázuriz writings, Amunátegui felt it unnecessary to answer these assertions, confident that he had proved his case.

Errázuriz appeared on firmer, if more unpopular, ground with his critique of Luis de Valdivia, which ran concurrently with his Amunátegui articles in the pages of *El Estandarte Católico*. He believed that Valdivia was overglorified, since his exaggerated renown put all others who fought for the glory of the Church in the shade, especially those who had opposed state interference in Church affairs. Valdivia actually was inferior to these unsung heroes, since, as Errázuriz claimed, he had actively supported the regalism of the state.[45] The charges were twofold. First Errázuriz claimed that Valdivia had arranged with Philip III for the removal of García Ramón as governor of the Kingdom of Chile and his replacement by Alonso de Rivera, whom Valdivia believed would be more sympathetic in his fight for Indian rights. Errázuriz asserted that Valdivia chose Rivera, a known enemy of the Church, for the position merely to further his personal goals.

But this error was minor compared to Valdivia's second flaw. Valdivia understood that he could be free to accomplish his plan of defensive warfare only if he had administrative power in both the political and religious spheres. Standing in his way for the latter was the obstinate bishop of Santiago, Juan Pérez de Espinosa, who opposed Valdivia's project. Errázuriz charged that Valdivia urged the king to write a letter of *ruego y encargo* which would force the local ecclesiastical tribunal to appoint Valdivia to the position of temporary bishop of Concepción, a post held at that time by Pérez de Espinosa. This plan was slightly changed by Valdivia after he realized the opposition of his superiors. He finally suggested that the king "request the Holy See to entrust the government of the diocese of Concepción to Father Valdivia for whatever period of time His Majesty deems convenient for the pacification of Chile . . . investing him with the powers of a bishop so that he might carry out His Majesty's plans for the pacification and conversion of the Kingdom of Chile."[46] He would exercise the "powers of a bishop" in the

---

45. Errázuriz articles: *El Estandarte Católico*, December 4, 11, 1875; November 21, 22, December 6, 14, 16, 23, 1876; and January 6, March 10–15, April 27, 28, 30, and May 1–3, 12, 1877. Zoilo Villalón articles: February 19–22, April 16–21, 23, 24, and May 6–11, 1877.

46. Korth, *Spanish Policy*, 125–26.

position of vicar-general, a position normally conferred on Jesuit missionaries in Japan and other distant lands. Thus, Valdivia would avoid the conflict with his superiors. Errázuriz sharply condemned Valdivia's scheming with the heads of state and his explicit sanction of the king's interference in the internal affairs of the Church. "Such ideas presented to any Jesuit would have been refused immediately, were he not totally blinded by his commitment to a cause. Unfortunately for the fame and renown of Valdivia, he was weak enough to take this step." While he hated to criticize such a great hero, Errázuriz noted that it was the duty of the Catholic historian in his search for truth. "It is my mission in writing history not to hide or censure evil where I find it."[47]

The leader of the Jesuits in Chile, Baltazar Homs, responded indignantly to the critique of Errázuriz and explained that he was presenting the articles and several important documents to a young Jesuit, Zoilo Villalón, a former secretary to Archbishop Valdivieso, who would answer these charges. Errázuriz coyly asserted that the Jesuits were attacking his works "because they disliked his newspaper" and were miffed that a young patron gave *Estandarte Católico* a large contribution which had been promised to the Jesuits.[48] Despite his attempt to belittle the importance of this challenge, the results of this confrontation were surprisingly dramatic.

Both Villalón and Errázuriz first attempted to criticize the other's use of the documents. Here Errázuriz appeared the victor. He had recently received newly discovered documents from Barros Arana and Vicuña Mackenna. After writing his initial articles he lent the documents to Francisco Enrich, S.J., who was writing a history of the Jesuits in Chile, and was therefore unable to make them available to Villalón. Villalón was forced to resort to the Jesuit chronicles of the colonial period in the attempt to prove his assertions. Errázuriz, however, found these documents of dubious value:

The only historians that lived at the same time as Valdivia were the Jesuits Ovalle and Rosales; the first entered the Jesuits in the year Valdivia went to Spain never to return, and the second wrote his work fifty years after the event we are discussing. Thus, you cannot claim that "contemporary historians who wrote what their eyes saw and their ears heard" contradict me, since they do not exist.[49]

47. *El Estandarte Católico*, December 14, 1876, and December 6, 1876.
48. *Ibid.*, February 19, 1877; Errázuriz, *Algo*, 210.
49. *El Estandarte Católico*, March 10, 1877.

When Villalón realized that the argument could not be won by the appeal to the facts, he resorted to another scheme. He recalled that Valdivieso himself had assumed the position of *vicario capitular*, acting as provisional archbishop of Santiago, by means of a letter of *ruego y encargo*.[50] He then queried: What would historians say about this fact two centuries from now? Would they allow this fact to stain his fine reputation? Crescente Errázuriz defended his uncle by noting that he had resigned as *vicario capitular* before the election of archbishop by the ecclesiastical council. However, this was a mere *pro forma* gesture, which did little to counter the charges of Villalón. Despite the disclaimer of Errázuriz, Valdivieso was deeply hurt by these debates. Errázuriz later recalled: "Villalón knew that nothing would hurt Valdivieso more than the charge that he was a partisan of regalism, which he had spent his whole life opposing. This was equivalent to saying that Valdivieso forgot his principles when he tried to obtain the nomination for Archbishop."[51] Although Errázuriz did not broach the question of Valdivieso's assumption of the Archbishopric himself, Valdivieso stopped talking to him. He rode past Errázuriz in his carriage without acknowledging his presence. Valdivieso died a few weeks later, without speaking again to the nephew he had so deeply loved.

It should not have surprised Errázuriz that a study of sixteenth-century Chile could offend a contemporary, for this was indicative of the type of history written by the Catholic historians. Their history existed on two levels: it was indeed a study of the past, but the importance of their history remained in the present to support claims of the independence of Church affairs from state interference. Thus, when the Church was least threatened, the clerical historians were able to explore the heroic exploits of missionaries during the colonial period. However, after the "affair of the sacristan," the defense of Church priorities was paramount, and the past was judged with the independence of the Church as the prime criterion. The clerical interpretation of Chilean history changed from the heroic and elegiac to the critical and the defensive as the position of the Church in Chilean society became threatened. Despite protestations to the contrary, the type of history envisioned by Valdivieso and Errázuriz was functional, an ideological weapon in the battle against the secularization of nineteenth-century Chilean society.

50. Encina, *Historia de Chile*, XII, 376–82.
51. Araneda Bravo, *Errázuriz*, 105.

6

HISTORIANS AS DIPLOMATS

THE CHILEAN BOUNDARY DISPUTES

WHILE HISTORIANS were often critical of the governments of nineteenth-century Chile, they were also willing to assist them if their goals coincided. For example, the boundary disputes with Argentina and Bolivia stimulated all of the major Chilean historians in the attempt to determine Chile's legal borders fairly. The usefulness of the historians in this situation resulted from the individual decisions of ten South American countries and the United States to use the rule of *uti possidetis juris* in the demarcation of their boundaries, which dictated that the colonial limits as determined by Spanish legislation would remain unchanged for the newly independent nations.[1] While all agreed to the principle, few were able to precisely determine their boundaries at the beginning of the Independence era. This dilemma forced several South American governments to turn to historians for aid, in the hope that they might have encountered documents which could definitively prove the nation's boundaries.

Unfortunately, all nations claimed to possess the appropriate documents, and Chile's task of asserting ownership of the mineral-rich Atacama desert in the North and the Patagonian region in the South became more difficult than

---

1. This concept, derived from Roman Praetorian law, was officially adopted by Colombia, Ecuador, Peru, Bolivia, and Chile at the Congress of Lima in 1847. Actual occupation of the lands (*uti posseditis de facto*) had no influence on the territorial boundaries. All that mattered was the colonial legislation (*uti posseditis juris*). See Valentín Abecia Baldivieso, *Historiografía Boliviana* (La Paz, 1965), 347, and John L. Phelan, *The Kingdom of Quito in the Seventeenth Century* (Madison, 1967), 38–40, 119–121.

Ministers Antonio Varas of Chile and Felipe Arana of Argentina could have imagined in their early negotiations. The search for a definitive document became an impossible quest. With hundreds of valuable acres of land at stake, each nation discovered that a remnant of the past might be interpreted in many ways, and possibly in a manner that would ensure the nation's annexation of new territory. As a result, the objective study of documents became an impossibility, as historians attempted to serve their governments' expansionary goals.

The Chilean claim to Patagonia, the Strait of Magellan, and Tierra del Fuego, at the southern tip of the continent, rested on the founding of a small colony, Fort Bulnes, in 1843. Manuel Bulnes, then president of the republic, had encouraged settlement in the Strait region both to give Chile access to the Atlantic and protect it against foreign invasion. Such fears were not illusory. British scientific expeditions had been snooping in the region since 1823, and Bernardo O'Higgins had been positive that the English were actually engaged in spying. A new fleet of British ships arrived in the area in 1843 which excited similar fears.

A small Chilean force of twenty-three sailors and six artillery men, two with their wives, set sail in early 1843 for the southern climes under the command of Juan Guillermos (John Williams), a British captain who had served in the Chilean navy since 1824. The crew raised a flag at Port Hunger in May of 1843. The site was aptly named since members of Pedro Sarmiento's previous expedition in the sixteenth century had starved to death while awaiting aid. Shortly thereafter, Williams renamed the site Fort Bulnes.[2]

The Argentine Confederation offered no immediate response to the occupation of the Strait of Magellan for a variety of reasons. First, Chile had emerged from the war against Santa Cruz and the Peru-Bolivian Confederation as the undisputed power of South America, and the chaotic domestic situation in La Plata was hardly propitious for a firm assertion of Argentine rights. When Juan Manuel de Rosas finally protested the Chilean occupation in 1847, he was also faced with the French blockade of Buenos Aires, and thus unable to shake the Chileans' complacency. The note of the minister of foreign relations, Felipe Arana, however, directed the path of all future nego-

2. Diego Barros Arana, *Un decenio de la historia de Chile* (Santiago, 1913), I, 358–66. See also Armando Braun Menéndez, *Fuerte Bulnes* (Buenos Aires, 1968).

tiations by claiming that "the territorial divisions of the South American re-
publics should be the same as those of the viceroyalties."[3] Unable to force
Chile to surrender control of the Strait, Rosas, satisfied with the Chilean acceptance of the doctrine of *uti possidetis juris*, entrusted the task of proving
Argentine ownership of the Strait to a young historian, Pedro de Ángelis.

The choice was indeed fitting. De Ángelis was an avid bibliophile and an
inveterate wanderer through the archives and libraries of Buenos Aires. Fascinated by the wealth of unedited documents, de Ángelis decided "to save the
past from being forgotten and prevent the destruction of documents which
had remained buried for centuries in remote corners of the world."[4] He then
convinced Rosas of the value of his project and was permitted to use the government press for his endeavor. He readily gathered 488 subscribers to his
work. Six volumes were printed before the French blockade prevented the
further importation of paper. Volume one of the collection of documents included several descriptions of the Patagonian region and the fourth volume
presented treaties between Spain and Portugal on the boundaries of the New
World territories. Rosas was impressed by these volumes of 1836 and 1837,
and proposed that de Ángelis undertake a defense of Argentine rights in the
Strait region. In 1852 de Ángelis published his study and claimed that Chile
had no right to the Strait of Magellan. He included 45 *cédulas reales* proving
the right of the Argentine Confederation to the region and 164 documents
demonstrating that the Argentines had established settlements in the South
prior to Fort Bulnes in 1843.[5]

The Chileans who had formerly asserted their right to the southern tip of
the continent without bothering to supply the appropriate documents were
disturbed by the de Ángelis tract, and they eagerly sought to counter the
Argentine claims. Claude Gay, who had published a multivolume history of
Chile in 1842, began noticing a strange flurry of activity in the Madrid archives as a result of the government's desire to discover historical support for
the Chilean occupation of the Strait. Gay noticed the Chilean agent in
Madrid, Colonel José María Sesé, taking an unusual interest in historical research. He then wrote to his friend Manuel Montt:

3. M. L. Amunátegui, *Títulos de la República de Chile a la soberanía i dominio de la estremidad austral del continente americano* (Santiago, 1855), 17. Henceforth cited as *Títulos*
(1855).

4. Elías Díaz Molano, *Vida y obra de Pedro de Ángelis* (Santa Fe, Argentina, 1968), 89.

5. *Ibid.*, 118–19.

In the past few days I met a gentleman in the archive who has been hired by Sesé to investigate the limits of Chile. I thought at first that it was a personal interest of Sesé and paid no attention to his studies. Somewhat later, however, I realized that the government desired him to undertake this investigation of Chile's northern and southern limits. I wish I had known, since I, too, might have directed my investigations toward this question.[6]

Gay himself was later approached by General José Francisco Gana and was requested to discover historical evidence proving Chile's right to the Atacama desert in the North. He again wrote to Montt: "If you believe that my great experience in the study of ancient manuscripts can be helpful, I will gladly return to Seville and Peru and review the materials in their archives and perhaps the question can be resolved. If not, I can study the documents in Madrid concerning South America which I have not yet examined because of their state of disarray."[7]

The efforts of Gay and Sesé bore little fruit, but Antonio Varas, then minister of the interior, entrusted the reply to de Ángelis' claims to a young and relatively inexperienced historian, Miguel Luis Amunátegui, and the resulting study firmly stated Chile's territorial claims. In 1853, Amunátegui published his defense of Chilean rights in the South, *Títulos de la República de Chile a la soberanía i dominio de la estremidad austral del continente americano*, and fully satisfied Varas' faith in him. Not only did he claim that Chile maintained full rights to the Strait of Magellan, but he also asserted that Chile owned Patagonia as well. Formerly there had been no discussion of Patagonia between Argentina and Chile, but Amunátegui's apparent discovery of new documents added a vast new territory to the boundary deliberations, and, certainly, proved the surprising value of the historian to the Montt government.[8]

In addition to presenting documents dating from Pedro de Valdivia's instructions on his arrival in Chile in 1541 as proof of Chilean territorial rights, Amunátegui also attempted to deflate de Ángelis' image as a historian. He wondered why de Ángelis did not discover the documents which proved Chilean assertions. They were readily available, since the *Recopilación*

6. Guillermo Feliú Cruz and Stuardo Ortiz (eds.), *Correspondencia de Claudio Gay* (Santiago, 1962), 115.

7. *Ibid.*, L.

8. Francisco Encina, *La cuestión de límites entre Chile y la Argentina desde la Independencia hasta el tratado de 1881* (Santiago, 1959).

de Indias (Lei 12, Tit. 15, Lib. 2) provided ample evidence. Rather, Amunátegui charged that de Ángelis deliberately overlooked documents: "It is not possible that de Ángelis forgot about these documents; more than likely, he did not take these titles into account since they decide the dispute in Chile's favor, and no reply would be possible. If he had discussed the laws that were included in my work, he would not have been able to write his study."[9]

Amunátegui's surprising challenge prompted a quick response from across the cordillera, and Rosas entrusted a young lawyer and professor of political economy at the University of Buenos Aires to review de Ángelis' work and respond to Amunátegui. Dalmacio Vélez Sársfield found de Ángelis' study an adequate survey of Argentine claims to the Strait, but noted that he had been unable to discuss Chilean claims since they were unknown at that time. Vélez Sársfield prepared a new study which refuted all Chilean claims to the South. The work was originally destined for Rosas' personal use, but the Argentine leader decided "it could be of some utility" and ordered it published by the government press in 1855.[10]

Varas learned of the new treatise and again urged Amunátegui to draft a response. In February, 1855, the government published a second Amunátegui study with the same name as the earlier work, but with a lengthy, but appropriate subtitle: "A Refutation of the *memoria* published in Buenos Aires by Doctor Dalmacio Vélez Sársfield entitled 'A Discussion of the Claims of the Chilean Government to the Lands of the Strait of Magellan.'" Amunátegui both repeated the assertions of his previous study and attempted to destroy the arguments of Vélez Sársfield by noting that he used false quotations and "had little knowledge of the history of America and of Chile in particular."[11] Despite several flippant attacks against Vélez Sársfield, Amunátegui's work was once again a well-reasoned defense of Chile's rights.

Amunátegui's latest arguments even impressed the Argentines. De Ángelis wrote Barros Arana that the "works of Señor Amunátegui ought to be known and appreciated by scientific societies in Europe." He also enclosed a letter written in French for Amunátegui, since he assumed that the author of

9. M. L. Amunátegui, *Títulos de la República de Chile a la soberanía i dominio de la estremidad austral del continente americano* (Santiago, 1853), 35, 71. Henceforth cited as *Títulos* (1853).

10. Abel Cháneton, *Historia de Vélez Sársfield* (Buenos Aires, 1938); Díaz Molano, *De Ángelis*, 120.

11. Amunátegui, *Títulos* (1853), 118.

such erudite treatises had to be one of the foreign scientists who had been brought to Chile during the Portales era.[12] The Argentines appeared concilia-tory after the latest Amunátegui work, but, most likely, the disorder follow-ing the fall of Rosas also explained the hesitancy to press their demands. The resulting Treaty of 1856 (the Benavente–La Marca Treaty) did little to re-solve the disputed claims. It was agreed that both nations would observe the 1810 boundaries, but, most important for the Argentines, the pact delayed discussion of the boundaries until a future date "when they may be discussed peaceably and amicably without resorting to violent means."[13] Although the resolution of the Argentine question was postponed until a future date, Amunátegui did not remain free to rest and return to his own university du-ties. A new debate with Bolivia concerning the Atacama desert again led Amunátegui to defend Chilean territorial claims.

During the last years of the Wars of Independence and the early years of the republic, neither Chile nor the Bolivian Confederation had bothered to claim or dispute the arid Atacama desert region. However, during the 1830s, Chileans began to discover both guano and nitrate deposits in the southern Atacama desert and especially in Mejillones. In 1843, President Bulnes decreed that Chile owned all land south of the twenty-third parallel, and Boliva was in no position to dispute the action. During the Montt years, Chilean and British capital entered the region, turning a formerly unpopu-lated desert area into a flourishing source of riches, thus exciting Bolivian desires to partake in the newfound wealth. The Chilean government refused all Bolivian claims politely but firmly until the beginning of the Pérez re-gime in 1861, when the Bolivian Congress voted to declare war on Chile unless the dispute were resolved. Suddenly, the Chilean government realized that the Bolivian claims had to be taken seriously.[14]

The daily papers accentuated the importance of the threat and noted that a Bolivian historian had been spotted in the Valparaíso library of Gregorio Beeche collecting documents to prove Bolivia's right to the Atacama. A cor-respondent warned: "We see that the government is taking no similar action and it appears satisifed with the titles to Atacama that it already possesses,

12. Diego Barros Arana, "Don Miguel Luis Amunátegui," in C. Morla Vicuña, *Don Miguel Luis Amunátegui* (Paris, 1889), 36.
13. Encina, *La cuestión de límites*, 21.
14. Agustín Edwards, *Cuatro presidentes de Chile* (Valparaíso, 1932), Ch. 18. See also Francisco Encina, *Las relaciones entre Chile y Bolivia, 1841–1963* (Santiago, 1963).

believing them quite sufficient. . . . We believe that our most famous historians should search the archives and libraries and write pamphlets that show the truth to the civilized world. The more abundant the information and documents, the more powerfully can we counter the arguments of the Bolivian government and press."[15] The article then recalled the great services of Amunátegui during the Argentine debates, but he did not need such encouragement. He was already at work.

By this time, Amunátegui considered himself the defender of Chilean territorial claims and undertook the latest study on his own initiative. He then printed *La cuestión de límites entre Chile i Bolivia* at his own expense and distributed it among his friends. Eventually Varas and Manuel Tocornal, the new minister of the interior, deciding that Amunátegui's work ably presented the government's position, bought all remaining copies and reimbursed Amunátegui for the publication costs.[16] The five-hundred-peso remuneration infuriated Amunátegui's friend José Victorino Lastarria, then on a diplomatic mission in Lima, since he felt the work was so valuable for Chilean claims. He wrote to his friend: "It is unfortunate that you have sent me so few copies of your book, since many people here are reading it. Fortunately, your work has called public attention to the question. . . . You perform an honorable service for Chile by proving her rights to the possession of the Atacama desert with these documents." He, too, began searching the archives for a missing *cédula*. The same day Lastarria wrote Tocornal chiding him for not appreciating Amunátegui's services to Chile. While the defender of Bolivia's rights received "national prizes" in Bolivia and "gold medals" in Peru, Amunátegui had received only "five hundred miserable pesos." He then urged Tocornal to correct this wrong and "innundate America with this work so the justice of our cause would be understood by all."[17]

Amunátegui again surprised his audience by arguing that Chile had titles to the whole Atacama desert, thus, as in the Patagonian case, claiming more territory than the government had ever dared. His response to Manuel Macedonio Salinas' *Derecho de Bolivia a la soberanía del desierto de Atacama* (1860) appeared more labored than the Argentine studies. While Amunátegui had no difficulty supplying the documents supporting Chile's cause, cer-

15. *El Mercurio*, June 4, 1863.
16. Barros Arana, "Amunátegui," 73.
17. Domingo Amunátegui Solar, *Archivo epistolar de Don Miguel Luis Amunátegui* (Santiago, 1942), I, 159, 160.

tain phrases could be open to varying interpretations. The Bolivians laid claim to the Atacama desert by citing a letter of Pedro de Valdivia to Charles V, which stated that "he had journeyed to the valley of Copiapó which is the beginning of this land, after passing the unpopulated Atacama desert." The Bolivians thus believed that Copiapó was the northern border of Chile. Amunátegui, however, considered this a misunderstanding, due to the "sloppy and incorrect grammar used by military men in the sixteenth century." He argued that Valdivia really meant that he was walking from the "unpopulated part of Chile (Atacama) to the populated part (Copiapó)." Also causing Amunátegui difficulty were the Constitutions of 1822, 1823, 1828, and 1833, which declared that Chile stretched from (*desde*) the Atacama desert in the North to Cape Horn in the South. Unfortunately, the word *from* was ambiguous. Did it mean "from, and including" the desert, as Chileans claimed, or, as the Bolivians argued "from, but excluding"?[18] Unlike the Argentines, the Bolivians were not as easily convinced or discouraged by Amunátegui's arguments. In 1864, Bolivia broke relations with Chile and war seemed imminent.

As in the Argentine affair, external events again delayed the resolution of the dispute, whether by peaceful or martial means. As Chile and Bolivia prepared for war, a so-called Spanish "scientific expedition" under Admiral Pareja rounded the Horn and soon after laid claim to the guano-rich Chincha Islands owned by Peru. The justification of the seizure was "revindication" of lands lost during the Wars of Independence, a euphemism for reconquest. Peru soon succumbed to Spanish demands and agreed to pay a three-million-peso "indemnification" for the islands. Pareja relinquished the islands, but remained determined to punish the Chileans, who had loudly criticized the Spanish activities. First, a blockade was declared, and soon after Valparaíso was bombed. Chile's diminutive fighting fleet, one eighteen-cannon corvette and a four-cannon steamship, could do little to counter the eight Spanish warships with 208 cannon. Chile then entered into an alliance with Peru, Ecuador, and Bolivia, and, as a result of a confidential agent's assurances to Bolivia, the Atacama boundary dispute was delayed until the threat of war was over. The Treaty of 1866, signed after Pareja had been forced to leave the Pacific, was a model of amity. The Chilean northern border was lowered to the twenty-fourth parallel, and both nations agreed on norms for taxing met-

18. M. L. Amunátegui, *La cuestión de límites entre Chile i Bolivia* (Santiago, 1863), 21.

als extracted from the other's territories. The treaty was as short-lived as the spirit of alliance dictated by the Spanish menace.[19] But, again, a delay occurred in the final settlement of Chile-Bolivian boundaries, and Chile was again able to turn its attention to affairs with Argentina in the South.

The revived Argentine question in the 1870s had to be treated more delicately than before. Argentina had emerged victorious from the five-year Paraguayan War and her booming economy, population growth due to immigration, and increased foreign trade gave Chile second thoughts about her own domination in the South. Already, Argentina had ignored the provisions of the 1856 treaty and had begun establishing small settlements in Patagonia. Fortunately for Chile, the new minister of foreign relations, Adolfo Ibáñez, a former judge, vigorously asserted Chile's rights to Patagonia. Contributing to his efforts was the separation of the ministry of foreign relations from the ministry of the interior, which allowed Ibáñez to devote all of his energy to the boundary negotiations.[20] Félix Frías, the Argentine representative in Chile, surprised Ibáñez by rejecting a generous compromise which would have divided Patagonia in half but would have given Chile total control of the Strait of Magellan. While Ibáñez offered to concede more land than ever before in hope of a quick settlement of the issue, Frías insisted on Argentine claims to all Patagonia, the eastern mouth of the Strait of Magellan, and half of Tierra del Fuego. Both representatives seemed intransigent in the extreme, and when Frías replied that his country would never allow Chile an outlet to the Atlantic, Ibáñez countered that he believed "Chile had a right to all Patagonia, and that when the occasion arrived, Chile would present the documents supporting its case."[21]

The search for these documents began anew. First, Ibáñez ordered the secretary of the Chilean Legation in France, Carlos Morla Vicuña, to travel immediately to Spain and begin searching the archives. Unfortunately, Morla Vicuña was not a trained historian. His literary experience was limited to a brief term as editor of the daily *La República* in 1869, and he had translated Longfellow's *Evangeline* into Spanish. For this reason, his task appeared unusually difficult. He soon wrote to the Chilean ambassador in France, Alberto Blest Gana:

19. Robert N. Burr, *By Reason or Force* (Berkeley, 1967), 97–99.
20. See Ximena Rojas Valdés, *Don Adolfo Ibáñez* (Santiago, 1970); Edwards, *Cuatro presidentes*, II, 136.
21. Encina, *La cuestión de límites*, 48.

In spite of my efforts and my desire to continue this task which I find more and more interesting each day, I am experiencing many difficulties. I do not have the training necessary for reading manuscripts, but the employees of the archive help me in this endeavor. I am trying to master the shapes of the letters and the most curious abbreviations. . . . My incompetence is complicated by yet another matter . . . the disorder of the documents and the lack of a classification system, indices, or inventories, which make me lose precious time.[22]

Also complicating Morla Vicuña's life in Spain were the street disturbances that often forced the archive to close early, as well as a broken arm, which hindered his ability to write. Despite the fact that he wrote a pamphlet in French in 1876 refuting an article of Emile Daireux which supported the Argentine claims, Morla Vicuña's slow working habits did little to aid the boundary negotiations.[23] The only result of his efforts was a large shipment of foreign documents for the National Archive in Santiago.

Amunátegui, who was again entrusted with preparing the exposition of Chile's rights to the southern lands, was also annoyed with Morla Vicuña's progress. He commented to a friend that "although Morla had compiled a vast portfolio of documents, no one knew exactly what it contained. He kept the documents so close to himself, that one would suspect that they brought dishonor to his family name." Adding to the pressure arising from Morla's handling of the documents was the rapidly accelerating pace of the negotiations due to the recent completion of a Santiago to Buenos Aires telegraph line.[24] Also, while Amunátegui had busied himself with other affairs, several new Argentine treatises had been written, all of which claimed to refute definitively the contentions of his 1853 and 1855 studies.[25]

While Ibáñez merely requested that Amunátegui prepare a new edition of his earlier studies since they were now out of print, Amunátegui had discovered several new documents since 1855 and found it necessary to rewrite his earlier works. Also, responding to a complaint of Manuel Ricardo Trelles, he decided to insert all documents in complete form, since the Ar-

22. Guillermo Feliú Cruz, *Historiografía colonial de Chile* (Santiago, 1958), 118–120.

23. Carlos Morla Vicuña, *Estudios históricos sobre el descubrimiento y conquista de la Patagonia y de la Tierra del Fuego* (Leipzig, 1903), 25; José Miguel Yrarrázaval Larraín, *La Patagonia* (Santiago, 1966), 88.

24. Amunátegui to A. Fierro, February 4, 1879, reprinted in *Anales de la Universidad de Chile* (1958), 55; John J. Johnson, *Pioneer Telegraphy in Chile, 1852–1876* (Stanford, 1948).

25. Yrarrázaval Larraín, *La Patagonia*, 85–90. See also Raúl A. Molina, *Misiones argentinas en los archivos europeos* (Mexico City, 1955), 75–126.

gentine had objected to the use of fragments "which made it difficult to judge the exactitude of the Chilean argument."[26]

Despite the renewed urgency of the affair, Amunátegui was not able to work as quickly as he had previously. During the 1870s he was a deputy from Talca, a presidential aspirant, and minister of justice, religion, and public instruction in the first cabinet of President Aníbal Pinto in 1876. However, he worked diligently and completed the first volume in *La cuestión de límites entre Chile i la República Argentina* in 1878. Two more volumes followed in 1880 which carried the work to the seventeenth century. The study was well received both by literary critics and those involved in the boundary negotiations. The Spanish critic Menéndez Pelayo considered it "a new display of Amunátegui's profound knowledge and erudition." Ibáñez was quite satisfied with Amunátegui's work and used his discoveries in letters to the Argentine representatives and in his Senate speeches. Lastarria had nothing but praise for his work, and took several copies on his diplomatic mission to Brazil. He gave copies to the prominent leaders of Brazilian political life, and even Pedro II was greatly pleased with the work.[27]

Despite the apparent success of Amunátegui's study, a completed fourth volume remained unpublished, since an agreement on the limits question was reached in 1881. Chile gave up all claims to Patagonia, half of Tierra del Fuego, and retained sovereignty only over the Strait of Magellan. Amunátegui's defense of Chile's rights was thus no longer needed. Patagonia was lost for Chile, and Amunátegui's studies never achieved their desired goal of reserving the tip of South America for Chile. Were the efforts of a historian trying to defend his nation's rights totally worthless? If the doctrine of *uti possidetis juris* was to govern the boundary negotiations, why, ultimately, was no heed paid to Amunátegui's advice? The bitter irony was due to the fact that Amunátegui was isolated in this affair, as the other major historians of the era—Lastarria, Barros Arana, and Vicuña Mackenna—thought it would be better if Chile ceded control of Patagonia to Argentina. What of the documents Amunátegui had discovered? Merely "wormy, moth-eaten pieces of

26. Amunátegui, *La cuestión de límites*, I, 11–12.

27. For the candidacy of Amunátegui, see *El Mercurio*, February 10, 13, August 3, October 1, 8, 1875, and Cristián Zegers A., *Aníbal Pinto: Historia política de su gobierno* (Santiago, 1969), 8–10; *Anales de la Universidad de Chile*, Nos. 109–110 (1958), 58; Ministerio de Relaciones Exteriores, *Cuestión de límites entre Chile y la República Argentina* (Santiago, 1874); Amunátegui Solar, *Archivo epistolar*, I, 183.

paper," Vicuña Mackenna replied.[28] While Amunátegui worked almost alone as a government historian in defending Chile's claims, the others worked for opposite goals, and, suddenly, the documents that Amunátegui discovered had no meaning or worth. Why, then, was Patagonia lost, and how and why did these historians, who had been taught the importance of original documents from Andrés Bello, freely dismiss them when they considered other goals of greater importance?

Although Amunátegui discovered the existence of documents proving Chile's right to Patagonia, few historians considered this area worthy of such an inordinate fuss. While any historian in Chile might know the streets of Madrid, the cafes of Paris, and the historical monuments of Boston or New York, none had actually been anywhere near Patagonia, and were therefore greatly influenced by the few published travelers' accounts of journeys to the South. The most illustrious of these voyagers was a rather young and naïve fledgling scientist, Charles Darwin. His ship, the *Beagle*, under the command of Captain Fitzroy, reached South America in 1832, and the young scientist was quite dismayed by what he saw. The region appeared a vast desert to him, and the only water he ever saw was saline, except in the rainy season. The land was rocky and vegetation scarce. He concluded his evaluation of Patagonia by noting that "the sterile land extended throughout the entire area as though it were a living hell."[29]

Few Chileans were prepared to counter Darwin's description of the South, and the myth of the sterility of Patagonia was widely accepted among intellectuals and political leaders. Barros Arana prepared a textbook, *Elements of Physical Geography*, for the National Institute, and described Patagonia as an "immense desert."[30] Vicuña Mackenna followed suit, and quoting an English traveler, Beerbohm, found Patagonia "a piece of petrified ocean, sterile, lonely, silent, and damned." Only one Chilean, Vicente Pérez Rosales, saw any hope for the Patagonian region, noting possibilities for agriculture, and acknowledging the existence of coal deposits. Unfortunately, Pérez Rosales, who had been hired by the government to encourage immigration from Eu-

28. Yrarrázaval Larraín, *La Patagonia*, 85.

29. Charles Darwin, *Mi viaje alredor del mundo* (Buenos Aires, 1970).

30. See Humberto Fuenzalida Villegas, "Barros Arana y la geografía," *Anales de la Universidad de Chile*, nos. 109–10 (1958), 272–82.

rope, published his opinions in a pamphlet designed to convince French families of the myriad of opportunities awaiting them in Chile.[31] The glowing portrait of Patagonia was no more convincing than an alluring travel brochure of today, and his optimistic views were given little credence.

However, the sterility of a disputed territory has never prevented nations from desiring it, and this was no exception. The supposed worthlessness of Patagonia served as a convenient rationalization for Chileans who wished to cede the disputed area to Argentina. The prime factor in the willingness to lose Patagonia was the realization that South American unity ought to be valued more highly than any strip of land. The "Americanism" of Lastarria, Barros Arana, and Vicuña Mackenna thus dictated the loss of Patagonia, and they summoned all the powers at their disposal, including the writing of history, in order to achieve their goal.

The ideal of American unity had rarely been discussed in recent years. Only the threat of European intervention in the New World managed to revive a proposition that Bolívar had stressed during the Independence era.[32] The reannexation of Santo Domingo by Spain in 1861, and the threat of French, British, and Spanish intervention in Mexico in 1861 and 1862, led a small group of Chileans to form a "Society of American Union." Former president Bulnes joined the group, along with Lastarria, Vicuña Mackenna, Domingo Santa María, and Alvaro Covarrubias. Almost immediately, the society began publishing pamphlets supporting their cause; and they soundly criticized anyone, such as President Bartolomé Mitre and Foreign Minister Elizalde of Argentina, who did not view the European activities "as a threat to American independence and democracy."

As the Spanish forces entered the Pacific waters and seized the Chincha Islands, the protest passed from the private level to the governmental. Cognizant of the threat, President Pérez circulated a letter to the other South American nations exhorting them to cooperate in every way.[33] The Pérez gov-

31. Vicente Pérez Rosales, *Ensayo sobre Chile* (Santiago, 1859).

32. Ricardo Donoso, *Don Benjamín Vicuña Mackenna: Su vida, sus escritos, y su tiempo* (Santiago, 1925), 143. For a discussion of the Lima Congress of 1847, see Barros Arana, *Un decenio*, II, 225.

33. Robert W. Frazer, "The Role of the Lima Congress, 1864–1865, in the Development of Pan-Americanism," *Hispanic American Historical Review*, XXIX (August, 1949), 319–48. See also Mark J. Van Aken, *Pan-Hispanism: Its Origin and Development to 1866* (Berkeley, 1959).

ernment also replaced Manuel Tocornal, minister of the interior, by Alvaro Covarrubias, a former member of the Society of American Union, who would be more capable of dealing with the rapidly changing situation.[34] The government also sent former president Montt to the Lima Congress of 1864, thus displaying its recognition of the importance of the event. While Colombia, Venezuela, and Ecuador argued for a compulsory confederation of all South American nations at the congress, Montt was unwilling to surrender Chile's sovereignty and proposed a voluntary arrangement, which suggested a governing body functioning as a clearing-house for the drafting of mutual assistance and arbitration treaties.[35]

The public initiative for unity was continued via private negotiations, as Lastarria was sent to Argentina to enter into an anti-Spanish alliance with Mitre in 1865. Covarrubias chose his friend from the Society for American Union for the diplomatic post, and reemphasized that "the primary object" of his mission was a treaty of alliance, while also explaining that he might attempt to resolve the Patagonian question, which was left in limbo by the inconclusive Treaty of 1856. Lastarria's mission was to be more difficult than he had expected. By the time he arrived in Buenos Aires the entire atmosphere had abruptly changed. Spain had announced that it would abandon the doctrine of "revindication" and would return the Chincha Islands to Peru for a price. Thus Mitre no longer conceived of the Spanish expedition as a threat. For this reason, Mitre and Elizalde immediately rejected Lastarria's project of alliance, and Lastarria then withdrew the proposal.

Lastarria, however, decided to display Chile's good intentions and resolve the Patagonian dispute. He then proposed to Mitre that Chile would surrender Patagonia and half the Strait of Magellan. Lastarria then wrote Covarrubias, explaining: "The transaction will be favorable to us since our rights to Patagonia are not sustainable, and, even if they were, we ought not to fool ourselves and believe that Patagonia is anything but a primitive land, uncultivable, and unfavorable to the habits and aspirations of industry." Covarrubias was quite shocked by Lastarria's attempt, and wrote that his terms were "far from favorable." Lastarria responded two days later, claiming that he was persuaded that Chile did not have a legitimate title to the lands. He added: "Sr. Amunátegui, in his attempt to provide Chile's control of Pata-

34. For the opinions of Covarrubias, see J. V. Lastarria, *La América*, in *Obras completas* (Santiago, 1909), VIII, 188–90.
35. Burr, *By Reason or Force*, 93.

gonia, uses pure induction based on ingenious interpretations of official documents as a means of proof."[36]

Covarrubias was irate and suggested that Lastarria reread Amunátegui's two works and see that his work "is not based on ingenious interpretations, as you think, but on the text of the documents of the Crown of Spain, the only irrevocable authority in this matter." Shortly thereafter, Lastarria drafted a letter to Amunátegui which claimed that his attempt "to prove Chilean ownership of the southern tip of the continent was completely useless." He added, "Perhaps I do not know as much as you, but the study of the situation convinces me that we are not masters of Patagonia."[37]

Lastarria's reversal appears strange. Just two years earlier he had praised Amunátegui's use of documents as proof of territorial claims and urged that he receive a national prize for his work. However, by 1865, Lastarria viewed Chilean claims to Patagonia as a hindrance to his dreams of American unity in this time of international troubles, and, consequently, he felt that the documents were hardly worth the paper on which they were printed. In order to counter the force of Amunátegui's arguments, Lastarria also resorted to history for support for his position. First, he attempted to construct a myth of long-standing Argentine-Chilean friendship which would override any divisions resulting from the Patagonian question. He noted to Covarrubias: "I call attention to (the hospitality) of the people of Buenos Aires, citizens whom Chile has titles to a great friendship from the days of the alliance of the Independence era, a friendship proven with historical facts, public monuments, and official acts."[38]

In addition to stressing this ideal in all public gatherings, Lastarria also attempted to spread his "Americanist" philosophy by writing books and contributing articles to newspapers. He also helped sponsor a newspaper "which argued the American cause" by contributing 3,000 Argentine pesos. Additionally, he wrote *La América* while on his diplomatic mission. He commented to Covarrubias:

Faithful to my instructions and the desire of Chile to promote American interests and a unified political position, I have worked incessantly since my arrival to achieve this goal. Being unable to convince the Argentine government to waver from its

36. Carlos Larraín de Castro, "La misión Lastarria," *Boletín de la Academia Chilena de Historia*, no. 10 (1938), 68, 77.

37. Amunátegui Solar, *Archivo epistolar*, I, 167.

38. Larraín de Castro, "La misión Lastarria," 68.

policy of treason to America, I have tried to form a public opinion favorable to American interests. For this reason, I have published and am sending you a book entitled *La América*. Its sole object is to make our interests known by showing the natural political antagonism which exists between our continent and the Old World.[39]

The intent of *La América* was both deceiving and confusing to the Argentines. The work assumed the form of a history of liberal ideals from Ancient Greece to modern Europe, and argued that the Old World had much to learn from the new South American nations. Lastarria claimed that despite the advanced liberal theories of Mill, Saint-Simon, and Tocqueville, despotism still reigned in Europe. Only in America had the rights of the individual triumphed before the rights of the state; only in the New World had liberalism come to fruition in the form of republican governments. Lastarria then argued that Europe was backward, not South America. The Argentines responded to the argument, but saw no lessons of value for their nation. They believed the work was intended primarily for a European audience in order to introduce them to the political systems of the New World.[40]

This dismissal of *La América* infuriated Lastarria. The true intended audience for the work was the Argentines, whom Lastarria called *europeistas*, since "they claimed that they owed more to Europe and had more to expect from it." He objected strongly to the European airs of the *porteños* and believed it strongly detrimental to their national interest. For example, he found that Argentine newspapers never defended American interests. He noted: "Their newspapers wrote of the Chincha question with their Spanish subscribers in mind, mentioned Mexico with an eye to their French subscribers, and stuffed their columns with puerilities which everyone approved but represented no national interest." The real audience for *La América* was thus not Europe, as the *porteños* thought, but the citizens of Buenos Aires themselves. Lastarria added: "I have written this work to convince the ignoramuses and the *europeistas*, who are plentiful here, that the political antagonism which exists between both continents obliges the Americans to consolidate our democratic organization and unite to prepare ourselves for European attack."[41]

39. *Ibid.*, 85.
40. Lastarria, *La América*, in *Obras*, VIII, 128–29; *La Tribuna* (Buenos Aires), November 22, 1865.
41. Lastarria to Covarrubias, February 25, 1865, reprinted in *Historia*, no. 7 (1968),

Despite Lastarria's attempts to achieve an American alliance by his historical writings and his offer to cede Patagonia, his efforts were to no avail. After the Paraguayan War erupted, Lastarria left Buenos Aires for Brazil and Montevideo. Soon after, he resigned his post in response to repeated reprimands from the Chilean government for exceeding his authorized bounds during negotiations. Although Covarrubias and the Chilean government refused to acknowledge or approve Lastarria's attempted cession of Patagonia, the damage was done, as Argentine diplomats used Lastarria's admission that Chile had no right to Patagonia as a precedent for future negotiations, much to Chile's detriment.[42] After Lastarria's return no diplomatic mission was sent to Argentina until 1876, when yet another historian-turned-diplomat, Barros Arana, attempted to resolve the problem of Chilean boundaries.

Diego Barros Arana appeared surprised when he discovered that he had been placed in charge of the Chilean legation in Argentina, confessing that he "had never concerned himself with diplomatic questions" and that the new position would take him from his "peaceful and tranquil profession" of writing history. However, this love for historical study was apparently the trait that attracted Barros Arana to the new minister of foreign relations, José Alfonso. The current minister of the interior, Alvaro Covarrubias, explained this attitude at Barros Arana's farewell dinner: "No better choice could have been made than this famous historian and distinguished geographer of Chile, Diego Barros Arana, who has made extensive studies of all the nations of South America. He has made a passion of study, a pleasure of hunting through public archives and private documents. We could entrust the tranquil examination and reasonable discussion of a question that involves ancient documents to no one but him."[43] However, this initial optimism was soon to be dashed by one of the most catastrophic diplomatic missions Chile had yet witnessed.

Barros Arana himself actually seemed an unlikely candidate to present strict terms to Argentine diplomats. Family ties on his mother's side bound

---

324; Lastarria to Domingo Santa María, June 1, 1865, reprinted in *Revista Chilena*, XIII (1921), 123−24; Lastarria to Covarrubias, January 6, 1866, reprinted in *Historia*, no. 7 (1968), 324.

42. Yrarrázaval Larraín, *La Patagonia*, 107−108.

43. Barros Arana to Juan María Gutiérrez, reprinted in *Revista Chilena de Historia y Geografía* LXXXVI (1939), 58; Luis Barros Borgoño (ed.), *Archivo Barros Arana: Misión en el Plata, 1876−1878* (Santiago, 1936), 16.

him closely to Argentine society, a fact which hastened his acceptance by the Argentines, but also produced a true sympathy within him for their cause. Like Lastarria, he was convinced that the historical and familial bonds uniting Chilean and Argentine society should not be ruptured by a relatively minor territorial dispute. He thus looked forward to "pleasant chats about letters, history, and geography" which interested him more than his official affairs.[44] Also complicating Barros Arana's diplomatic posture was his strong belief that Patagonia was nothing but a worthless piece of land. Despite the fact that he had never seen the southern tip of America, he followed Darwin's opinions without hesitation. His *Elements of Physical Geography*, a textbook used in the National Institute, condemned Patagonia as a living hell, "an immense desert where only cacti grow amid salty streams, salty lakes, and salt rocks."[45]

However, despite Barros Arana's willingness to resolve the dispute quickly and amicably, his efforts were hopeless from the first days of his mission. Just before he arrived in Buenos Aires, Chilean vessels seized the *Jeanne Amélie*, a French merchant ship with an Argentine permit to collect guano near Patagonia, for infringement of territorial rights. The move infuriated the Argentines, and Barros Arana's ship was forced to wait in the harbor outside Buenos Aires until the furor had dissipated. The affair was to complicate all future negotiations, since the Argentines insisted the matter be resolved along with the boundary disputes. Once Barros Arana arrived on shore, he fared no better. The new Argentine president, Nicolás Avellaneda, further complicated the situation by welcoming Barros Arana, "not as the representative from Chile, but exclusively on his personal merits," which offended Chilean government officials who viewed this act as an insult to their national honor.[46]

Barros Arana's adeptness at historical study did little to aid his mission. He found the discussion of the historical documents concerning territorial claims "sterile and wearying," and privately confessed to Minister Alfonso that "people laugh with marked disdain when we say that Chile has rights to

44. Ricardo Donoso, *Diego Barros Arana* (Mexico City, 1967), 117; *Revista Chilena de Historia y Geografía*, LXXXVII, no. 94 (1939), 58.

45. Barros Arana, *Revista bibliográfica*, in *Obras completas* (Santiago, 1905–1906), IX, 205–206; Yrarrázaval Larraín, *La Patagonia*, 16.

46. Barros Borgoño, *Archivo Barros Arana: Misión en el Plata*, 178; M. L. Amunátegui, *Discursos parliamentarios* (Santiago, 1906), II, 227.

Patagonia, and they get angry when we speak of titles." Also, Barros Arana found Amunátegui's documents and the Chilean case "inconclusive," noting that Chile's Constitution of 1833 and the Treaty of Independence from Spain suggested that Argentina might indeed have the right to Patagonia.[47]

Also weakening Barros Arana's attempt at negotiation was the unity of the Argentine spokesmen. While the extremely vocal Americanists influenced the Chilean government position on Patagonia both privately and from cabinet positions, the Argentines firmly asserted their right to the disputed territory. Due to pressure from the Americanists within Chile, the ardent defender of Chilean claims to Patagonia, Adolfo Ibáñez, had been replaced in the cabinet by José Alfonso, who believed in conciliation, while in Argentina no one contested government policy on Patagonia. Even public opinion staunchly supported the official position. As negotiations broke down, rioters burned the house of the Chilean legation, and Barros Arana fractured his arm and lost his household goods during the tumult.[48] Even the "historical discussions" that Barros Arana had so anxiously anticipated turned sour, as Argentine historians and speakers at public occasions vilified Chileans at every possible opportunity. Suddenly, the Argentines alone had freed South America from the yolk of tyranny, despite "the fact that two-thirds of the Army of the Andes were Chilean, and that the Chileans accomplished the liberation of Peru by themselves." Barros Arana then urged his friend, President Aníbal Pinto, to publish a historical article refuting these outrageous errors.[49]

Barros Arana, like Lastarria before him, finally exceeded his instructions and offered most of Patagonia and the Strait of Magellan to Argentina. The Chilean government, despite its willingness to compromise on Patagonia, still desired an outlet to the Atlantic. It thus refused Barros Arana's proposal and an attempt to resolve the *Jeanne Amélie* affair, and recalled Barros Arana to Santiago. Again, the results of a diplomatic mission by a historian were essentially fruitless.[50] As relations deteriorated, the Chilean fleet seized yet

47. Barros Borgoño, *Archivo Barros Arana: Misión en el Plata*, 178; Encina, *La cuestión de límites*, 169; Barros Borgoño, *Archivo Barros Arana: Misión en el Plata*, 63.

48. Encina, *La cuestión de límites*, 172.

49. Amunátegui Solar, *Archivo epistolar*, I, 42–44.

50. For Barros Arana's view of the negotiations, see his *La cuestión de límites entre Chile i la República Argentina* (Santiago, 1895), 1–9. The debate whether Barros Arana was responsible for the loss of Patagonia continues to this day. See Ricardo Donoso, *Hombres e ideas de antaño y*

another vessel, the *Devonshire* of the United States, whose explorations had been authorized by the Argentine government. Both nations organized for war, but last minute negotiations prompted the Fierro-Sarratea Treaty of 1878, which solved none of the boundary of disputes but, again, provided for peaceful settlement in the future. A threat of war with Bolivia in early 1879 allowed the treaty to pass swiftly through Congress. As Barros Arana departed for Europe after his harried attempt at negotiations, Benjamín Vicuña Mackenna was the only great nineteenth-century historian left to oversee the ultimate resolution of the boundary disputes. However, unlike Lastarria and Barros Arana, he did not act as a diplomat abroad, but urged his position on his Chilean comrades as senator from Coquimbo and as an ardent proponent of Americanist dreams.

Vicuña Mackenna had been defending the ideal of American union since 1862 and the first threat of European intervention in the New World during his youth. He was elected director of the Society of American Union and became its most ardent propagandist. He published *Estudios históricos sobre confederación americana* in the afternoon newspaper *La Voz de Chile* in order to explain previous attempts at union, and, at the end of the first year of the club's existence, he compiled a lengthy *Colección de ensayos y documentos relativos a la unión y confederación de los pueblos hispanoamericanos*, which attempted to explain why previous confederations had failed. Furthermore, he argued that France constituted the greatest threat to the New World, and in *La nueva Santa Alianza*, he displayed documents which revealed France's insidious activities during the Independence era. After the Spanish invasions, Vicuña Mackenna was selected confidential agent to the United States in order to "promote warm and open sympathy for the Chilean cause in that Republic" and also to secretly purchase new battleships for Chile's navy.[51]

This long history of Americanist ideals caused Vicuña Mackenna to view the prospect of impending war with Argentina in 1878 with horror. After

hogaño (Santiago, 1936), and *El Mercurio*, March 15, 21, April 1, 1931. See also Ernesto Greve, "Diego Barros Arana en la cuestión de límites entre Chile y la República Argentina," *Anales de la Universidad de Chile*, nos. 109–110 (1958), 263–306. For Barros Arana's European letters, see *Revista Chilena de Historia y Geografía*, no. 70 (1930), 49*ff.*

51. Donoso, *Vicuña Mackenna*, 144; Vicuña Mackenna, *Miscelanea* (Santiago, 1872), II, 349–68; Vicuña Mackenna, *Diez meses de misión a los Estados Unidos de Norte América como agente confidencial de Chile* (Santiago, 1867).

the break in diplomatic relations resulting from the recall of Barros Arana and the capture of the *Devonshire*, Vicuña Mackenna personally attempted to divert the two neighboring nations from their disastrous course. Vicuña Mackenna arranged a meeting between Mariano E. de Sarratea, Argentine consul-general, and Colonel Saavedra, minister of war, helping to pave the way for the Fierro-Sarratea Treaty, which Vicuña Mackenna tenaciously defended in the Senate. Despite the fact that the pact had once again done nothing to settle the boundary situation, it had avoided war, and Vicuña Mackenna defended it as "good, noble, just, patriotic, advantageous, and equally beneficient to both countries."[52] The treaty met only one dissenting vote in the Senate, that of Ibáñez, whose assertion of Chile's claims to Patagonia in 1873 had become a dead issue due to ministerial shifts and the rising influence of the Americanists.

Although a war had been successfully averted, Vicuña Mackenna was not satisfied with leaving the boundary dispute in limbo, and he published *La Patagonia*, a collection of speeches and historical essays designed to "bring some light to the Patagonian question." Actually, the work was designed to cause Chile to renounce all claims to Patagonia by uniting all previous arguments to this effect. He again revived the historical argument of a longstanding friendship between Chile and Argentina which ought never to be betrayed. He repeatedly stressed the inferiority of Patagonia, using Darwin as his prime source. But, most important, he bitterly attacked the "Pandora's Box" of *uti possidetis juris* and argued that direct arbitration between Chile and Argentina should provide the final solution to the limits dispute.[53]

Again, a historian argued that historical documents had no importance when more vital interests were at stake. Suddenly, the historians who defended Chile's territorial claims (Amunátegui, Morla Vicuña) were involved in the "sterile vanity of gathering soporific or impertinent notes."[54] The documents themselves became "wormy and motheaten *cédulas reales.*" Vicuña Mackenna believed that the countless volumes produced by the historical defenders of Chile's rights were wholly worthless in this situation. He then presented an anecdote to support his contention. One day someone had asked

52. Vicuña Mackenna, *Discursos parlamentarios* (Santiago, 1939), III, 167–93; Donoso, *Vicuña Mackenna*, 371.

53. Vicuña Mackenna, *La Patagonia* (Santiago, 1880), title page, 2, 62, 9.

54. *Ibid.*, 51.

Juan Batista Alberdi of Argentina if he had ever read Amunátegui's study of the Patagonian question. Alberdi replied:

The author has sent me his book, but I have not read it and probably will never read it. It is probably a very interesting work as are all of Amunátegui's writings. However, I believe that these territorial questions which are bloodying the soil of America ought not to be resolved by ancient and worthless customs, but by the common interests of the nations involved, by the demands of progress and civilization, and by political and geographical rights.[55]

Thus Vicuña Mackenna also repudiated the documents that as a historian he had been taught to revere because a more important goal so dictated. His study was welcomed by no one more than the Argentines, who used Vicuña Mackenna's assertion of Argentine rights in their future negotiations.[56]

The Treaty of 1881 marked the ultimate ascendance of the Americanist argument. This position was bolstered by certain political and military factors, since Chile's successes in the war with Peru certainly influenced Argentine opinion. Yet, Chile seemed unable to quell guerrilla activity in the Peruvian countryside. Reluctantly, both countries accepted United States mediation. Chile surrendered Patagonia, but retained sovereignty over the Strait of Magellan. Terms were also discussed for the division of Tierra del Fuego and the arbitration of any future dispute arising from the treaty.

The documents that Amunátegui had discovered had proved worthless, despite the fact that Argentine Minister Irigoyen confessed privately that if the issue should ever be submitted to arbitration, Argentina's claims would prove unacceptable.[57] Ironically, Amunátegui's arguments were not deflated by Argentines eager to defend their nation's right to Patagonia, but were sabotaged by the greatest Chilean historians of the nineteenth century, who were willing to disregard unfavorable documents when they deemed it necessary to fulfill political or personal goals.

55. *Ibid.*, xvii.
56. Santa María to Lastarria, May 25, June 19, 1880 in *Revista Chilena*, VIII (1916), 38–44.
57. Encina, *La cuestión de límites*, 252.

7

A QUESTION OF HONOR

HISTORIANS DEFEND THEIR PROFESSION

LOFTY QUESTIONS of international diplomacy and domestic politics often shaped the direction of historical studies in Chile. Yet, personal and private passions also came to the forefront as historians attempted to defend their veracity before the reading audience which would judge the merit of their works. While Bello and his followers insisted on the noble motives of the historian, virtually everyone else began to view this occupation with profound distrust.

This suspicion of the historical profession became apparent as early as 1857. Narciso Desmadryl, a renowned artist, assembled aspiring young historians to contribute brief biographies of the famous heroes of Chile's past to accompany his drawings in the *Galería nacional o colección de biografías i retratos de hombres célebres de Chile.*[1] Amunátegui and Barros Arana provided most of the biographical information, but the latter soon found that his study of the Conde de la Conquista, Don Mateo de Toro Zambrano, was going to be eliminated in the second edition of the *Galería*, since the count's grandson, Bernardo José de Toro, decided to prepare a new study of his illustrious ancestor.

This abrupt change angered several of the subscribers who had praised Barros Arana's original sketch as "written without passion or hate" and "faithfully following the interpretations of the most eminent historians of the country." However, the descendants of the count were displeased by the

---

1. Narciso Desmadryl (ed.), *Galería nacional o colección de biografías y retratos de hombres célebres de Chile* (Santiago, 1854).

work, and his grandson pressured Desmadryl to insert his new biography into the second edition of the *Galería*. The subscribers were furious at this "betrayal of the past," since all previous historians had condemned the count to mediocrity. José Javier de Guzmán, a relative of the count, found him "docile." Padre Melchor Martínez had written that the count was "a pliable little man who could easily be influenced by revolutionaries to achieve their own perverse ends." Claude Gay considered him "limited, lacking energy and will," and Barros Arana followed suit and dismissed the count as a man "without talent, energy, or firmness." Yet, the count's grandson noted: "The Count was of slight stature, extremely affable, with a frank character and noble sentiments. . . . His principles were solid and his virtue sincere and humble. He cultivated dignity, modesty, energy, moderation, generosity, and prudence. He was always loved and respected by his family."[2]

What may appear a minor incident actually set the pattern for many future debates on historical works. The past was always seen as a potential betrayer of a higher ideal, that of honor. "History is the conscience of a nation," wrote Manuel de Olazábal, an Argentine colonel, to Vicuña Mackenna. "It allows the names of heroes and villains to live forever and be judged by future generations."[3] Since an ancestor's transgressions held the prospect of living forever in the pages of a history book, a relative often found it necessary to rise to his defense and whitewash the past in order to protect the family name. This preoccupation with honor pervaded the small aristocracy of Santiago society which had long defended its right to noble titles and *mayorazgos*. But, interestingly, the same attitudes also were demonstrated by almost anyone reading a historical work which discussed a living relative or ancestor. Soldiers, their wives, newspapermen, and even the wife of the last pirate to threaten Chilean waterways resented an unflattering depiction of their ancestors as much as any aristocrat. In the face of this critique of the treatment of the past, the honor and rectitude of yet another individual, the historian, was challenged. If indeed the historian had viewed the past incorrectly or had used the past to slander an individual and destroy his reputation, his own professional standards became threatened. Thus, in the countless debates on historical works in the nineteenth century, this question of honor affected all participants.

2. "Una cuestión literaria," *El Ferrocarril*, September 5, 1856.
3. *La Asamblea Constituyente*, November 19, 1858; Guillermo Matta, "Manuel Rodríguez," *Galería nacional*, 117.

Benjamín Vicuña Mackenna became involved in several of these controversies for a variety of reasons. First, he was prolific and his works were widely disseminated in newspapers and pamphlets. Secondly, he discussed contemporary history, wherein most of the participants, or at least their children, were still alive. Until Vicuña Mackenna, most Chilean historians had avoided discussions of the recent past. They preferred to follow the suggestions of historians from Plutarch to Bello who cited the dangers of contemporary history. Guillermo Matta followed the warning in the *Life of Pericles* that "contemporary history is blinded by hate and envy," and Marcial Martínez listened to Bello's advice that he desist from writing a study of Portales because "it would renew passions not yet extinguished and provoke debates that might divide along party lines."[4]

Vicuña Mackenna, however, considered the study of the recent past a challenge. He argued in a letter to Santos Tornero, editor of *El Mercurio*, that his next work "would be the history of a time that we have created ourselves, our *civil* history. Until now, historians have only written the history of the Spanish domination in its three phases of conquest, plunder, and emancipation. The history of our organization as a *free* people began only when the last battle of the Independence period ended."[5] However, while responding to the challenge of contemporary history, Vicuña Mackenna never seemed to realize the dangers it might entail.

Vicuña Mackenna's problems stemmed from the fact that, unlike other Chilean historians, he was consistently interested in the "great men" of Chile's past. While Lastarria, Barros Arana, and Amunátegui tended to emphasize entire epochs or social groups, Vicuña Mackenna was fascinated by the individual, the personality that was able to change the course of destiny. Following Carlyle, he argued that: "Mankind advances like an army on the march toward the unknown. It marches for a day or for a century according to its needs, led by the daring explorer along the pathways which he lights with his spirit or the tribute of his blood."[6] Unfortunately, Vicuña Mackenna never realized that while depicting these grand figures of Chile's past, he was often forced to belittle the contributions of all those surrounding an O'Higgins, a Carrera, or a Portales, and thus offend and alienate many of their supporters and their descendants.

4. *El Mercurio*, November 2, 1864.
5. *Ibid.*, March 18, 1861.
6. Vicuña Mackenna, *La independencia en el Perú* (Buenos Aires, 1971), 21.

One of Vicuña Mackenna's first works, the *Vida del General Mackenna*, led to a controversy which was characteristic of the furor that was to greet the publication of each of his succeeding studies. Vicuña Mackenna realized the difficulty of discussing the life of his grandfather, General Juan Mackenna, objectively. For this reason he differentiated the "life" and the "biography" as the two methods of considering the history of a single man. The biography was to be written with "impartiality and tact, a difficult task for a descendant," while the "life" was to be filled with the "sentiment" and personal feeling that only a relative could supply. Although finally calling his study a "life" of General Mackenna, Vicuña Mackenna also wished to satisfy those demanding an impartial biography. For this reason, this work assumed a curious form: "Whoever wishes to read the biography of a public figure can read the documents which are presented in the footnotes. Whoever desires to study the life of a famous gentleman and understand his feelings may read the narrative portion of the work."[7] Again the question of objectivity in historical writing was raised, and Vicuña Mackenna seemed to have solved it in a unique manner, by leaving the impartial study to the footnotes, and the personal viewpoint in the narrative section. However, this clever division failed to satisfy those who read the study and were involved with General Mackenna.

An anonymous critic, "an elderly soldier who served with the valiant Colonel Balcarce," attacked Vicuña Mackenna soon after the fifty copies of the work were printed by the *El Ferrocarril* press. He claimed that the historian had praised his grandfather so highly that he offended all of his compatriots who fought at his side.[8] A sister of José Santiago Muñoz, who was killed in battle with Mackenna, echoed the same complaint. Although professing her modesty, proclaiming that it was unusual for a woman of such a lowly position to challenge such a successful writer, Muñoz Bezanilla chided Vicuña Mackenna: "You have deflated the claims of my brother in order to glorify General Mackenna without realizing that you have deeply wounded the hearts of four orphans who have inherited only their father's good name. José Santiago Muñoz has no son or grandson to protect his memory, nor to

7. Vicuña Mackenna, *Vida del General Mackenna* (Santiago, 1902), note 1. See also Barros Arana, "Historia," *Retórica i poética*, in *Obras completas* (Santiago, 1905–1906), III, Ch. 2 and p. 221.

8. Ricardo Donoso, *Don Benjamín Vicuña Mackenna: Su vida, sus escritos, y su tiempo* (Santiago, 1925), 77; *El Ferrocarril*, January 4, 10, 1857.

satisfy his own vanity by writing a biography, nor to defend the honor of the father that you have scorned."[9]

Vicuña Mackenna responded to these challenges claiming that "to glorify a name at the expense of historical truth would be a scandal worthy of the highest scorn." He further commented that he judged his grandfather severely and criticized him "the only time he strayed from the exceptional path of his glorious career, when he signed the Treaty of Lircay in 1814," which provided for a tentative compromise with the mother country during the fight for independence. In order to prepare an unbiased work, Vicuña Mackenna asserted that "he had never written a single line of the history of the national period without a document at hand." But from these first writings, the reader had a basic distrust of Vicuña Mackenna's appeal to the documents as the guarantee of truth. The "old soldier" complained that anyone could find an "original document" to prove a point. Vicuña Mackenna could easily find "a letter from General So-and-So" to prove any assertion he presented. The mere existence of a letter or document did not necessarily constitute proof to the readers.[10]

Similar critiques also greeted Vicuña Mackenna's next major work, a study of the Carreras, the audacious and irascible heroes of Chilean independence. The work was first published in serial form in the daily *El Ferrocarril*, beginning in August, 1857, but did not appear in book form until December 10. Vicuña Mackenna then wrote Mitre and complained:

Do you realize what has been the result of my labor and sacrifices of an entire winter in order to prepare these documents? . . . The generous owner of *El Ferrocarril* printed 2,000 copies of the work, spent 1,000 pesos for the printing, and then sold it at 3 pesos, which was almost the cost of printing the work. Do you know how many copies have been sold in our capital? Hardly 30 have been sold, which gives the editor 90 pesos in return for 3,000 pesos in total costs. . . . Despite this fact, there are more than 300 in circulation, because I have received so many requests for *gifts* of this *very interesting* book.[11]

Despite the small number of copies sold, the *Ostracismo de los Carreras* received ample criticism. These letters appeared in the daily papers before December 10, and were thus responses from people who had read the study

9. *Ibid.*, January 6, 1857.
10. *Ibid.*, January 4, 1857, January 10, 1857.
11. Mitre disagreed with Vicuña Mackenna on the so-called genius of Carrera. See their debate in *El Correo Literario*, August 7, 12, 14, 1858.

in the newspaper, and not in the book form. A "Chilean and a relative of the Carreras" who desired "the truth be known" asked for the facts which allowed Vicuña Mackenna to call Juan José Carrera "cowardly, greedy, and envious." The relative further warned that "it was still impossible to write a history of the independence movement with the necessary impartiality."[12] Yet, this relative paid little attention to the tone of Vicuña Mackenna's study, which actually tended to vindicate the Carreras' actions during the Independence era. An Argentine colonel similarly ignored what Vicuña Mackenna actually said and printed *A Refutation of Certain Opinions in the "Ostracism of the Carreras," a Work Published in Chile by Sr. Mackenna*. Manuel Olazábal, fearful of "public opinion,"[13] disputed the claims of Benavente and Amunátegui,[14] who suggested that he had visited Carrera on the day of his execution and claimed he had been pardoned, merely to unnerve him when he discovered it was not true. Vicuña Mackenna responded kindly to Olazábal's letter, simply because he had agreed with him, never having printed the charge in the first place. Thus both writers used the printing of Vicuña Mackenna's work as an opportunity to defend their honor, although the historian had done little to offend them.

Thus far, complaints against Vicuña Mackenna's interpretation of the past and use of documents consisted of merely a few letters to the editor. His next book, *El ostracismo del General Bernardo O'Higgins*, caused an even greater stir, resulting in a charge of slander, since Vicuña Mackenna had supposedly stained the memory of O'Higgins' minister of finance, José Rodríguez Aldea. As in *El ostracismo de los Carreras*, Vicuña Mackenna was attempting to rehabilitate the image of a great hero of the Independence era, Bernardo O'Higgins. O'Higgins' reputation had become tarnished of late. Faced with the difficult task of organizing the newly independent state in 1817, after the Spanish Reconquest had been dispelled, Supreme Director O'Higgins assumed much of the responsibility on his own shoulders and attempted to reform the colonial society with several proposals directed against the Church and the aristocracy. While O'Higgins' goals may have been applauded, several Chilean liberals objected to the means, as they disapproved of the intense

12. *El Ferrocarril*, September 12, 1857.
13. *La Asamblea Constituyente*, November 19, 1858.
14. Diego José Benavente, "Don José Miguel Carrera," *Revista Chilena de Historia y Geografía*, XL (1930), 296–310; and M. L. Amunátegui, *La dictadura de O'Higgins* (Santiago, 1914).

concentration of power in one man, be it O'Higgins, Portales, or Montt. Even Miguel Luis Amunátegui had used the O'Higgins' era in his study *La dictadura de O'Higgins* (1853) in order to prove that a tyrant could never maintain himself in power in the new South American nations. O'Higgins himself had died in exile in Peru and it was not until 1869 that his remains were returned to Chile, thanks to the dogged insistence of Vicuña Mackenna in the Chamber of Deputies.[15]

Vicuña Mackenna began his study of O'Higgins while he too was in exile as a result of the abortive revolt against Montt in 1859. While in Lima, he met O'Higgins' son, Demetrio, and, after expressing the desire to write the biography of the great Chilean patriot, was given lodging and complete access to the family archive at the O'Higgins' estate at Cañete. The relationship between Demetrio and Benjamín was not always easy-going, for, while desiring to clear the name of O'Higgins', Vicuña Mackenna also expressed the desire to "write a serious, impartial, and complete work." He added that he "would praise his successes and criticize his faults," and "all the facts would be religiously documented."[16]

But perhaps Vicuña Mackenna was going about his task with too much impartiality. Vicuña Mackenna wrote to Demetrio claiming that O'Higgins "had also committed grave errors, and at times exhibited a weakness of character which has caused his name to become blemished."[17] He later wrote that he expected to clear O'Higgins' name of these criticisms, but expressed surprise when Demetrio "expected him to explode *all* harmful myths which still clouded O'Higgins' name."[18] Perhaps, Vicuña Mackenna explained, Demetrio's expectations were driven by the ties of blood which united him to his father. But Demetrio rested assured, in a later letter from Hamburg, that Vicuña Mackenna would put the documents to a "noble use." He added: "I am quite pleased to have given you access to my archive so that you might discover the misconceptions concerning my father's rule. I hope that with a little more study, you shall present your hero as good, noble, and grand."[19]

15. Simon Collier, *Ideas and Politics of Chilean Independence, 1808–1833* (Cambridge, 1967), 233–34; Amunátegui, *La dictadura de O'Higgins*; Donoso, *Vicuña Mackenna*, 187, 189, 235.

16. *Archivo Nacional: Archivo Benjamín Vicuña Mackenna*, November 5, 1860, T. 167.

17. "Mi respuesta a un pasquín de Manuel Bilbao," *El Ferrocarril*, May 5, 1863. The letter itself is dated September 14, 1860.

18. *Ibid.*, September 29, 1860. Italics mine.

19. *Ibid.*, October 28, 1860.

Demetrio finished reading the first fifteen chapters in Milan and praised his friend for the strict impartiality of his work. However, Vicuña Mackenna later noted that Demetrio stopped writing after this date. Almost two years later, Vicuña Mackenna wrote a common friend, José Manuel Zabala, to inquire why Demetrio stopped writing to him, believing that "he was not content with certain points in *El ostracismo del General O'Higgins.*"[20]

Despite the informal pressures of Demetrio O'Higgins to force Vicuña Mackenna to praise his father without limits, Vicuña Mackenna professed to have maintained a strict objectivity. However, these assertions appeared dubious to Francisco de Paula Rodríguez Velasco, son of O'Higgins' finance minister, who exploded when he read Vicuña Mackenna's account of his father's activities in *El Mercurio* from December 12, 1860, to March 13, 1861. Irate, Rodríguez Velasco wrote the editors to protest: "Anyone who has read *El ostracismo del General O'Higgins* should be indignant at the gross insults and audacious lies that the author has used to blemish the beloved memory of my father."[21] Velasco's anger stemmed from the fact that Vicuña Mackenna argued that O'Higgins himself did no wrong while in office, but was betrayed by his ministers, and, in particular, the crafty José A. Rodríguez Aldea. Rodríguez Velasco then threatened to sue the editors of *El Mercurio*, who promptly denied all responsibility, since, they claimed, they only printed the work and did not write it. Besides, they argued, Article II, Section 5 of the *Ley de Imprenta* of 1846 allowed that "any writing will not be found slanderous if it relates historical facts, as long as the study is written as a historical investigation or literary work and not with the intention of defamation."[22]

But Rogríguez ignored this provision of the 1846 law and chose instead to invoke Article 24, which allowed lawsuits for "all injuries against individuals which do not refer to their conduct in public office."[23] Rodríguez therefore chose to challenge only one paragraph of Vicuña Mackenna's work which painted his father in a very unflattering light: "With regard to his professional morality, the common folk say that when a client arrived at his law

20. *Archivo Nacional: Archivo Benjamín Vicuña Mackenna*, T. 168, 71: May 10, 1863.

21. *El Mercurio*, February 26, 1861. For a complete account of this episode, see Gustavo Labatut Glena, *Juicio de imprenta seguido a Benjamín Vicuña Mackenna con motivo de la publicación del "Ostracismo del Jeneral O'Higgins"* (Santiago, 1921), and M. G. Carmona, *Vicuña Mackenna ante el jurado de Valparaíso* (Valparaíso, 1861).

22. See Labatut Glena, *Juicio*, Ch. 2. See also Ricardo Donoso, *Las ideas políticas en Chile* (Santiago, 1967), 261–66, for a discussion of the 1846 law.

23. Vicuña Mackenna, *El ostracismo del General O'Higgins* (Valparaíso, 1860), Ch. 12.

office for the first time, he would point to his shelves of books and say, "On this side are all the books that will win your lawsuit, and on the other are all the laws that will lose your case." Whether true or not, it appeared so clever and characteristic that it was repeated all over Santiago." [24]

Vicuña Mackenna attempted to avoid the lawsuit with a compromise, whereby the public could submit all documents pertaining to the issue, but Rodríguez refused. On June 19 the first jury was called to decide the merits of the charge and whether it should be brought to trial, and on June 22 a second jury was chosen by lot to decide Vicuña Mackenna's guilt. Interest was aroused in the trial, and the largest hall in Valparaíso was selected for the event. The audience began gathering at 11:30 on June 24, and the first argument was heard at 12:15. The attorney for Rodríguez, José Eduardo Cáceres, argued that Vicuña Mackenna deliberately wished to slander the memory of Rodríguez Aldea, since he chose to first publish the work in *El Mercurio*, so it could be diffused faster and read by a larger audience than if it were in book form. He further argued that Vicuña Mackenna's concern for historical impartiality was a mere "disguise for his blind mania and savage hatred of the most revered figures of our history." [25] He concluded at one o'clock after reading ten statements attesting to Rodríguez Aldea's ability as a lawyer.

Vicuña Mackenna's defense was a well-reasoned response to the charges of the prosecuting attorney. He argued that this was not a mere question of slander, the transitory result of an argument in the daily press, but, rather, a more important issue. History itself, not a man, was on trial that day in Valparaíso. Vicuña Mackenna decided to present the history of the era to the gentlemen of the jury, and allowed them to "decide an historical question" Further, he argued, the jury must decide whether a historian may investigate the past impartially, with "truth and justice." He compared the historian to a judge and a priest, emphasizing his honor, severity, and love of truth. Was the historian to be denied his desire to present the past as it really was merely to cater to the whims of aristocrats wishing to protect their families' reputation? He added: "We live in an aristocratic society . . . which believes that a name is worth more than the truth, even more than one's country. For this reason we must attack this preoccupation with lineage and vanity which

---

24. Labatut Glena, *Juicio*, Ch. 4.
25. Vicuña Mackenna, "Mi defensa ante el jurado de imprenta que tuvo lugar en Valparaíso el 24 de junio de 1861," *Revista Chilena de Historia y Geografía*, LXX (1931), 35, 47, 90, 130, 73.

closes every door to progress. . . . There are men among us, who, although accepting the truth of the facts, exclaim, 'But why bother to write such a history? Why embarrass the children? Why say such things about these families?'" Finally, Vicuña Mackenna, like all historians of his day, appealed to the importance of the documents which could never lie. He had at his service "the authentic archive, with all the confidential remarks of all of the famous men we are discussing. It contains their own words, their acts, their mysteries, and their guilt laid before you in evidence. All letters were written by the authors and signed by them."[26]

These two themes, that the historian exercised a priesthood and that the documents never lied, served Vicuña Mackenna well. He was absolved, and never forgot the arguments that had convinced the jury of his innocence. Rodríguez Velasco, however, wished to appeal the decision, but Vicuña Mackenna threatened to release several documents concerning Velasco's father which had been too scandalous to present either in the trial or in the book. A mutual friend arranged a private meeting wherein Vicuña Mackenna surrendered the documents and Rodríguez agreed not to renew the suit. Soon after Vicuña Mackenna wrote to Rodríguez Velasco: "At least the *historical* question is completed. All that remains is a domestic question, that of a son's love for his father and of a person's honor. This is your job now, and I would be pleased to do whatever I can to help you."[27]

The debate was not yet ended. In order to save his father's honor, the son began to write a biography himself, just as the grandson of the Conde de la Conquista had done eight years earlier. The *Biografía del Doctor D. José Rodríguez Aldea* (1862) only partially considered past history, as Rodríguez Velasco continued his attack on Vicuña Mackenna and the trial decision. He argued that it was foolhardy for a jury of businessmen to decide a historical question in two hours that would have taken an academy of history two months to decide. He then slowly proceeded to vindicate his father and demolish Vicuña Mackenna's image of O'Higgins, which "presented a man lacking a conscience or will, a mere toy for all who surrounded him."[28]

The debate on *El ostracismo del General O'Higgins* may have been stilled for

26. Reprinted in Donoso, *Vicuña Mackenna*, 508–13.
27. Francisco de P. Rodríguez Velasco, *Biografía del doctor D. José Rodríguez Aldea* (Santiago, 1862), introduction.
28. Vicuña Mackenna, *Historia de los diez años de la administración Montt* (Santiago, 1862), I, 9, 17, 19.

the moment, but the controversy over Vicuña Mackenna's succeeding works continued. *La historia de los diez años de la administración Montt* bore a deceptive title. Despite such lofty aims, the five-volume work, begun in 1858 in Vicuña Mackenna's newspaper *La Asamblea Constituyente*, but interrupted by his exile, remained a history of the 1851 revolt against Montt. The work ended with the Battle of Loncomilla and the Treaty of Purapel, which marked the beginning of Montt's rule and the definitive consolidation of his power. Vicuña Mackenna again expressed his impartiality at the beginning of this work: "History is justice—As a writer I am a judge—The historian has no friends—The judge bears no grudges. . . . I believe I have a sublime impartiality, that bulwark of history, the impartiality of conscience." Furthermore, he believed his history of the abortive revolt would counter "those that discuss the same facts for a certain purpose, whose histories are confused, mutilated, and riddled by a thousand contradictions." [29]

Yet Vicuña Mackenna expected controversy: "I have promised in the preface of my work that I will print all corrections that are supported by the truth. Therefore all letters will be included in the last volume of my work where I shall leave ample space for all the correction of errors. Can I give you more sincere proof of the good faith and loyalty of a historian?" Despite protestations of his impartiality, Vicuña Mackenna probably expected that many might not completely trust his work as an unbiased report of the revolt against Montt. Barros Arana noted that people were saying: "This is not a history; it is the result of passion." This distrust came as no surprise since Vicuña Mackenna himself had participated in the revolt, been arrested, and forced to escape by night dressed as a woman. While in prison he wrote a lengthy diary as well as a biting diatribe against Montt, *Tablas de sangre de la candidatura Montt*. After the defeat of the rebellious troops, Vicuña Mackenna found it prudent to leave Chile and visit Europe and the United States. [30]

While this episode alone might harden anyone's resistance to a political regime, it was not to be an isolated incident. In 1858, as opposition to the Montt regime and the possible succession of Antonio Varas to the presidency

29. *La Voz de Chile*, October 9, 1862; *El Correo del domingo*, May 18, 1862; Donoso, *Vicuña Mackenna*, 35, note 1.

30. Pedro Félix Vicuña chided his son Benjamín for not being sympathetic to the rebel troops, and thus defended his own interests, since he also had joined in the revolt against Montt.

was increasing, Vicuña Mackenna began publishing *La Asamblea Constituyente*. This newspaper called for the reform of the Constitution of 1833, which gave so much authority to the president that the legislative branch became powerless. Additionally, it freely criticized Montt, comparing him unfavorably to Portales. In November the paper called for an open meeting to discuss constitutional reform, and the intendant of Santiago promptly prohibited the gathering. Vicuña Mackenna was again arrested, the printing office was closed, and, after three months in prison, he found himself involuntarily enroute to Europe in the comany of a disreputable English captain who had been given 3,000 pesos by the Chilean government to deposit several rebels in Liverpool.

Thus a certain sympathy for the rebellious troops and their leaders might be expected in Vicuña Mackenna's work.[31] Indeed, several charged that he had written an "impassioned work." Yet, Vicuña Mackenna offered his standard response, without changing any of the original opinions expressed in his work. "Remember," he answered, "the proof of my faith as a historian lies in the fact that the only reward for my efforts is seeing the light of truth shine in the eyes of our children as they learn to understand the troubled life of our Republic."[32] Again, the historian could do no wrong.

His critics, however, remained adamant. They were divided in two groups, all military men: those defending their own conduct during the revolt and those defending the conduct of a relative. Two brothers defended the memory of their father, former governor of Curicó, whom Vicuña Mackenna alleged to have been a coward. A regiment captain claimed that his battalion acted independently of all other divisional commanders in an attempt to bolster his own image. Metaphors of war and battle filled the letters of these military men to Vicuña Mackenna: One must "combat" accusations, and facts must be used to "demolish" faulty interpretations.[33]

Interestingly, anyone who wrote to Vicuña Mackenna, and thus had read the work, found himself or a relative discussed in the book. Therefore, as can be seen in most public debates on historical works, people tended to read works which discussed themselves or a near relative. Vicuña Mackenna himself noticed this trend. He sent out requests to agents to sell his book noting

31. *La Voz de Chile*, October 9, 1862.
32. *Ibid.*, October 6, 9, 14, 21–22, 1862.
33. *Archivo Nacional: Archivo Benjamín Vicuña Mackenna*, T. 168, 90–91.

that 500 copies had to be sold to insure the work's financial success. Yet, despite the greater concentration of a reading public in Santiago and Valparaíso, the largest urban centers, the historian pinned his hopes for the best sales in the provinces because "these men figured most prominently in the book."[34]

By this date, the practice of public debates on historical works became commonplace for a variety of reasons. Pedro Félix Vicuña, Benjamín's father, expressed this lofty notion: "When contemporary history is discussed, it is necessary that the men who participated in the events attempt to discover the truth by means of their testimony and a rational polemic between those expressing differing interpretations. In this manner the knowledge of the past becomes complete and a ready source for the actions of nations and their governments."[35] However, yet another factor encouraged these public debates in the daily press. All this hullabaloo served to increase public interest in the new historical works, and possibly increase future sales. Vicuña Mackenna's next book, a controversial history of Portales, served to illustrate this fact.

Merely the expectation of a polemic seemed to heighten the excitement surrounding the publication of *Don Diego Portales*. When Vicuña Mackenna noticed that letters began to appear on the editorial pages of both *El Mercurio* and *El Ferrocarril*, he published the following reply, in a move to increase the anticipation of the inevitable controversy: "Since several critiques of *Portales* have already been printed in Santiago and Valparaíso, and many others are in preparation, I believe it is my duty to inform these people that I shall not reply to these articles until most of them have been published. This is not due to discourtesy or tardiness on my part, but, rather, to save myself from endlessly repeating my ideas."[36] Two months later, a series of editorials by Isidoro Errázuriz in *El Mercurio* continued to heighten the interest in *Portales*. Although Errázuriz bitterly attacked Vicuña Mackenna's flattering picture of Portales, he also confessed to his friend Vicuña Mackenna that his editorials had "done little to speed the sales of *Portales*" and "he would continue to mention the work from time to time."[37]

Again Vicuña Mackenna faced several criticisms of his now famous im-

34. *El Mercurio*, March 4, 1863.
35. *Ibid.*, March 18, 1863.
36. *Ibid.*, May 9, 12, 20, 1863. See also *La Voz de Chile*, May 11, 1863; *Archivo Nacional: Archivo Benjamín Vicuña Mackenna*, T. 171, ff. 59, May 22, 1863.
37. Barros Arana, *Un decenio de la historia de Chile* (Santiago, 1913), XVI, 371ff.

partiality. Fernando Urizar Garfias, former intendant of Aconcagua, undertook the double task of defending his father and himself from the charges in *Portales*. Vicuña Mackenna had claimed that Urizar's father had been the right-hand man of Marcó del Pont, the sadistic ruler of Chile during the Spanish Reconquest, and found that Urizar Garfias himself had carried out the execution of the assassins of Portales too quickly, without waiting for a trial.[38] As a result Urizar Garfias was forced to claim that his father had left Chile after the Battle of Rancagua (1814), making it impossible for him to have conspired with del Pont from 1814 to 1817, and further insist that the assassins deserved the strictest sentence possible since theirs was a premeditated act of murder, not a sudden act of passion. Urizar then commented that Vicuña "lacked the loyalty of a historian and a gentleman by slandering my father so blatantly."[39] This comment angered Vicuña Mackenna, who had realized the potentially scandalous nature of this interpretation, so he had delivered all of the documents in his possession to Urizar before publishing the book. Vicuña Mackenna asserted that his own conduct had been perfectly correct, explaining that "these are the actions of a man who seeks the truth at all cost with his conscience as his only guide. I hide nothing when I speak to future generations from the *tribunal of history*, and yet someone has the audacity to call me disloyal and a liar."[40]

Thus far Vicuña Mackenna had been able to maintain a lofty position both personally and professionally. The moral standards of the historian and the man remained unscathed until a second trial for libel in the midst of the *Portales* debates. Again the accusation stemmed from a historical dispute. While in London in 1859, Vicuña Mackenna read the first volume of the memoirs of Lord Cochrane, the naval hero who had greatly aided Chile during the Independence era. Vicuña Mackenna had two reservations about the work, objecting to Cochrane's charges that the Chileans did not pay him enough for his services, and to his intense dislike of San Martín, whom Vicuña Mackenna considered "a great man, a great soldier, and, especially, a great American." Vicuña Mackenna promptly wrote to Cochrane, explaining his criticisms, and requesting permission to prepare the Spanish edition of the work, since "his narration occupied a distinguished position in Chile's

38. *El Mercurio*, August 14, 1863.
39. *El Ferrocarril*, August 20, 1863.
40. Collier, *Ideas and Politics*, 231; Vicuña Mackenna, *La independencia en el Perú*, xxxiii, xxix.

national history."[41] Cochrane's reply was curt, thanking Vicuña Mackenna for his "worthy observations," but saying nothing about a future meeting to discuss the translation of his memoirs. Soon after, Cochrane left for the continent and never met with Vicuña Mackenna.

The incident might have ended here except for two reasons. First, Vicuña Mackenna decided to prepare a refutation of Cochrane's memoirs, which, although entitled *La Revolución de la Independencia del Perú desde 1809 a 1819*, managed to remain an extremely personal attack on the naval hero and a defense of San Martín. He felt compelled to undertake the task because he found Cochrane's work "an attack on Chile's dignity" and because no one else seemed disturbed by the affair. *El Ferrocarril* merely reprinted a review from the *Times* of London which called San Martín a "coward and a braggart." Vicuña Mackenna found Cochrane's work "an attack on history itself" and was determined to vindicate San Martín, whom, like Carrera, Portales, and O'Higgins, he considered one of the great men of history.[42] Interestingly, the use of a work of history to frame a personal attack against Cochrane did not seem foreign to Vicuña Mackenna's conception of the functions of history.

Despite the fact that Cochrane had died by this time, Vicuña Mackenna's work soon elicited an irate response from Manuel Bilbao, an old acquaintance who had finally managed to obtain the translation rights for Cochrane's memoirs. Within the text of the work, Bilbao proceeded to insult Vicuña Mackenna whenever possible. Two footnotes offended him deeply. One suggested that he wrote his study of O'Higgins as a favor to Demetrio, presenting a flattering portrait of his father merely to repay the son for his generous offer of room, board, and the use of the family archive.[43] A second footnote criticized Vicuña Mackenna's attack of Cochrane in his study of the Independence era in Peru. Bilbao later commented: "We protest in the name of history against a writer who has based his career on the defamation of character and the scorn of the truth. We, however, render profound gratitude to the foreigners, Cochrane, Miller, and (Juan) Mackenna, who have helped our nation."[44]

41. Vicuña Mackenna, *La independencia en el Perú*, xxxv, xxxix.
42. See Donoso, *Vicuña Mackenna*, 157–160, for a full account of the insults.
43. *El Ferrocarril*, May 5, 1863.
44. *Archivo Nacional: Archivo Benjamín Vicuña Mackenna*: T. 144. See the winning essay: Manuel Bilbao, "La rejeneración i el porvenir," *La Tribuna*, September 26, 1849.

Vicuña Mackenna angrily responded to the charges in the pages of *El Ferrocarril*, claiming that Bilbao had sold his soul to Peru by becoming a member of the secret police and a special agent for President Castilla during the revolt of General Vivanco in 1856. Vicuña Mackenna's vicious attack on Bilbao was not merely a response to the insults contained in the Cochrane translation, but the inevitable result of a long enmity between the two. In 1849, Vicuña Mackenna discovered that he had lost the prize in the Literary Society competition to Bilbao, because the latter's work maintained "a more Christian tone."[45] Their relationship worsened during their companionship in the Academy of Laws in 1850 and deteriorated further during the revolt of 1851, wherein Bilbao supposedly "turned tail and retreated as scared as a rabbit," while Vicuña Mackenna "succeeded gloriously against magnificent odds."[46]

Lastarria read Vicuña Mackenna's article and wrote him on June 5, 1863: "Bilbao is going to accuse you of libel. I am very sorry, but don't you understand, fatso? You shouldn't get so excited. You have a just complaint, but it is necessary that you put up with the insults. . . . Must a writer of your stature be constantly fighting with everyone? Let these attacks pass, dear fellow."[47] And, indeed, Bilbao did sue, claiming "the first to last word" of Vicuña Mackenna's article were libelous.

The trial occurred as the intentions of other works of history were being challenged in the press. The acid-tongued Antonio José de Irisarri was claiming Melchor Concha y Toro's recent *memoria* had erroneously charged that he had acted without authority when he had obtained a loan from Britain during O'Higgins' rule, a debt that Chile had yet to repay due to its highly unfavorable terms.[48] At the same time, Vicuña Mackenna was also replying to yet another Irissari work, *El charlatanismo de Vicuña*, which claimed that Vicuña Mackenna had also treated the debt episode unfairly in the pages of *El ostracismo del General O'Higgins*. And in the midst of these historical debates on the front pages of *El Ferrocarril*, came the Bilbao accusation, which, ironically, had nothing to do with the historical questions that had begun the argument. Rather, the main objection was to Vicuña Mackenna's treatment

45. *El Ferrocarril*, May 5, 1863.
46. *Archivo Nacional: Archivo Benjamín Vicuña Mackenna*, T. 171.
47. See Antonio José de Irisarri, *Escritos polémicos* (Santiago, 1934), 269–318.
48. *El Ferrocarril*, May 6, 1863; Vicuña Mackenna, *Diez años*, 15.

of Bilbao himself, namely, the charges of cowardice in Coquimbo in the 1851 revolt and the insinuations that he acted as a spy in Peru.[49]

The public flocked to the trial on June 25, much as they had done at Vicuña Mackenna's Valparaíso trial. *El Ferrocarril* reported that the final hearing would "take place at 11:00, and, judging from the number of people that attended today, it appears that the crowd may not fit in the courtroom." While Bilbao's charges were not directed against Vicuña Mackenna's historical works per se, Vicuña Mackenna used a tried-and-true argument once again, claiming that as a historian his impartiality in all matters was guaranteed, almost by definition: "I have never been an agent provocateur in the press . . . nor a libelist. On the contrary, my only goal as a writer has been a social mission. If you doubt it, then look at my works."[50] He then noted that he had written an impartial biography of the Carreras even though Luis Carrera had killed his grandfather in a duel. Also, he had prepared an impartial biography of Portales, even though he had removed the Mackenna family from power. And still further, he presented an impartial study of the Montt regime even though he had been persecuted for over ten years by the government. He then invoked the image of the priesthood of the historian which had served him so well in an earlier trial, and then rested his case. Unfortunately, the jury was not entirely convinced, absolving him on one count of libel, but charging him with the minimum sentence (fifteen days in prison and twenty-five pesos) on another count.

Although Vicuña Mackenna felt himself entirely vindicated, the "historian as priest" argument seemed less successful than before. Vicuña Mackenna himself noted that his comparison "had become an ironic remark for sharp-tongued wits." Irisarri suggested that the "sa" be removed from *sacerdote* (priest), thus converting a priest to a pig (*cerdo—te*), "the name you historians deserve."[51] Yet Vicuña Mackenna continued to insist on the impartiality of the historian, a position which the literary wits and the reading public found less and less defensible as the years progressed.

When Vicuña Mackenna returned from his secret mission to the United States during the war with Spain with an outdated man-of-war, his critics

49. *El Ferrocarril*, June 24, 1863, July 1, 1863.

50. "Carta a Don Pedro Ugarte sobre la acusación de Bilbao," reprinted in Donoso, *Vicuña Mackenna*, 514–17; *El Ferrocarril*, July 1, 1863; Irisarri, *Escritos*, 269.

51. *El Ferrocarril*, September 12, 1868, September 22, 1868.

heaped abuse on him as never before. *El Ferrocarril*, which had often supported him earlier, now was the official organ of the National party, the followers of Montt. After Vicuña Mackenna heartily encouraged the challenge to the Supreme Court, with Montt as the chief justice, *El Ferrocarril* presented a lengthy editorial which charged that Vicuña Mackenna had made a healthy profit in his deals with the United States for the warships. Vicuña Mackenna then promptly accused the newspaper of libel, and at the same time charged two new satirical magazines, *La Linterna del Diablo* and *Charivari*, with the same offense. The latter magazine may not have repeated the charges of deceit in Vicuña Mackenna's foreign dealings, but rather concerned itself with a weekly deflation of Vicuña Mackenna's ego, by including a biting caricature which for obvious reasons depicted him in priest's garb.

Whereas the affair of the ship purchases should have been the main item of discussion during the trials, the issue of whether a historian could be trusted emerged again and again. José Francisco de Godoy, editor of *El Ferrocarril*, claimed that "the historian's profession is defamation," and Vicuña Mackenna's studies were the best example of this trend. He then asked the jury if there "was one family of high reputation that had escaped his shameful attacks? Not a single one," he replied. Irisarri's son, Hermójenes, read Godoy's defense in *El Ferrocarril* and seconded his opinions: "If Vicuña Mackenna ever said anything favorable about anyone, he must have had personal motives for doing so."[52] The charges against Godoy were dismissed, leaving Vicuña Mackenna to face the editors of *Charivari*, who also challenged his professional conduct.

A bizarre aura of *déjà vu* pervaded the *Charivari* trial, since it became almost an exact repetition of the Valparaíso trial of 1861. The poem which Vicuña Mackenna was objecting to attacked him as a "writing machine" and criticized his lies about the past. The poet was Alcibiades, a pseudonym for Luis Rodríguez Velasco, brother of Francisco who had accused Vicuña in 1861, and, naturally, also the son of O'Higgins' finance minister. Both repeated the arguments of seven years earlier. Vicuña Mackenna asked: "Who have I ever defamed? I only glorify those who are deserving. I have honored all those in political life whom I have found worthy of honor by future generations, and my only criteria have been *justice* and *truth*." Luis Rodríguez re-

52. Vicuña Mackenna, *El castigo de la calumnia* (Santiago, 1868), 74–75, Ch. "Juicio de Charivari."

plied, calling him "this so-called priest of history, the man who had poisoned the life of any family who has had a famous ancestor."[53] While the jury again supported Vicuña Mackenna's claims in the case, the audience of 4,000 apparently thought otherwise, carrying Rodríguez to the doors of the publishers of *El Ferrocarril*. Only one unidentified woman accompanied Vicuña Mackenna to his home.[54]

To this date Vicuña Mackenna never admitted his critics could have been correct. He remained steadfast in the argument he developed during the early 1860s, that the historian, by definition, wrote objectively, and without hidden motives. While the "historian as priest" argument had seemed appropriate in 1861, by 1868 it had become a target for bitter jokes. However, Vicuña Mackenna insistently repeated his argument. Only in the 1870s did he admit that a historian might be proven incorrect. Only then did he abandon his argument of the 1860s.

Vicuña Mackenna's prolific pen slowed slightly in the early 1870s, since he was occupied with a trip to Europe, a term as intendant of Santiago, and a futile attempt to become president.[55] His historical works of this period were shorter than those of the 1860s, and often composed at a frenetic pace. *Cambiaso* was no exception to this trend. Santiago had recently been informed of a military revolt at Punta Arenas, and it had reminded Vicuña Mackenna of the bloody exploits of the pirate Cambiaso in the same area in 1851. The book was completed with his "pen at a gallop in nearly a week and without any pretensions but an honest opportunity to show a terrible drama full of useful lessons." The press greeted the work accordingly. Rómulo Mandiola, in *El Estandarte Católico*, noted that "from the historical point of view, the works of Vicuña Mackenna are quite lacking. They lack the maturity of prolonged investigation, and one can easily discover errors resulting from superficial study."[56]

Yet, more important than the critical barbs of Mandiola was the threat of yet another lawsuit. *La República* first noted this possibility publicly: "A reputable source informs us that the famous writer Vicuña Mackenna is about to

53. Donoso, *Vicuña Mackenna*, 255.
54. Cristián Zegers A., *Aníbal Pinto* (Santiago, 1969), Chs. I.1, I.2., and Vicuña Mackenna, "Impresiones de viajes," in R. Donoso and R. Silva Castro (eds.), *Páginas olvidadas: Vicuña Mackenna en El Mercurio* (Santiago, 1934), 23–164.
55. *El Ferrocarril*, April 14, 1878; *El Estandarte Católico*, January 2, 1878.
56. *La República*, January 29, 1878.

be sued by the widow of Cambiaso."[57] The cause of the widow's dissatisfaction was based on Vicuña's aspersions on her character in *Cambiaso*. Dolores Borquéz Severino Pérez wrote Vicuña Mackenna two weeks after the publication date, expressing her sadness when she found the historian had called her a "prostitute, a concubine, and an evil woman." She expressed disbelief that "the great writer Vicuña Mackenna who so enjoys injuring peoples' reputations" could attack such a "poor and unfortunate woman." She then demanded that he print a retraction in "every newspaper in Chile," remove all remaining copies from bookstore shelves, and prepare a new book based on documents that she would supply. Vicuña Mackenna then attempted to assuage her wrath by sending her a personal letter acknowledging his errors, but this remained unacceptable to her. Dolores' present husband, Severino Pérez, then replied to Vicuña Mackenna, urging him to present a public statement admitting that he had erred. He then claimed that all he desired was "the whole truth which should be presented in all historical works." Further, he expected Vicuña Mackenna to depict his wife in a new work as a woman "pure and free of all blemish, because this is the truth."[58]

Vicuña Mackenna submitted a new study to *El Ferrocarril—La juventud y el proceso de Cambiaso*, based on the new data he had acquired, and also on the desire to avoid a lawsuit. After proving that indeed Cambiaso and Dolores were legally married, Vicuña Mackenna gave a complete reversal to his first image of Dolores: "Her later life demonstrates her honor and her beauty. . . . She married the honorable Jorge Coms after the death of Cambiaso, and when Coms died, she married her third husband, Severino Pérez, an intelligent printer. Cambiaso's widow remains beautiful even today, and lives in her honorable home with her third husband in Ancúd."[59]

Despite this remarkable portrait of this "honorable" woman, Vicuña Mackenna did not submit weakly to printing the rectification. First he defended his writing of contemporary history as "the only true history," since it can be continually corrected by the accumulation of new data given by the participants in the events themselves.[60] Thus despite efforts to avoid printing this new work, Vicuña Mackenna still attempted to depict himself as an im-

57. *Archivo Nacional: Archivo Benjamín Vicuña Mackenna*, T. 29, ff. 55, 43.
58. *Revista Chilena de Historia y Geografía*, LXIV (1927), 54.
59. *Ibid.*, 44.
60. *El Ferrocarril*, November 18, 19, 1878; January 1, 1879.

partial historian who willingly accepts all new information. Thus he still remained on the offensive, although forced to print a correction of *Cambiaso*. However, his reputation for impartiality was soon to crumble as six months later he was to become involved in yet another polemic in which he was to be proven wrong once again.

The surprising news of the assassination of Manuel Pardo, former president of Peru, had shocked Chileans, and Vicuña Mackenna in particular since he had known the ex-president since he was a child. Vicuña Mackenna immediately began writing a heartfelt eulogy for Pardo which praised his spirit of Americanism, his pacific nature, and his use of wise advisers. He compared him to Portales, noting that Pardo "was the genius who accomplished the national reorganization of his country" and "one of the most enlightened heads of state" that Vicuña Mackenna had had the privilege to meet. While the warm praise of Pardo impressed the members of the Faculty of Letters and Political Science at the University of San Marcos in Lima, causing them to rush Vicuña Mackenna's nomination for honorary membership through committee with uncustomary speed, others were not as satisfied with his depiction of Pardo's rule.[61]

Justiniano de Zubiria, a Colombian who had lived in Peru when Pardo was president, immediately attacked this eulogy, claiming Vicuña Mackenna had blatantly distorted the facts. He asserted that the eulogy, printed in *El Ferrocarril*, "pretended to be a page of history" and for this reason "the veracity of the facts must be established." Vicuña Mackenna decided not to answer the "ravings" of Zubiria, who claimed that Pardo "implanted violence and the will of one man as law" in Peru, until he received a letter from Augusto Orrego Luco. Orrego asked Vicuña Mackenna "not to tolerate the display of these vile passions under the cloak of the love of justice and truth. As a writer, as a Chilean, and, as a friend, you must reveal these deliberate misrepresentations of history."[62] Vicuña Mackenna reprinted this letter in *El Ferrocarril*, but still abstained from debate with Zubiria, claiming that any errors in his study of Pardo were mere misprints which should be blamed on the printer.

Zubiria immediately responded noting that Vicuña Mackenna had taken

61. *Ibid.*, November 23, 1878, November 24, 1878.
62. *Ibid.*, November 26, 1878, November 27, 1878, January 8, 1879, February 24, 1879.

the question at hand "from the point of view of history and the facts" and had removed it to "the scandalous domain of personal recriminations, impassioned judgments, and pathetic appeals to the sentiments." Vicuña Mackenna then read Zubiria's latest article, which claimed that Pardo had betrayed Chile by a secret alliance with Bolivia, and resolved to defend the name of Pardo "before justice and history." Vicuña Mackenna's *La justificatión del ex-presidente del Perú Don Manuel Pardo* repudiated all charges that Pardo "did not love Chile" by presenting several letters from Peru which attested to this fact. He tersely concluded saying that "history and truth have spoken their last word." Zubiria hammered away at Pardo's betrayal of Chile, and ended his study more "modestly," by "humbly asking the American people who have read these articles to compare them, judge for themselves, and decide the truth."[63]

Ironically, the positions of Vicuña Mackenna and Zubiria represented a reversal from the debates of the 1860s, as here Vicuña Mackenna became the defender of a friend's historical image, while his opponent struggled to keep the debate in the terrain of "history and the facts." The assertions of Zubiria eventually proved correct. Pardo indeed had been allied with Bolivia in a mutual defense treaty, their goal being the possible acquisition of Chile's rich nitrate lands in the North.[64] The revelation shocked Vicuña Mackenna deeply, and he felt compelled to print a retraction on his own accord, as well as resign his honorary memberhsip from the University of San Marcos. He wrote to Sebastián Lorente, dean of the faculty, that his resignation "affected him deeply," but, he hoped that the future would bring American unity, and the passions of the past would be forgotten.[65]

In this manner, one historian, Benjamín Vicuña Mackenna, admitted that perhaps a historian could be incorrect in the interpretation of the past, misled by haste, disinterest, or even his own passions. Thus, the image of the historian as infallible arbiter of the facts became deflated as the century progressed. It became evident that the mere protestation that a work was based

63. Francisco A. Encina, *Las relaciones entre Chile y Bolivia, 1841–1963* (Santiago, 1963), Ch. 1.

64. *El Ferrocarril*, April 16, 1878.

65. For Lastarria on Vicuña Mackenna, see Domingo Amunátegui Solar, *Archivo epistolar de Don Miguel Luis Amunátegui* (Santiago, 1942), I, 149–50; *Archivo Nacional: Fondos Varios*, T. 171; and *El Ferrocarril*, November 15, 1871. For Barros Arana on Vicuña Mackenna, see *Anales de la Universidad de Chile*, nos. 109–110 (1958), 82.

on a careful study of the facts did not exempt it from criticism, nor establish its veracity. Vicuña Mackenna may have ideally believed in the objectivity of the historian, thus following Bello's views on historical writing, or he may have deliberately attempted to construct the image of the "historian as priest" in order to convince his audience of his truthfulness, whether it existed or not. The audience was not to be fooled. While Vicuña Mackenna's fellow historians felt free to joke of his prolific pen, his highflown imagination, and his exaggerated passion for the study of great men, they rarely attacked the basic assumptions of the historical profession. Only the audience, admittedly for highly specific motives, was able to question the possibility of a historian's bias. This soon led to the realization that history, despite the claims of Andrés Bello, could be, and often was, an object of the passions.

8

FOR GOD OR COUNTRY

HISTORY AND EDUCATION IN CHILE

AT FIRST THE DAILY PAPERS warmly praised the efforts of the University of Chile to encourage historical writing because they were convinced that "there was nothing more useful for a man destined to serve his country than the knowledge of history." For this reason, the opening of a course of history in the colegio was an event of prime importance. The first class of José María Núñez at the Colegio de Santiago received front-page coverage in *El Progreso*. The newspaper lauded the teaching of history as the "ideal means to bind an individual's loyalties to his nation."[1] In addition to the belief that the knowledge of history could induce a man to become a "first-rate patriot," the ideal was widespread that the lessons of the past would aid those in political affairs in the making of day-to-day decisions.

The glowing optimism of these reports presented the teaching of history as a cure for the ills that troubled the young Republic of Chile. José Victorino Lastarria had argued that self-interest was the prime characteristic of Chileans.[2] He reasoned that education could erase this trait and encourage an allegiance to one's fellow man and the nation. Others noted that Chile lacked trained leaders and scientists. Again, an intensive program of education could fill this gap. Education became a panacea for both Chilean Liberals and Conservatives, although each envisioned a different educational system. Las-

---

1. *El Progreso*, February 14, 1843, April 10, 1843. See also *El Ferrocarril*, June 13, 1863.
2. Lastarria, *El manuscrito del diablo* (Lima, 1850).

tarria, Barros Arana, and fellow Liberals demanded vigorous state action in the financing of public education and the licensing and control of schools, teachers, and textbooks. They argued that education was a right and an obligation for every citizen. Lastarria believed that "the state should demand that all members of society should learn the first elements of human knowledge so they might know and comply with their social duties."[3] Conservatives favored private initiative in the formation of an educational system, and they argued that the number of schools in Chile would increase if cumbersome regulatory controls were abolished. In the meantime, they expressed their satisfaction with the primary and secondary educational facilities that had been supplied by the Church.

However, despite the widespread optimism that education would be beneficial for Chilean progress, there existed a growing sense of inquietude. A parish priest warned: "The mind of a child is incapable of guarding itself against error and bad faith; it is susceptible to deceit as well as error."[4] A child could just as easily be educated to become a patriot as a traitor. It depended on who educated the child and how. Thus, the educational process could just as easily become a danger as a savior to the state. In Chile this threat was realized as the Liberals perceived the religious schools advocating the political ascendancy of the Church to the children, while Conservatives and fervent Catholics recognized a similar danger in public schools which urged the supremacy of the state in a secular society. Concerned educators discovered that history textbooks were the most guilty of this covert attempt at persuasion. A curiously ambivalent debate on this practice resulted as Conservatives and Liberals alike condemned this subjective approach to historical writing in textbooks written by their political opponents. However, both were unable and unwilling to eliminate the practice among those of their own political stripe since they found history an able ally in the continuing controversy between Church and state.

The acerbity of the textbook debates grew in direct proportion to the diffusion of primary and secondary education and the increasing impositions on the prerogatives of the Church. When only 10 percent of the school-age children attended class by 1848, the textbook issue was rarely discussed. However, during the presidency of Manuel Montt, the leader who gave the

3. Luis Oyarzun, *El pensamiento de Lastarria* (Santiago, 1935), 136.
4. *Revista Católica*, IX, 575.

greatest impetus to educational reform, the number of students attending primary school more than doubled, and the number of schools more than tripled (see Chart I). Secondary private education experienced a similar boost. Montt argued that the state should take complete control of the educational system and provide free, if not obligatory, instruction. While the final legislation governing the public financing of the school system was not approved until the last year of his rule, the amount spent on education from 1850 to 1854 almost doubled the expenditures of the previous decade (see Chart II). With the increased numbers attending school, the textbook issue acquired new importance. Additionally, Montt's assertion of civil authority in the internal affairs of the Church in the "affair of the sacristan" and his refusal to place a cleric in charge of the National Institute, accentuated a division between Church and state which had remained muted since the time of Portales.

A sharp division in historical interpretations was not apparent during the 1830s and 1840s. Vicente Fidel López, the Argentine émigré, presented the first Chilean history textbook to the University Council for approval in 1845. The decision process was often a slow one. After the author presented his textbook to the council, an eleven-member board which included the deans of the five faculties would refer it to the dean of the appropriate faculty. He would then appoint one or two faculty members to prepare a critique of the text and compare it with similar works available in Chile. The criteria for final approval were decided in an 1845 meeting of the Faculty of Philosophy and Humanities, which ruled that "a work should be *approved* if it contained no prejudicial or erroneous doctrines; it should be *recommended* if it were notable for a special reason; and *adopted* if its outstanding advantages made it deserving for use as a textbook in public schools."[5] The approval had no absolute effect, since previous textbooks were not eliminated by this choice. The final decision on textbook use was still left to the director of the school, who, however, was often receptive to the decisions of the faculty council.

López' textbook posed a dilemma for the University Council since it seemed to present ideals more characteristic of Argentines than Chileans. The *Manual de la historia de Chile para el uso de las escuelas primarias* agreed with Chilean writers that the "state should teach students what they must know in order to be worthy citizens of a civilized republic," but this was the

5. *Anales de la Universidad de Chile*, II (1843), 61.

Chart I: PRIMARY SCHOOLS IN CHILE, 1850–1861

Year	Total Schools	Total Students
1850	300	21,000
1853	571	23,131
1854	660	27,550
1855	680	28,822
1856	758	30,613
1857	857	33,351
1858	740	33,701
1859	764	33,730
1860	950	39,633
1861	919	43,368

Source: Luis Galdames, *La Universidad de Chile, 1834–1934* (Santiago: Universidad de Chile, 1934), 62–66.

Chart II: PUBLIC EXPENDITURES ON EDUCATION

Year	Pesos Allotted	Pesos Spent
1836	7,621	
1837	7,717	
1840	8,635	
1841	8,635	
1842	20,785	
1843	20,609	
1844	37,013	
1845	41,163	
1846	48,503	40,039
1847	42,523	37,000
1848	43,823	38,585
1849	47,832	41,568
1850	93,581	87,050
1851	71,003	44,942
1852	89,169	65,782
1853	99,321	89,504
1854	149,322	145,639
1855	165,407	—

Source: Julio César Jobet, *Doctrina y praxis de los educadores representativos chilenos* (Santiago: Andrés Bello, 1970), 215. Jobet notes that the expenditures remained small with respect to the total budget, i.e., the 1852 education budget was only 1 percent of the total government expenditures.

only note to strike a responsive chord. López presented a lengthy study of the nature of race which defined the Spanish "race" as civilized and the Indian "race" as barbarous, thus following the argument of his compatriot Sarmiento's *Facundo*, which was printed in Santiago in the same year. While scorning the Indians, López mildly praised the Spaniards by noting that "Spain was not always the enemy of the philosophic spirit and the freedom of thought." Such an interpretation countered the "Black Legend" and the myth of the "heroic Araucanian savage" which formed a vital part of Chilean revolutionary rhetoric. The text was returned to López for corrections after the University Council meeting, and the secretary suggested that "the writer should call attention to the mixture of the Spanish race and the Indians which formed the *mestizo* class which comprises the majority of our people."[6] Argentines preferred to ignore such thoughts at this time, and apparently López was no exception. He submitted the work again with minor corrections a week later, and it was accepted, partially because no other textbooks had been presented.

A satisfactory textbook for primary schools as well as for *colegios* seemed years in coming. Until that time professors managed as best they could. Antonio García Reyes, a member of the University Council, attended the South American history examinations in 1853 at the National Institute and noted: "The exams were satisfactory, considering the troubles the professor and the students had with the text they chose. They chose it not because it was approved by the University Council, but because more copies of it were available than of any other text. . . . As a matter of fact, the class in American history does not have a textbook now. You well know the inconveniences this causes: slow and imperfect learning of the lessons."[7]

The lack of texts often necessitated a lecture system for the teaching of history which allowed the teacher to stray, if he wished, from the text approved by the University Council. This variance from approved texts irritated Diego Barros Arana, a member of the Faculty of Philosophy and Humanities, when he attended the modern history examinations of 1857.

6. Vicente Fidel López, *Manual de la historia de Chile* (Valparaíso, 1845), 117; Simon Collier, *Ideas and Politics of Chilean Independence, 1808–1833* (Cambridge, 1967), 192–200, 207–17.
    7. M. L. Amunátegui Reyes, *Don Antonio García Reyes* (Santiago, 1930), V, 187–88, 182.

The examination period became the only time when the University Council might exercise some control over the education presented in private schools, and, in particular, the *seminarios conciliares*, schools under the direction of the local diocese. Every year, students from both public and private schools took exams before a board of three professors from the National Institute, which decided whether the students should receive their degrees. Barros Arana listened to the students' responses and became irate when he learned what these students were being taught at the *seminario conciliar* of Santiago: "[The texts, written by the professors] are presented with an ultracatholic zeal, and are conceived with the express purpose of inciting terror in the young students whenever they hear the words *Protestant Reformation*. The text is a diatribe against the Protestant kings and a panegyric to the Catholic monarchs. Philip II of Spain, Mary Tudor of England, and many other luminaries of the sixteenth century who prostituted religion to serve their bastard ambitions, are depicted as models of virtue."[8]

Barros Arana repeated his charges in the daily *El Ferrocarril* and soon received a stinging rebuke from the rector of the Seminario de Santiago, Joaquín Larraín Gandarillas, who defended the 118 students who took the history examinations that year. He scoffed at Barros Arana's complaint that "the future of the republic was compromised by these history exams, denied that his establishment was training "narrow-minded and intolerant priests," and refused to accede to the demand that he "appoint a professor of history whose spirit was free of sectarian hate." Barros Arana then wondered why the students from the *seminario* were unable to answer his simple questions which were taken from the chapter summaries of Michelet's writings used in the National Institute.[9]

Larraín Gandarillas explained that he resented the anti-Catholic bias of Michelet, and, for this reason, he preferred the text of Drioux, a work of "secure doctrine, which countered Michelet's ideas that Luther's reforms were the most important event in the modern world." He then added that the students should know the "vices and errors of the fathers of the Protestant Reformation." Barros Arana then countered: "But shouldn't they also know their merits and virtues?" Larraín Gandarillas replied: "We feel that the Ref-

8. *Anales de la Universidad de Chile*, January 4, 1857.

9. *Revista Católica*, VIII (1857), 2137, 2188–90, 2196–98; *El Ferrocarril*, March 14, 1857.

ormation paralyzed the progress of European civilization. Without this en-
cumbrance, England would be the leader of all nations in the prosperity of
the moral, intellectual, and spiritual order. We teach that Protestantism was
just a rebellion of human pride against the Divine principle of authority in
the realm of human faith." He then slyly queried: "Perhaps, Sr. Barros
Arana, this divergence of opinions is due to the books we have consulted.
After all, De Maistre believed that in certain hands history is only a conspiracy against the truth." [10]

Barros Arana resented this remark and noted that it might be true of the
professors in the *seminario* itself. He argued that the directors of the *seminario*
"wanted books written only by clerics, and not sensitive and enlightened
clerics, but those who see the past through a telescope that disfigures all they
see. They would rather use the text of Drioux, composed of bits and pieces of
other writers, chosen with an eye to defending Catholicism and the Monarchy, which are the goals of the professors of the *seminario conciliar*." [11]

Larraín then attempted to prove that "passion (not reason) moved the
pen" of Barros Arana, by noting that former reports on the history examinations had been unanimously favorable, even that of Barros Arana himself! [12]
Why should there be such a difference one year later unless he were attacking
the *seminario* for other motives? Barros Arana's previous report had indeed
been flattering, but there was one important qualification. Formerly, he had
praised the professor for his reliance on the "text adopted by the University
Council which aided him immeasurably in his teaching." Thus, the shifting
of textbooks to the work of Drioux would seem to supply sufficient reason for
Barros Arana's change of heart. It is also interesting to note that the textbook
shift and the increased controversy over the history examinations occurred in
the year following the "affair of the sacristan," which once again brought the
question of the relations between Church and state to the forefront.

At the same time that Barros Arana was criticizing the bias in the history
textbooks at the *seminario conciliar*, he was also involved in the editing of
another textbook for the Society of Primary Instruction. These privately fi-
nanced societies began in 1856 with the desire to "encourage primary instruction in the department of Santiago and reach those men, women, and

10. *Ibid.*, March 18, 1857.
11. *Ibid.*, April 3, 1857.
12. *Revista Católica*, VIII (1857), 2196–97.

children who had not learned to read but expressed the desire to learn." [13]
Two hundred students attended these classes in 1856, and more than eight
hundred in 1857. The choice of Barros Arana, Miguel Luis Amunátegui, and
Guillermo Matta to compile "a gallery of famous men examined in the light
of truth and justice" was designed to ensure strict impartiality in the "Popular Biographies of Famous Chileans." An editorial in *El Ferrocarril* praised the
work: "Until now only the passion of the moment or the narrow interests of
the aristocratic have led to the writing of biographies of the great men of our
country. The nation does not know who its greatest heroes are since no one
has directed attention to them. This book will lead the nation to know and
judge its heroes and perhaps imitate them." [14]

Yet, while strict impartiality was supposedly guaranteed, a marked anticlerical bias filled the pages of the work. Although Benjamín Vicuña Mackenna expressed his desire to discuss the lives of the three most famous
Chilean Jesuits without bias, he noted: "Perhaps the contrast between these
men and the ridiculous *farceurs* who are now invading our country with the
name of Jesuits will help persuade our citizenry that the days of Loyola are
gone forever." [15]

Although Vicuña Mackenna claimed that he wrote for the love of "truth
and justice," the Catholic press found his writings laden with slurs against
these famous Jesuits and the Church as well. Vicuña Mackenna summarily
dismissed Alonso de Ovalle's account of the early colonial era, *Histórica relación del Reino de Chile* (1646), as a "simplistic and barbarous mishmash," and
criticized the Inquisition's persecution of men of independent thought. [16] Isidoro Errázuriz, who had criticized the Jesuits since his high school days in a
strict Jesuit institution in Washington, D.C., concluded this anticlerical attack with a sketch of Caupolicán, the Indian chieftain, in which he lambasted the Spaniards and the missionaries: "The Spaniards invaded the Indian
territory in the name of civilization and a false Christianity. What could the

13. Alberto Velásquez, *Reseña histórica de la Sociedad de Instrucción Primaria, 1856–1873*
(Santiago, 1873); and José Alfonso A., *La Sociedad de Instrucción Primaria de Santiago de Chile*
(Santiago, 1937).

14. *El Ferrocarril*, April 20, 1857.

15. *Ibid*. The Jesuits were reestablished in Chile on July 10, 1854.

16. "Revista de errores publicados por el diario de Santiago y de sus agresiones contra el
clero en la presente semana," *Revista Católica*, VIII, 2247. See also "Biografías populares,"
ibid., 2273–76.

Indian think of this Christianity and civilization? The same missionary who preached charity, love, and the existence of a beneficent deity, also blessed the vile sword, encouraging murder and plunder by the conquistadors." [17]

Two new textbooks were also submitted to the University Council in 1857, and Barros Arana found them hardly satisfactory. While praising the work of Orestes Tornero as "the best educational text written thus far," he lamented the author's tendency to borrow full paragraphs from the works of William Robertson and insert them unchanged into the text. Miguel de la Barra's *Compendio de la historia del descubrimiento i conquista de América* offered similar defects and "lacked the order necessary to provide a clear narrative style." [18]

In order to provide some order in this dizzying mélange of history textbooks, Barros Arana suggested to the University Council that the same text be used in all public institutions of instruction. Once this had been achieved, an informal pressure would exist for the private schools to adopt the same text since the university controlled the examination system. Students using the standard text would naturally perform better than those lectured by their professor or those using outdated or biased textbooks. Barros Arana, who had recently been appointed to the University Council, chose a committee of Amunátegui, Jean Gustave Courcelle-Senouil, a French economist residing in Chile, and himself, to examine the textbook situation. The committee soon decided that the six-volume *Course of Universal History* by Victor Duruy would be an ideal text. [19] Duruy, an energetic young historian of the Lycée Napoleon and soon-to-be minister of education under Napoleon III, had begun this project with the aid of thirty collaborators in 1848. Duruy, also a former secretary of Michelet, contributed two volumes, those on Greek and Roman history, to the final work.

The choice was not surprising since the committee chose a work in sharp conformity with its views. Duruy's work differed greatly from the texts Barros Arana had found so disagreeable in the *seminario conciliar*. Duruy presented a secular view of history which considered the Bible primarily as a work of literature. He once commented that "je ne crois pas que des légendes

17. Isidoro Errázuriz, *Historia de la administración Errázuriz* (Santiago, 1935), xx; *El Ferrocarril*, May 22, 1857.

18. *El País*, October 20, 1857.

19. Diego Barros Arana and Miguel Luis Amunátegui, *Nuevo plan de estudios para el curso de humanidades* (Santiago, 1857).

soient matìere d'Histoire." Catholic writers in Chile found the choice offensive and dangerous. They claimed that "while Duruy does not belong to the school of irreligious enthusiasm of Voltaire, we believe that he belongs to a new rationalist and liberal school which sees Christianity as a human fact, not as an event of divine origin. From this viewpoint, Duruy arrives at many false ideas about the Church hierarchy." [20]

The Catholic opposition also found the greater emphasis on history in the "new plan of studies," prepared by Barros Arana and Amunátegui, as yet another threat to their values. After 1858, Duruy's work would be presented to all students, whether they were studying to become doctors, priests, or businessmen. Everyone would be required to take a common humanities course in the mornings, before proceeding to their specialized work in the afternoons. Every student would study Duruy's works for four out of the five years in the *colegio*. The only exception was a one-year history of America and Chile, for which, naturally, the work of Duruy was insufficient. Thus history was no longer a freely elected subject.

Yet, despite the swift passage of the reform and the high praise of Duruy's works in university circles, years passed before the reforms were implemented. Problems of translation and printing plagued the project. Duruy's work was originally accepted on the provision that it be printed in two different sizes of type, one large, designating the sections of most importance to the student, and, one small, providing points of lesser interest for the professor's background reading. This specification resulted in considerable delay for the project. By 1863, when Barros Arana was appointed rector of the National Institute by President Pérez, he reported that the reforms of 1858 had yet to be implemented: "The disorganization of historical studies in Chile and the use of confusing or completely inadequate texts make a solution to this problem extremely difficult. The students still learn a great quantity of names and dates by memory, but they still have no idea what history really is. The necessity of standardizing the texts becomes more apparent every day. The continuous approval of textbooks by the council and the use of others which have not been approved produce inconveniences which must be avoided." [21]

20. Jean Rohr, *Victor Duruy, Ministre de Napoleon III* (Paris, 1967); *Revista Católica*, IX (1858), 576.
21. *Anales de la Universidad de Chile*, March 7, 1863, May 2, 1863.

Despite the desperate appearance of the situation as Barros Arana assumed his post, ten years later the works of Duruy were taught in all public institutions. Similarly, Barros Arana's own *Compendio de historia de América* and Amunátegui's *Compendio de la historia política i eclesiástica de Chile* became the standard texts in all American history classes in Chile's public schools. Yet, the implicit purpose of the reform, that private schools adopt the same textbooks, had yet to be realized. Only the *seminario conciliar* at Ancud taught Duruy's course, and only the *seminario* at La Serena taught the Barros Arana history of America (see Charts III and IV). The failure of the reform in the private schools was not suprising since the Church hierarchy stubbornly resisted all attempts at change by the new rector, who, they claimed, represented the new secular attitudes that were entering the schools. Their opposi-

Chart III: HISTORY TEXTBOOKS USED IN PUBLIC AND PRIVATE SCHOOLS—1871

		History Textbooks	
Seminarios Conciliares	*World*	*American*	*Chilean*
Ancud	Duruy	—	—
Concepción	Drioux	De la Barra	—
La Serena	Drioux	Barros Arana	—
Santiago	Drioux	—	—
Valparaíso	Drioux	—	—
Liceos			
Ancud	Duruy	Barros Arana	Amunátegui
Cauquenes	Duruy	Barros Arana	Amunátegui
Concepción	Duruy	Barros Arana	Amunátegui
Copiapó	Duruy	Barros Arana	Amunátegui
Curicó	Duruy	Barros Arana	Amunátegui
Chillán	Duruy	—	—
La Serena	Duruy	Barros Arana	Amunátegui
Los Angeles	Duruy	Barros Arana	—
San Felipe	Duruy	Barros Arana	Amunátegui
San Fernando	Duruy	Barros Arana	Amunátegui
Santiago	Duruy	Barros Arana	Amunátegui
Talca	Duruy	Barros Arana	Amunátegui
Valdivia	Duruy	Barros Arana	Amunátegui
Valparaíso	Duruy	Barros Arana	Amunátegui

Source: *Anales de la Universidad de Chile* (1872)

Chart IV: CHILDREN STUDYING HISTORY IN PUBLIC AND
PRIVATE SCHOOLS

	Liceos	Seminarios	Total
Spanish Grammar	1,466	488	1,954
Arithmetic	1,275	281	1,556
HISTORY:			
Ancient	19	158	177
Roman	15	62	77
Medieval	191	137	328
Modern	147	40	187
American/Chilean	227	123	350
Sacred	946	161	1,107
TOTAL STUDYING HISTORY	1,545	681	2,226

Source: *Anales de la Universidad de Chile* (1872)

tion eventually led to the removal of Barros Arana from the rectorship in 1873.

The threat that Barros Arana represented in the minds of Catholic writers was primarily to their religion. He soon suppressed the daily mass, the rosary, and confession in the National Institute. Parents and educators also worried because the new rector allowed their children to read books that attacked the virtues of religion. Barros Arana answered this complaint by installing two card catalogues in the library, one for students, which lacked the writings of Voltaire, Condillac, and others, and a second catalogue for professors. His actions were to no avail, for Catholic writers saw threatening ideas everywhere in the institute, and especially in the textbooks written by Barros Arana. His *Nociones de historia literaria* provoked a series of fifteen front-page articles in the *Revista Católica*: "We deplore anyone who puts textbooks that weaken religious principles in the hands of our youth. Unfortunately, this book is not the first that we have noticed of this nature. For several years textbooks of this type have been used in our schools. Barros Arana's work criticizes the belief that Divine Providence constantly influences the direction of earthly events, that ideal enshrined by Vico and Bossuet which so clearly follows Catholic dogma." [22]

Barros Arana's *Compendio de historia de América* (1865) also brought clerical complaints, despite the author's attempt to appear impartial. Barros

22. *Revista Católica*, May 16, 1868.

Arana's criticism of Lucas Alamán in the bibliography of his work revealed a subtle irony. While Barros Arana considered the Mexican historian's inability "to hide his sympathy for the Spanish cause" a "grave defect," he himself was unable to remain impartial when discussing the role of the Church in Chile's history. Barros Arana established that the "ecclesiastical authority always paid its respects to the royal authority" in Chile's past, thus placing the Church in its proper and subordinate position in a secular state. He also viciously attacked the clergy in this historical text. He noted that they "enjoyed a great influence in the Spanish colonies due to their great wealth and the popular respect for religion." He added that the clerics' faith "in their own prestige was the cause of their corruption and ignorance."[23]

Others added infractions of the university rules to their charges against Barros Arana. Zorobabel Rodríguez claimed in his column in the Conservative literary magazine, La Estrella de Chile, that the rector was making a 400 percent profit on every copy of his Manual de composición literaria that was sold. The deputy from San Carlos, Luis Martínez Rodríguez, noted that the Historia de América textbook had been approved by the University Council before it had been published. Why should people bother to write textbooks if the university clique decided in advance which works would be chosen? Barros Arana responded that the work had been read to the University Council and had been approved in that form. The publication had been delayed due to the Spanish blockade in 1865 which prevented shipments of paper from Europe.[24]

Despite the criticism of Barros Arana in the 1860s, his position seemed secure after he had achieved several successful reforms within the institute. He allowed the professors of humanities to specialize and teach the subject they knew best, where formerly they had taught "Latin, mathematics, geography, cosmography, Spanish grammar, and all fields of history, except American and Chilean" all in the same semester. He allowed students to take examinations without taking the course itself if they could prove that they had mastered the subject matter. He worked diligently, writing seven textbooks comprising all realms of thought: rhetoric, grammar, American history, literary history, literary composition, and physical geography.[25]

23. Barros Arana, Compendio de la historia de América (Santiago, 1865), II, 167, 265.
24. La Estrella de Chile, November 5, 1871; La República, December 21, 1876.
25. El Mercurio, March 19, 1862; Antonio Ruíz Urbina, "Barros Arana, educador,"

The reason for Barros Arana's dismissal from the institute was based more on a difference of educational philosophy with the new government than the petty rumors of loose discipline, rampant syphilis, and declining morals in the classroom. Initially Barros Arana had received the warm support of President Pérez, who had found in the historian and scholar a man of trust and independence. However, the situation changed abruptly with the election of Federico Errázuriz as president in 1871 and his selection of Abdón Cifuentes, who had been chosen to attract Conservative elements, as the minister of education. Cifuentes and Barros Arana espoused sharply differing views of the state's role in encouraging education. Barros Arana insisted on strong state action in the field of education: "I do not have to repeat that no public instruction existed in Chile before the state assumed responsibility. Individual action as well as the activity of religious groups were fruitless. If the state had not founded the National Institute and the provincial *liceos*, Chile would be today what it was prior to 1810: the model of ignorance." Cifuentes echoed the Conservative position and insisted on the "liberty of education" and the ending of the state monopoly in educational matters. Liberals considered this call for liberty a tricky maneuver, a mere rhetorical device to achieve the Conservative goal of a return to Church control over education.[26]

The action that was going to bring these debates to a head was the declaration of the "freedom of examination." The examination system had remained unchanged since the establishment of the University of Chile in 1842. The exams, half-written, half-oral, were administered yearly by professors of the National Institute. The student picked his questions from a hat placed in front of the secretary of the Faculty of Humanities. He then had two hours to write the exam, using only a dictionary for assistance. The exams were then classified as good, fair, or poor by three professors from the institute. A poor examination prohibited the youngster from taking the oral exam and he had to wait six months before he could repeat the test. Six days after the written exam, the student appeared for his oral exam. Again he was asked to pick a card from a hat. Each card had a list of nine discussion questions. The examiners, however, were not limited to these questions, and

---

Anales de la Universidad de Chile, nos. 109–110 (1958), 173–74; and Rolando Mellafe, "Barros Arana, americanísta," *ibid.*, 260–69.

26. *El Ferrocarril*, December 21, 1871; Abdón Cifuentes, *Memorias* (Santiago, 1934); Barros Arana, *Mi destitución* (Santiago, 1873), 21.

could, if they desired, ask the student whatever they wished. Whereas the exams were public, the decision whether the student passed or failed was made in private. The system could be subject to abuse. Students in the National Institute knew their examiners and might be familiar with the type of questions they might ask. Students from out of town might have to take all of their exams within three days, while those living in Santiago were given the full examination time required by the university rules. Also, the examination schedule was sent only to the two liberal dailies, *El Ferrocarril* and *La República*, thus leaving the readers of the Conservative *El Independiente* out in the cold.[27]

Barros Arana never wavered in his defense of the examination system, since he believed that to allow the private schools to survey their own exams would produce chaos and worthless degrees. An event which occurred during the December, 1871, examinations served to confirm his beliefs. Nine students from the Colegio de San Ignacio, a Jesuit institution, failed their Spanish grammar examinations. There was no denying that the students were unprepared, since Gregorio Amunátegui had quizzed the students in advance and advised them not to take the exams that year. Complicating the affair was the fact that "Padre Mújica, professor of grammar at San Ignacio, sat on the sidelines and made gestures and whispered to the students in order that they would give the proper response to the questions. However, it was most unusual when Mújica tried to correct the students even when they gave the right answers." But the greatest irony occurred when, despite the dismal performance on the exams, over 265 prizes were distributed at the San Ignacio graduation ceremonies. Barros Arana laughed and remarked that it reminded him of a similar school near Paris, where "all the students in the school received prizes. If the students were children of the rich or high political figures, they received two prizes, but if their father was *very* rich or occupied a *very* high political position, they received three or more prizes."[28]

Barros Arana was not to laugh for long, for Cifuentes abolished the examination system at the beginning of 1872. Arguing that the present system imposed great hardships on the students of private schools and demanded growing amounts of time from professors of the National Institute which could be better spent teaching, he declared that private schools would no

27. *El Ferrocarril*, October 25, 1872; *El Independiente*, November 10, 1871.
28. *La República*, January 2, 1872, January 9, 1872.

longer be subject to state examination. Also, the private schools were "free to adopt whatever plan of studies, methods, or educational texts that they believed preferable, with the only restriction being that they taught the minimum requirements demanded by the university for a degree." [29]

Liberals feared that the loosening of the requirements would lead to the growth of "degree mills" where students could purchase their degrees or attend only a few classes and answer simple questions on their exams. The Conservative press, however, welcomed the recent flurry of new school openings as a sign of educational progress. Three had already opened within thirty days of Cifuentes' decree. The chaos predicted by the Liberals soon developed. Two hundred students withdrew from the National Institute in order to take simpler exams elsewhere. Classroom discipline declined. R. A. Philippi, an eminent biologist, complained: "For the third time in a row, no students have attended my botany class, although I have seen them walking about only two hours before. I have been teaching nineteen years and this has never happened before. I refuse to go back to my classroom unless I am guaranteed that I will find my students there." [30]

Yet, while some students were enjoying the "vacation" decreed by Cifuentes, others vigorously supported Barros Arana. Two minor uprisings at the institute directed against an inspector appointed by Cifuentes were used by the government as proof of the laxity of the rector. Students even attacked Cifuentes' home. Barros Arana was suspended from his job after these disturbances and was judged before a tribunal which prohibited him and professors from the institute from speaking. Only his accusers were heard. [31]

The protests of professors and students were to no avail, as the government divided the rectorship of the institute, giving Barros Arana the inferior position. Soon afterwards, he was relieved of all responsibilities, but he did not quit his post. Finally, a decree of March 12, 1873, removed him from office. He saw this as the "final result of the clerical campaign against him that began in September 1871." He later wrote to his friend Bartolomé Mitre and explained why he was fired from the institute: "I lost my job be-

---

29. Decree of January 1, 1872; reprinted in *La República*, January 17, 1872.

30. *El Independiente*, February 18, 21, 1872; *Anales de la Universidad de Chile*, November 22, 1872, 383; *ibid.*, June 26, 1872.

31. *El Instituto i el Ministro Cifuentes por varios alumnos* (Santiago, 1873); Cifuentes, *Memorias*, II, Ch. 19; Barros Arana, *Mi destitución*.

cause I taught history without miracles, literature without calling Voltaire a thief and a fool, and natural history without mentioning the whale that swallowed Jonah. This manner of education infuriated the clergy, who tried their best to cause me trouble."[32]

Although Barros Arana was later vindicated, since Cifuentes resigned his position in 1874 and the freedom of examination decree was repealed, he still felt embittered against what he believed was a clerical campaign against him. He received a letter from his friend Courcelle-Senouil in 1873 which he forwarded to Miguel Luis Amunátegui, claiming that it expressed his own sentiments exactly:

Actually, this vice of lying under the pretense of a system is more ancient than the Jesuits who perfected it. It is a Christian habit, admitted to be true by the first great historian of the Church, Eusebius of Caesarea. He claimed that Christianity purified our morals, abolished slavery, etc., and made us believe it without any examination or discussion . . . and this is how history is taught.

This is how I understand history. Am I mistaken? I know that it would be dangerous to publish this, but I believe that it will become necessary to teach it very shortly.[33]

Despite Barros Arana's dislike of the way Catholics wrote history in an attempt to buttress their position in society, both he and his friend Amunátegui engaged in a concentrated effort to place the Church in disrepute by the use of scandalous historical revelations. Their turn to anticlerical history was quite timely, since it occurred when the Liberal position on education was most threatened by the Church, after Barros Arana had lost the rectorship, and the Conservatives, led by Cifuentes, had gained control of the Errázuriz cabinet. Before 1872, the anticlerical bias of Barros Arana and Amunátegui was confined to a few sentences in their historical works. However, after the assault of Cifuentes and the Conservatives, this viewpoint obsessed them, coloring all of their historical articles of the period. Their writings may have first been limited to the literary journals, but soon after they found their way to the pages of the newspapers supporting Liberal principles during the National Institute affair.

32. *El Ferrocarril*, June 25, 1872; Letter to Bartolomé Mitre, August 28, 1875, in Museo Mitre, *Correspondencia, literaria, histórica, i política* (Buenos Aires, 1912), II, 281.
33. Domingo Amunátegui Solar, *Archivo epistolar de Don Miguel Luis Amunátegui* (Santiago, 1942), I, 31–32.

Barros Arana first attacked *Las riquezas de los antiguos jesuitas de Chile* (1872) and claimed that the order dominated the colonial governments by means of its fabulous wealth and power "which seems so incredulous to us in this day and age." He argued that the only wish of these "capitalist" missionaries was earning money—their interest in religion was only a clever guise. While others hailed the importance of the Jesuits in the establishment of the colonial educational system, Barros Arana countered: "It was only a business to them—They only founded schools where they were given salaries, buildings, and maintenance costs. Why they even sold candles at prices high above cost during religious festivals!"[34]

Adding to the critique of the materialistic Jesuits, Barros Arana also charged that their historians were traditionally biased: "Chilean historians have often attempted to discuss the Jesuit experience, but, unfortunately, they have studied the documents in a one-sided manner by using only those chronicles written by the Jesuits. If you read these chronicles, you will see Jesuits marching heroically to the spiritual conquest, preaching fraternity and scorn for material wealth, and making Indian slavery disappear. . . . However, if you read the few documents written by others, you can see the other side of the story, namely . . . that the Jesuits were only interested in lining their own pockets."[35]

Barros Arana continued these attacks on the clergy in the pages of *Revista Chilena*, which he founded with his friend Amunátegui in 1875. *La acción del clero en la revolución de la independencia americana*, which appeared in the first issue, surveyed the antirevolutionary activity of the clergy in Chile, Mexico, Peru, Nueva Granada, and Caracas. With the sole exception of Hidalgo in Mexico, Barros Arana proclaimed that priests and bishops everywhere in South America had worked against American independence. Soon afterwards, Barros Arana prepared a treatise on the burial of the dead during the colonial period. While it may have appeared harmless at first glance, it was actually a biting diatribe against the Church's control of funeral practices in the colonial era. The author condemned the ostentation of the funeral ritual and the unhealthy practice of burying the dead within the walls of the Church, which had been continued to the present day. Adding power to the

---

34. *Revista de Santiago* (1872), Ch. 2. This is quite a change from his opinions of nine years earlier. See Barros Arana, *Compendio*, 265.
35. Barros Arana, *Obras completas* (Santiago, 1905–1906), X, 80.

work was the fact that debates on Church control of the cemeteries were occurring at that very moment in Congress.[36]

Joining Barros Arana in this historical critique of the Church's activities was Miguel Luis Amunátegui in a profound change from his lengthy biographical works of the 1860s.[37] While Barros Arana preferred the literary magazine as the vehicle for his articles, Amunátegui chose the front pages of *El Ferrocarril*. To increase the readability of his historical writings, Amunátegui developed a new format, short historical fiction. Amunátegui chose a real incident for the basis of his moral tale and provided imaginary dialogue, vivid detail, emotional confrontations, and even sex and violence, when necessary, in order to interest his readers. The format closely resembled that of the *Tradiciones peruanas* of Ricardo Palma. Amunátegui had met Palma in Valparaíso in 1861, and afterwards they corresponded frequently and often exchanged works. Palma, on one occasion, asked for the latest copy of Amunátegui's "tradiciones."[38]

Yet, these were not merely lurid historical romances, for each *cuento* possessed a moral lesson. Barros Arana explained:

In order to spread his social and political ideals, Amunátegui used the novel form, that is, he used a true fact or an instance created from his imagination in order to explain the ideas and preoccupations of another era, and establish the advantages that modern civilization offers, and those that can be expected with a complete reform of old institutions.

These stories [*historietas*], told with great simplicity and color, were read with great curiosity and were reprinted in the newspapers and magazines of almost all the South American countries. There was more to these works than the ordinary novel, because underneath one could easily discover the liberal or political principle which Amunátegui espoused.[39]

Amunátegui's articles, which appeared biweekly in *El Ferrocarril* in early 1874, emphasized the superstitious nature of religious beliefs and the harmful aspects of religious rituals. The colonial era appeared as an endless pro-

36. Barros Arana, "El entierro de los muertos en la época colonial," *Revista Chilena*, III (1876), 224–45; Ricardo Donoso, *Las ideas políticas en Chile* (Santiago, 1967), 173–207.

37. During the 1850s and 1860s Amunátegui completed biographies of O'Higgins, José Joaquín Vallejo, Ignacio Domeyko, Salvador Sanfuentes, and others. See J. Abel Rosales, "Bibliografía," in C. Morla Vicuña, *Don Miguel Luis Amunátegui* (Paris, 1889).

38. Palma to Amunátegui, *Revista Chilena de Historia y Geografía*, LVI (1926), 28. See also Ricardo Palma, *Tradiciones peruanas completas* (Madrid, 1964), 1528, 1542.

39. Barros Arana, "Don Miguel Luis Amunátegui," in Morla Vicuña, *Amunátegui*, 107.

cession of saints and devils, inquisition officials and individuals, stripped and beaten, as they carried heavy wooden crosses during religious festivals. Yet, Amunátegui always admonished his readers not to forget that the events depicted were historically accurate. Those who supported the prerogatives of the Church easily saw through Amunátegui's intentions, and contended that his *Narraciones históricas*, compiled from *El Ferrocarril*, was not merely a collection of harmless fables. Rómulo Mandiola argued: "Sr. Amunátegui writes in order to teach, to propagate certain types of ideas, to serve a cause. The gifts of the historian and literati are easily put to the service of a lawyer and propagandist. He insists that our ancestors professed blind obedience to the Spanish monarch, and the clergy supported the monarch without limits, and, for this reason, became the prime enemy of progress and liberty during the colonial era." He argued further that Amunátegui's fables were not an "innocent game, but a conscious attack on our religious sentiments."[40]

While this attack on the historical bases of the Church's power in Chile may have exacerbated the debates on the liberty of education, there is no evidence that these works led directly to a weakening of the Conservative position. These attacks were less successful in another manner, for they elicited a series of responses from Catholic writers who once again adopted the same method of writing history that Barros Arana and Amunátegui professed to condemn, but, in reality, used quite frequently. Thus, despite their annoyance with the Catholic manner of using history to defend a political position, the repeated attacks of these Liberal writers fueled the debates and forced the Catholic writers to continue as before.

Barros Arana wrote Amunátegui from Argentina, where he traveled on a diplomatic mission soon after his removal from office:

As I was leaving Chile, I discovered that the Normal School in Santiago was using the cleric Muñoz Donoso's history of America as a textbook. It is an uneven work filled with countless errors and written with the worst possible spirit. He defends the Inquisition and apologizes for the activity of the Jesuits. This work has not even been approved by the University Council. . . .

The Chilean clergy has sent copies of this work to their colleagues in this city [Buenos Aires], but they have decided not to use it because of its exaggerated ultra-

40. Amunátegui, "El Templo de la Compañía de Jesús en Santiago de Chile," *Revista de Santiago*, May 15, 1872; "Lo que hace el diablo en Chile según el Padre Jesuita Miguel de Olivares," *El Ferrocarril*, April 19, 1874. See also *El Ferrocarril*, February 15, 27, March 8, 15, May 25, 1874; *El Estandarte Católico*, July 29, August 5, 1876.

montane ideals. You can no longer tolerate the fact that a state institution uses a book that has not been approved by the university, and which teaches doctrines contrary to the state and the progress of our own era.[41]

La República, a liberal daily, began the attack on Esteban Muñoz Donoso's *Compendio de historia de América i de Chile escrito para los seminarios i los colejios católicos* (1875) in its book review column. After the critic praised the texts of Barros Arana and Amunátegui, which he believed were written "seriously, without preconceived system, with the sole object of discussing well investigated facts," he challenged the cleric's manner of writing history. He noted that "the clergy of today does not wish to present a serious and well-reasoned history text. They are more interested in making this science [history] a weapon of their party in order to support their absurd attempts to hinder the progress of modern civilization."[42]

Muñoz Donoso's new text praised the Jesuit's efforts and lauded the Inquisition as the "prime means of prohibiting the influx of evil books which had done so much harm in Europe." *La República* ridiculed these claims: "Is this the opinion that Catholic children should form of the holy tribunal that bloodied the soil of Spain for two centuries? . . . This is self-evident proof that the clergy teaches history in a shameless manner by changing the facts and maliciously hiding all that does not favor its present interests."[43]

The *Estandarte Católico* quickly replied to the attack on Muñoz Donoso's textbook, partially because he was a frequent contributor to the newspaper. First, it criticized Barros Arana's portrayal of "some bishops as veritable monsters" and decried the Liberal author's harmful influence on the opinions of his friend Amunátegui. The critic thus attempted to deflect the criticism of the new textbook by explaining that Liberal authors had committed similar offenses. He added: "Under the guise of impartiality, there are some authors of history texts [of the ultra-liberal school] who plant the first seeds of doubt in the minds of children first studying this science (history). They bring to light every priest unworthy of his position and hide the names and deeds of those the world praises. This system could not be more harmful, for

41. *Anales de la Universidad de Chile*, Nos. 109–110 (1958), 83.
42. *La República*, May 27, 1875.
43. Esteban Muñoz Donoso, *Compendio de historia de América i de Chile escrito para los seminarios i los colejios católicos* (Santiago, 1875), 222; *La República*, May 27, 1875.

the youth are incapable of judging the facts correctly. . . . In this manner the ultra-liberals are trying to make our children non-believers."[44]

While both Liberals and Conservatives thus recognized the other's attempts to use history to influence the youth to support their own political philosophy, neither would admit that they themselves wrote history with these goals in mind. Both continued to profess that they presented a true and objective vision of the past, but they could no longer disguise the fact that their interpretation of history was primarily a well timed response to the current debates on the secularization of Chilean society.

Muñoz Donoso's textbook was the last to excite such passions in Chilean educational circles. As might be expected, the bitter debates concerning history textbooks stilled as the question of Church and state relations became slowly resolved by the 1880s. By this date, the Church's privileged position in Chilean society began to crumble as the Congress legislated the civil registration of births and deaths, the abolition of the ecclesiastical *fueros*, the strengthening of the *patronato*, and the alteration of Article Five of the Constitution which declared Catholicism the official state religion. Consequently, the final textbooks of the nineteenth century paid no attention to the question of Church-state relations, since the issue had been tentatively resolved.[45] Also contributing to the muted passions in these later textbooks was the influence of a Chilean educational mission to German universities, which advocated a scientific approach to the writing of history.[46] As a result these texts revealed a greater concern with purity of method and educational philosophy than with the resolution of political disputes. Therefore, the conflicting interpretations based on political considerations receded from the history textbooks for the time being, until yet another major issue divided Chilean society with the Revolution of 1891, when, once again, the objective writing of history became impossible.

44. *El Estandarte Católico*, May 29, 31, June 2–5, 12, 1875.

45. See Julio Bañados Espinosa, *Historia de América y de Chile para el curso medio i las escuelas públicas* (Santiago, 1883); Anon. *Lecciones de la historia de Chile para el uso de las escuelas públicas* (Santiago, 1887); Ambrosio Valdés, *Historia general de Chile dedicada a las escuelas primarias* (Santiago, 1888); Domingo Villalobos B., *Lecciones de la historia de Chile arregladas en círculos concéntricos* (Santiago, 1893).

46. See Gustavo Adolfo Holley, "Los estudios secundarios en Chile," *Revista del Progreso*, II (1889), 34–58; Luis Barros Borgoño, *La enseñanza de la historia* (Santiago, 1892).

9

KEYS TO THE FUTURE

POSITIVISM AND HISTORICAL THOUGHT IN

CHILE

AS EARLY AS 1842, both Chileans and Argentines viewed the study of history as the key to their nations' destinies. If one could understand the past, argued Vicente Fidel López, one might plan for the future. Although this was often vaunted as the most important use of history, few historians examined this link between past and future until the philosophy of Auguste Comte reached South America's shores. Comte seemingly had formulated a system which might fulfill the promise of historical studies.

Auguste Comte's attempt to construct a stable social order from the political unrest of Napoleonic France appealed to Latin American *pensadores* who faced similar problems.[1] These intellectuals believed that the wars of independence left a heritage of political chaos which often brought the progress of these new nations to a standstill. Elites also found domestic industries stagnating, constitutional guarantees violated, and a large mass of non-hispanized Indians and blacks threatening the survival of traditional Western culture. Latin American intellectuals from Mexico to Argentina turned to Comte's positive philosophy which heralded a society offering both "order and progress" as a solution to their domestic difficulties. Comte's new system appealed to science in the endeavor to discover the laws that governed man's social and political progress. Once these general laws were discovered, man would then be able to "modify, but not control" his future, and avoid the

1. D. G. Charlton, *Positivistic Thought in France in the Second Empire* (Oxford, 1959), 35.

political, social, and economic strife which threatened present-day Europe and Latin America.[2]

Yet, how could these universal laws be discovered? Comte first suggested experimentation, a technique which had hastened the progress of natural science during the previous hundred years, but he then discarded it as impractical. Society could not be manipulated as easily as light waves or falling objects in the scientific laboratory. Comte believed that an alternative method of discovering these laws might be the careful analysis of man's history. He argued that a new history should be founded which analyzed social causes for specific events. Formerly, according to Comte, history remained a prisoner of theological, fatalistic, or personalistic theories. That is, if a war were declared, historians would have attempted to attribute it either to the will of God (Bossuet), an act of fate (Vico), or the personal whim of a great leader (Carlyle). No one would have attempted to search for social, economic, or political causes of the war. This old-fashioned historical writing lacked practical utility, thought Comte, since it depicted man as a helpless creature with no opportunity to control his destiny. Comte foresaw a new history which promised man the ability to plan his future. This new scientific history was to be freed from all theological and metaphysical frameworks and subject to purely objective criteria. Comte warned that this would be a difficult task, and that it must be entrusted to the "best trained minds."[3]

Thus, from England (Henry Thomas Buckle's *The History of the Civilization of England*) to Mexico (Justo Sierra's *The Political Evolution of the Mexican People*), newly converted positivists turned to their own national histories in the search for the root of the difficulties that plagued their countries and the possible solutions to them. Chile was no exception to this pattern as a small group of intellectuals flirted with positivism as the means to plan Chile's future path. Again it was hoped that an analysis of Chile's past would provide the key to the direction of future policy decisions. Yet, ironically, positivism and history failed to join forces in the search for the general laws governing mankind's development. Although nine of the twenty initial members of

2. For Mexico, see: Leopoldo Zea, *Apogea y decadencia del positivismo en México* (Mexico City, 1944); for Argentina: Ricuarte Soler, *El positivismo argentino* (Buenos Aires, 1967); for Brazil: João Cruz Costa, *A History of Ideas in Brazil* (Berkeley, 1964). Auguste Comte, *The Positive Philosophy*, trans. Harriet Martineau (London, 1893), II, 79.

3. Comte, *The Positive Philosophy*, 83, 55, 82.

José Victorino Lastarria's Academia de Bellas Letras, which first introduced positivist thought to Chile, were practicing historians, none of their future works owed any debt to Comte's philosophy of history. Only Lastarria, perhaps the first Chilean to spread Comte's doctrines, Juan Enrique Lagarrigue, and Valentín Letelier devoted their works to an analysis of how positivistic history should be written, but no one adopted the Comtian method to a study of Chilean history. Why did positivism and history, so basic to Comte's philosophy, fail to join forces in Chile?

The acceptance of merely a part of Comte's philosophy should come as no surprise. While Comte's initial work, the *Cours de philosophie positive*, advocated a scientific approach to the study of society, his later studies preached of a society based on "love." Comte formed a new Religion of Humanity and became its high priest, while his dead lover, Clothilde de Vaux, became its Virgin Mother. The sight of the former rationalist clutching a lock of Clothilde's hair while kneeling in prayer before her empty red velvet throne revolted some of Comte's followers both within France and abroad. John Stuart Mill objected to this bizarre turn in the philosophy he had previously championed, and Émile Littré formed a society of heterodox positivists which followed the doctrines of the *Cours*, but rejected the new religion.[4]

Comte's favorable view of the coup of Louis Napoleon in 1851 similarly repulsed several of his early followers. Comte reasoned that a truly positivistic society could only be institutionalized under a dictatorship. He detested the bickering of rival political parties and scorned their inability to introduce positive reforms. Louis Napoleon appeared as the only solution. Thus, Comte's philosophy, taken in toto, remained rational and emotional, anticlerical, but religious, and favorable to both dictatorships and the aspirations of an intellectual elite.

As positivism crossed the Atlantic, it was not unusual for *pensadores* to accept only certain aspects of Comte's eclectic potpourri of philosophic thought. Latin American Positivism, in its many varieties, would have no doubt appeared incomprehensible to Comte and his disciples. Consider Lastarria's suggestion that the motto "Order and Progress" be changed to "Liberty and Progress." Comte's Religion of Humanity was ignored in Mexico,

4. Frank E. Manuel, *The Prophets of Paris* (Cambridge, Mass., 1962), Ch. 4; John Stuart Mill, *Auguste Comte and Positivism* (Ann Arbor, 1961). See also W. M. Simon, *European Positivism in the Nineteenth Century* (Ithaca, 1963).

exalted in Brazil, and accepted by a small group of Orthodox Chilean positivists. Therefore, the relative unimportance attached to a positivistic analysis
of Chilean history should not be surprising in the spread of Comtian doctrines to the Americas, since it was quite common to accept one tenet of
positivism and not another. Accordingly, Arturo Ardao has argued that
Positivism was "adapted, not adopted" in Latin America in order to fit the
political necessities of certain social groups.[5] Thus, the reason why national
histories and the positive method remained separated must be sought in the
social, political, and intellectual context of Chilean life in the quarter century of Positivistic influence (1873–1900).

José Victorino Lastarria first read Comte's *Cours* in 1867 and was amazed
by its similarity to his own ideas. Although he attempted to popularize the
work among his friends during the next few years, he met with little success,
as empty lecture halls greeted his discussions of Comte's philosophy. While
Lastarria considered Comte "the greatest philosopher of the century, comparable to Descartes and Leibniz," he was unable to accept the totality of his
philosophy. He promptly dismissed Comte's "absurd religion and his political system which defied all common sense." However, Comte's search for the
general laws which governed man's actions pleased Lastarria greatly. He believed that he himself had advocated similar ideas since 1844, and it flattered
him to realize that he had developed such theories independently of Comte.
Ironically, neither Lastarria nor Comte had revealed anything entirely new in
this attempt. Both had read Montesquieu's *L'Esprit des lois*, which regarded
"political phenomena as subject to invariable laws," and Condorcet, "who
discovered the idea of social progression." Yet, Comte chose to refine these
suggestions of the Enlightenment philosophers and attempted to turn the
study of human society into a science—a sociology. However, despite Lastarria's approval of a considerable portion of Comte's thought, he made few
converts in the years following his acceptance of positivism.[6]

The turning point for Chilean positivism is generally considered the

5. Arturo Ardao, "Assimilation and Transformation of Positivism in Latin America,"
Journal of the History of Ideas, XXIV (1963), 515–22.
6. Leopoldo Zea, *The Latin American Mind*, trans. James H. Abbott and Lowell Dunham
(Norman, Okla., 1962), 150; J. V. Lastarria, *El progreso moral*, in *Obras completas* (Santiago,
1909), IX, 429; Comte, *Positive Philosophy*, II, 44–51. There are other examples of Chilean
antecedents to positivistic thought. See J. G. Courcelle-Seneuil, "Ciencia social," *El Correo
del Domingo*, May 25, 1862.

foundation of the Academia de Bellas Artes in the wake of the government's "freedom of education" decree which allowed Church schools to be established without state supervision. The immediate spur to action was the removal of Diego Barros Arana from the rectorship of the National Institute. Barros Arana who had taught "history without miracles," had incurred the wrath of Catholics and Conservatives alike as a result of his attempt to introduce modern scientific philosophy into the institute.[7] In response, Lastarria encouraged fellow intellectuals to gather and "formulate a fixed set of philosophical principles" to counter those "perpetuated by the ecclesiastics." The assembly of luminaries offered a sharp contrast with the youthful and inexperienced members of Lastarria's first Literary Society in 1842. Twelve politicians (including two senators, four deputies, the intendant of Santiago, and a Supreme Court justice) joined with prominent journalists and educators in answer to Lastarria's request. From the academy's statutes to the opening speeches, members proclaimed their support for scientific positivism, by encouraging "a spirit of independence in the investigation of the truth," and "a reliance on the positive truth of the laws of nature." Lastarria, the director, presented a forceful speech which seemed almost a declaration of independence from the "Church and its attempt to enslave men's minds" by the removal of Barros Arana from the institute. While the academy strongly encouraged members to prepare works of science for the weekly meetings, Lastarria also added that works of literature would be acceptable. He proclaimed that "even literature ought to correspond to the true idea of the positive progress of humanity" by its "ability to bring men together."[8] Comte's Religion of Humanity was never mentioned in the opening ceremonies, as it would have seemed incongruous in the context of this anticlerical campaign which would ultimately limit Church influence in the educational system in Chile.

The political crisis which brought together the nation's most eminent intellectuals quickly dissipated of its own accord. In the wake of scandals resulting from the "freedom of education" decree, President Federico Errázuriz dismissed his minister of education, broke with the Conservatives, and

7. Thomas Bader, "Early Positivistic Thought and Ideological Conflict in Chile," *The Americas* (February, 1970), 376–93.

8. Lastarria, *Recuerdos literarios* (1968), 389–402. For the opinions of Barros Arana, see *La República*, September 17, 1866.

definitively fractured the shaky Liberal-Conservative alliance that had brought him to power. As a result, the academy lost its sense of urgency and turned to more mundane affairs. Lastarria scheduled a series of weekly meetings during which members could present works of literature, science, politics, and history. He hoped that these works would achieve a political result since he claimed that "the necessity of reform came from the literary progress of the nation, not necessarily from the transaction of parties." Unlike many previous intellectual societies in Chile, this academy was unhindered by questions of finance and thus able to continue its meetings without worries about rent and other expenses. Federico Varela, who had earned a fortune in mining ventures in the North, donated 4,000 pesos to the group, thus proving to Lastarria "that works of the mind were no longer viewed with indifference by the men who possess the material wealth to encourage culture."[9]

After the academy had settled into a weekly regularity, Lastarria again attempted to convince his fellow members of the importance of Comte's philosophy with a new work, *Lecciones de política positiva* (1875), essentially a rewording of his 1868 essay *El progreso moral*. Lastarria reiterated his support for Comte's Law of Three Stages and his concept of the ranking of the sciences, but again denied positivism's authoritarian strains and the Religion of Humanity. He also urged his fellow members to consider Comte's insistence on the importance of historical study in the search for the laws governing human society. He added that "the roots of these laws could be found in each society, and the national history must be studied in order to verify them."[10]

Lastarria's new study met with a singular lack of enthusiasm in this supposed hotbed of Positivism. Actually, from May, 1875, to May, 1876, only seven meetings were devoted to discussions of positivism. In June, Juan Enrique Lagarrigue gave the academy a gift of Comte's *Principles of Positive Philosophy*, which he had translated. He returned a month later to lecture "on vulgar errors about positivism which are commonly heard in Chile."[11] Only one debate about positivism interrupted the tranquillity of the academy. A visiting Cuban, Antonio Zambrana, voiced his intention to criticize Comte's

9. Francisco A. Encina, *Historia de Chile desde la prehistoria hasta 1891* (Santiago, 1942–1952), XX, Ch. 4; Lastarria, *Recuerdos*, 382; Gonzalo Izquierdo F., *Un estudio de las ideologías chilenas* (Santiago, 1968), Ch. 1; *El Ferrocarril*, May 7, 1873.

10. Lastarria, *Lecciones de política positiva*, in *Obras*, II, 17, 22.

11. *Archivo Nacional; Fondos Varios*, T. 306.

philosophy. Lagarrigue took copious notes during the lecture in order to challenge his contentions. Lastarria described the event in his yearly report to the academy:

> The attack on positivistic philosophy brought to our attention some of the objections of the experimental school to certain conclusions of the great French philosopher [Comte] without denying or rejecting the bases and the criterion of the positivistic philosophy; and he [Zambrana] moreover attempted to cast doubt on this philosophy with the malicious recriminations which the metaphysicists and theologians have directed against it. . . . But the defenders of the philosophy which guides our studies rejected and explained those attacks by demonstrating the advantage of the scientific or positivistic method. [12]

However, personal recollections of this event are somewhat deceiving. Lagarrigue credited himself with a brilliant defense of Positivism in his own memoirs, and his report to Émile Littré swelled with self-praise. [13] However, Lastarria's minutes of the meeting revealed that Lagarrigue had originally intended to counter Zambrana in the following session, but had to request a delay until March of the following year. He did not actually give his rebuttal until the following May. In the interim, only one comment on Zambrana's lecture, on December 4, led to a brief discussion of Positivism in the academy.

Thus, the Academia de Bellas Letras discussed the positive philosophy infrequently. They held literary competitions and discussed "yellow fever (27 June), Norwegian literature (17 July), the Chilean tax system (7 August), and Motley's *History of the Republic of Holland* (14 August)." However, no histories of Chile, let alone positivist histories of Chile, resulted from the academy's efforts. The members and visitors to the meetings seemed to display a similar lack of enthusiasm for discussions of positivism, and the Zambrana-Lagarrigue debate failed to spur attendance. An average crowd of one hundred people attended meetings concerning positivism, while considerably more attended the discussions of yellow fever and Motley's history of Holland. As a matter of fact, attendance had decreased so drastically by June, 1876, that a special meeting was called to decide whether the academy should continue. The directors, led by Lastarria, decided to lower the price of

12. Lastarria, *Recuerdos*, 428–29.
13. See Lagarrigue's accounts in *La Philosophie Positive* (Paris), Huitieme année, no. 5 (March–April 1876), 312–15; and Nuevieme année, no. 3 (November–December 1876), 440–42.

admission to lectures, increase the number of members, and write members who failed to attend meetings in order to discover why they were not coming. Despite these measures, the academy never recovered the enthusiasm manifested in its early meetings, and, by 1876, positivism still failed to excite the members of the academy.[14]

Although interest in positivism waned as the decade progressed, Lastarria never abandoned his devotion to selected portions of the positive philosophy. Although Comte's political ideals proved ephemeral in the Chilean context, his philosophy of history continued to fascinate Chilean intellectuals. Lastarria, in particular, succumbed to Comte's historical thought without question since he claimed that he had discovered similar theories at the same time as the French positivist leader. Lastarria recalled: "We had not heard of Auguste Comte's positive philosophy until 1868. . . . [At the time of our 1844 debates] Comte had finished his *Cours de philosophie positive*, yet we had not the slightest knowledge of this famous philosopher, his book, or his philosophy of history, which was *the same as ours*. We do not believe that anyone in Chile owned a copy of Comte's works at this time."[15]

Despite Lastarria's glowing assertions, his belief in the simultaneous development of a positive philosophy of history in both Chile and France must be viewed with caution. His memoirs, the *Recuerdos literarios*, written ten years after Lastarria had read Comte, were actually an attempt to reassert his own primacy in the cultural progress of Chile. The memoirs depict Lastarria as single-handedly leading the intellectual renaissance of 1842 and founding the Liberal party against considerable odds. Recent historical works had tended to ignore Lastarria's contribution to Chilean culture. For example, a recent study by Isidoro Errázuriz, the *Historia de la administración Errázuriz*, neglected to mention that Lastarria had edited *El Semanario* in 1842, but gave credit to "his collaborators and even those who did not participate in the publication of the journal."[16]

Therefore, Lastarria's desire to resurrect his image as a father of Chilean culture, coupled with a thirty-four-year lapse between the events and the

14. See Lastarria's minutes of this meeting in *Archivo Nacional: Fondos Varios*, T. 306. For an opposing viewpoint, see Bader, "Early Positivist Thought," 382.

15. Lastarria, *Recuerdos*, 227, 210 (Italics mine).

16. *Ibid.*, 20. For Benjamín Vicuña Mackenna's opinion in his *Cartas del Guadelete*, see *El Ferrocarril*, February 5–6, 11–12, 14, 16, 18, 1870, and Lastarria's caustic reply on February 15, 1871.

preparation of his memoirs, led to a hazy reproduction of the facts of the earlier era. Eager to prove himself equal to Comte, Lastarria claimed that he rebelled against Herder's *Ideen zur Philosophie der Geschichte der Menscheit* in 1844 because it presented a philosophy of history which limited man's liberty. Yet, Lastarria's historical work actually proclaimed Herder "the wisest philosopher of the eighteenth century" and borrowed his concept of divine causation in a slightly altered form.[17] Similarly, Lastarria stressed that he rejected Michelet's "subjective metaphysical system" in 1844, although Michelet's major historical works did not begin to appear in France until 1845 and did not reach Chile until 1847. Then, in that year, Lastarria defended Michelet before the University Council, claiming that his textbook should be used in university history classes.[18]

Lastarria's memoirs, a fuzzy mixture of fact and fiction, professed a great respect for Comte's philosophy of history, yet the author never attempted a history of Chile written according to this scheme, nor did any other members of the Academia de Bellas Letras. While other Chilean positivists, such as Eduardo de la Barra and Juan Enrique Lagarrigue, admired Comte's philosophy of history, they remained content to follow or be identified with the ideas of the French philosopher, but hesitant to carry his ideas any further.[19] Thus, despite the impetus of positivist thought in Chile, historical methodology actually stagnated in the years following the foundation of the academy. As a result, a young Chilean, Valentín Letelier, found it necessary to write a study in 1886 which asked *¿Por qué se rehace la historia?* He then replied, "Because it is not yet a science."[20]

Letelier, leader of the second generation of heterodox positivists, followed a process of intellectual growth similar to that of Lastarria. Educated

17. See Chapter 3 herein.

18. Universidad de Chile, *Memorias de egresados, Actas de la Facultad de Filosofía y Humanidades* (1957), I, 132.

19. Eduardo de la Barra, "De los elementos de la lei del progreso," *Sud-América* (1873), 735, and Juan Enrique Lagarrigue, "Las leyes de la historia," *Revista Chilena*, III (1875), 491–510; IV (1875), 317–36; VII (1877), 5–19; and "La enseñanza de la historia," VII (1877), 484. For a biography of the Lagarrigue brothers, leaders of Chilean orthodox positivism, see Pedro Pablo Figueroa, *Diccionario biográfico general de Chile, 1550–1887* (Santiago, 1888), 282–83.

20. Valentín Letelier, *¿Por qué se rehace la historia?* (Santiago, 1888). For an excellent bibliography of Letelier's works, see Peter J. Sehlinger, "El desarrollo intelectual y la influencia de Valentín Letelier," *Revista Chilena de Historia y Geografía*, no. 136 (1968), 250–84.

at the National Institute during the rectorship of Barros Arana, he noted that the works which influenced him most were Montesquieu's *Considérations sur les causes de la grandeur des Romains et de leur décadence* and *L'Esprit des lois* and Condorcet's *Esquisse d'un tableau historique des progrès de l'esprit humain.*[21] After graduation, while teaching history at the Instituto Americano and philosophy at the Liceo of Copiapó, he first read the works of Comte, Lastarria (*Lecciones*), and Buckle. Trained as a lawyer, he was reluctantly swept into the politics of the turbulent era prior to the Revolution of 1891 when President Balmaceda was deposed and a parliamentary system of government was established. During this period Letelier broke with the Liberal party and the liberalism espoused by Lastarria and joined the new Radical party.[22]

Letelier's disenchantment with Chilean liberalism stemmed from its visionary illusions. Lastarria had recently presented plans for a Chilean constitution modeled after that of the United States. Letelier found such an ideal ludicrous. He argued that a constitution must consider the current realities of a nation, rather than copy foreign models in the hope that the system of laws would change the Chilean people into counterparts of their North American neighbors. For this reason, Letelier praised the wisdom of the Portalean Constitution of 1833. Authoritarian in nature, it recognized the chaos prevalent in Chilean society and adopted harsh measures to counter it. The 1833 Constitution had long been anathema to Lastarria and Chilean Liberals, and Letelier's approval of Portales' moves signaled his sharp ideological break with the Liberals.

Furthermore, Letelier found the Liberals hypocritical and ineffectual. At times, they rigidly adhered to their laissez-faire principles, and, by denying civil marriage, unwittingly allowed the Church to increase its power. Yet, on other occasions, they deviated from their ideals by supporting state control of education in the attempt to limit the power of the Church. Hence, by their wavering adherence to their principles, Letelier found that they accomplished little of importance.[23] Therefore, he joined the newly formed radical

21. Letelier, "Emilio Littré," *El Heraldo*, August 8, 1881; Galdames, *Valentín Letelier y su obra, 1852–1919* (Santiago, 1937), 23–24.

22. For Letelier's opinions of the event, see "La correspondencia de Don Valentín Letelier," *Revista Chilena de Historia y Geografía*, no. 140 (1972), 200–202. See Luis Palma Zuñiga, *Historia del partido radical* (Santiago, 1967), and Angel C. Espejo, *El partido radical, sus obras y sus hombres* (Santiago, 1911).

23. Galdames, *Letelier*, 306. J. E. Lagarrigue is somewhat more sympathetic to the Liberals' dilemma. See "La teología i el positivismo," *Revista Chilena*, XV (1887), 309–24.

party, an outgrowth of the Liberal left, which supported scientific education, a parliamentary system of government, total separation of Church and state, obligatory vaccination, and public health measures.

Letelier, like Lastarria, refused to accept Comte's political principles, as his opposition to President Manuel Balmaceda (1886–1891) indicated. Ideally, Balmaceda should have epitomized a positivist leader. He believed in a presidential system of government and was unwilling to allow a recalcitrant Congress to hinder his plans for Chilean progress. He abandoned the laissez-faire principles of his predecessors and actively encouraged the transformation of the Chilean economy from its export-oriented and agrarian base. Congress, desirous to assert its authority over cabinet choices, refused to pass the appropriations bill in 1890. Balmaceda counterattacked while Congress was in recess and decreed that the previous year's appropriations bill would remain in force for 1891. Congress revolted against this supposed unconstitutional act, and a majority of members declared the president deposed, and, with naval aid, led an attack on those forces still loyal to the president. More than ten thousand died in the seven months of battle, and on September 18, 1891, the last day of his presidency, Balmaceda shot himself.

While orthodox positivists, such as the Lagarrigue brothers, would have approved of Balmaceda's assertion of presidential authority as the model of Comte's teaching, Letelier objected to the president's usurpation of power as "unconstitutional." Similarly, following in Lastarria's footsteps, he feared "concentration of powers in the hands of the executive."[24]

Although certainly not a positivist in the political sphere, Letelier did not wholly deny Comte's system. He believed that Comte's works laid the basis for a science of human society. While Lastarria argued that such a science already existed, as in the works of Comte and Mill, Letelier countered that these men had only laid the foundations for a scientific study of society. These earlier writers, while stressing their objectivity, entered their studies with a new bias, either that of positivism or liberalism. They sought past traditions or trends that could be used to support their current ideas, and thus committed the same crime that led Bishop Bossuet to search for the hand of God in historical development. Therefore, Letelier felt his first task was to refine the ideas presented by Comte, Lastarria, and others before "sociology" or positivism could assume the position of a science. In order to

24. Reprinted in Zea, *The Latin American Mind*, 163–65.

reach this level, Letelier, like Comte and Lastarria, insisted on the importance of the study of history as the laboratory in which the "scientist-historian" could discover the laws governing human society. The reason that positivist philosophy had not yet become a science was due to the faulty manner in which histories had been written. He argued in his second published work, *De la ciencia política en Chile*, that "histories, as they are written today, do not put into perspective any regularity in human events; they treat them all as if they were individual facts without any causal inter-relation."[25] Thus Letelier defined his first task as the redefinition of the methodology of historical writing.

Letelier's main premise was that "social phenomena, like natural phenomena, are subject to laws of a general character." In order to discover these laws, he insisted, there must be a strict objectivity in both the verification and selection of the facts as well as in their interpretation. Letelier differed from earlier historians, both Chileans and Europeans, who insisted that the selection of the facts was the objective phase of historical study, and only their analysis was subject to the influence of personal or political interests. Letelier replied that the process of fact collection could be as arbitrary as their interpretation. He then commented: "What commonly happens is that the historian finds it impossible to relate all the events; he only takes into account those which fit his own criteria and neglects to mention the others or only refers to them in an incidental manner. For example, Bossuet goes into ecstasy when discussing Martin, an obscure monk of Tours, and makes no reference to Mohammed or the influence of Córdoba and Bagdad on the intellectual developments of the Middle Ages." Interpretations based on facts selected with a certain bias were also unscientific because opposing conclusions could be reached from the same data, as "passions led the *philosophes* to view the Middle Ages as the 'Dark Ages' and the Catholics to view it as the 'Golden Era.'"[26] Thus Letelier argued for strict objectivity in all aspects of historical writing so that similar conclusions might be ineluctably drawn from the same data.

His second criterion was that historians should not be blinded by the actions of "great men" and concentrate on the actions of the individual rather than the society. He reacted against European historians such as Carlyle and

---

25. Quoted in Galdames, *Letelier*, 261. See also Henry Thomas Buckle, *History of Civilization in England* (New York, 1926), introduction, for a similar statement.

26. Letelier, *¿Por qué?*, 52, 13–14, 12.

Cousin who argued that: "Les historiens ont fort raison de ne s'occuper que des grandes hommes. Les grands hommes résument et représentent l'humanité." Letelier believed the contrary. When considering the French Revolution, Letelier commented that without Mirabeau, Danton, and Robespierre, the Revolution would still have run its full course, because "it was not the revolutionaries who engendered the Revolution, but the Revolution which engendered the revolutionaries."[27] Other men would have been thrust into positions of power had these revolutionary leaders never existed.

The emphasis on the "Great Man" theory and on the individual's ability to control his environment blinded historians to the basic factors operating within a society. For example, most analysts considered marriage a result of individual whim. If X meets Y and they fall in love, they will get married. Therefore, by the laws of chance, the marriage rates within a society should be constant. Yet, rather than accepting this well-worn aphorism, Letelier went to the *Anuario estadística de Chile* and compiled a table of the number of marriages celebrated between 1871 and 1880. He noted that many more marriages occurred during the first half of the period than the second. Letelier suggested that the economic prosperity of 1871 to 1875, followed by the economic crisis of 1876 to 1878 and the War of the Pacific (1879–1883), may have affected the rate of marriages in Chilean society. Then he presented a law explaining that the number of marriages in a society was a function of the population size, the state of the economy, and domestic customs. He further argued that such statistical studies could be extended to an analysis of suicide and crime. While he never claimed that he could predict whether a certain person would marry or commit suicide in a certain year, he asserted that if he were given certain data about a society, he would be able to predict relative rates of marriages or increases and decreases in numbers of crimes.[28]

This series of observations had two ramifications. First, the initial step had been taken in the development of a "science" of society in Chile. The general laws of Comte and Lastarria, primarily of a descriptive nature, were now being replaced by observations based on statistical evidence. Secondly, these studies opened the doors to new policy decisions. When it was shown

27. Quoted in Leonardo Fuentealba H., "Filosofía de la historia en Letelier," *Revista Chilena de Historia y Geografía*, no. 127 (1959), 338; Letelier, *La evolución de la historia* (Santiago, 1900), I, 265.
28. Letelier, *De la ciencia política en Chile* (Santiago, 1886), 61–67.

Chart V

Year	Marriages/1000 inhabitants
1871	7.10
1872	7.90
1873	8.57
1874	8.07
1875	8.19
1876	7.14
1877	6.41
1878	6.14
1879	6.78
1880	6.46

Source: Valentín Letelier, *De la ciencia política en Chile* (Santiago: Imprenta Gutenberg, 1886), 61–67.

that the crime rate was proportionally related to economic conditions rather than to the severity of punishment, crime-fighting could become preventive. At the Radical Party Convention a small group of delegates adopted this argument in their attempt to alleviate the government's harsh penal system and argue for social welfare measures.[29]

Yet, Letelier considered his first works as merely sketches for his classic *La evolución de la historia*, a critical analysis of historical methodology from the time of Herodotus to the present day. While received favorably in the world press, the work was approved by few Chileans. Bickering on a faculty committee delayed the presentation of an award for two years, from 1899 to 1901. Letelier eventually received the 400-pesos award, but several committee members presented dissenting opinions.[30]

The unfavorable reviews concentrated on the irreligious nature of *La evolución*, and one cleric condemned it as a "direct attack on the Catholic conscience."[31] Formerly, Chilean historians had challenged either the actions of individual clerics or the practices of the Church, but no one had dared attack

29. Francisco de Paula Taforó, *El libro de las cárceles o rehabilitación del presidario* (Santiago, 1884).

30. See the review in the *American Historical Review* (June, 1902); Carlos Risopatrón, *et al.*, *Juicios sobre "La evolución de la historia" de Valentín Letelier* (Santiago, 1901).

31. Carlos Silva Cotapos, *Algunas erratas de la "Evolución de la historia" de Valentín Letelier* (Santiago, 1901), 3.

religion itself.[32] Letelier had argued quite simply that no historical fact should be accepted unless it was analyzed scientifically. Myth, tradition, or faith offered no definitive proof of a fact's veracity.[33] Thus, science came into direct conflict with religious tradition, as Letelier claimed that Veronica, who helped Christ on the way to the cross, never existed,[34] nor was the earth created in seven days and seven nights. Letelier argued that there could be no proof of the latter since there were no witnesses present. Science could also demolish this sanctioned belief since geologists had recently proved that "certain rock formations had taken more than a million years in formation."[35]

Thus, by the turn of the century, science became the enemy, threatening to sap the Church of whatever power it retained. The state had effectively stripped the Church of the remaining colonial *fueros* by the declaration of civil registration of births, deaths, and marriages, and by the abolition of the ecclesiastical court system. The power of the Church had withered to such an extent that the threat of excommunication of the president and the Congress failed to deter the state from its determined path of the secularization of Chilean society.[36] As the Church slowly lost its civil powers, the scientific discoveries of the late nineteenth century threatened to destroy the Catholic religion itself. As early as 1874, the Church began a weekly lecture series on evolution, "The Bible and Archeology," in an attempt to reconcile scientific and Catholic thought. Science had become a threat to religion, argued Luis Vergara Donoso, "as it had escaped from the laboratories," and "made its way into magazines, books, and newspapers, where the common folk could only confuse these high matters of thought." He further stressed that "the new sciences of anthropology and archeology were offensive to the Church because they claimed that history did not begin with Adam."[37]

32. Francisco Bilbao was one of the few exceptions. See his *Boletines del espíritu* (Santiago, 1851).

33. For a contrary opinion, see *El Estandarte Católico*, July 8, 1876.

34. José Ramón Saavedra, "Verónica y los Santos Inocentes y don Valentín Letelier," *Juicios*, 27–56. Saavedra had often criticized liberal historians who had attacked the Church and the clergy. For an account of the debates with Vicuña Mackenna on the Inquisition, see Saavedra, *La Inquisición: Rápida ojeada sobre aquella antigua institución* (Santiago, 1867). See also Zorobabel Rodríguez, "La Inquisición de Saavedra," *La Estrella de Chile*, March 22, 1868, and "Francisco Moyen," June 28, 1868.

35. Letelier, *El hombre antes de la historia* (Copiapó, 1877), 4–5.

36. See Miguel Guzmán Rosales and Octavio Vio Henríquez, *Don Francisco de Paula Taforó y la vacancia arzobispal de Santiago, 1878–1887* (Santiago, 1964).

37. *Revista Católica*, April 23, 1874. Similar arguments were voiced in the United

Letelier's *La evolución de la historia* continued this trend, as a new scientific history threatened to join "the new sciences of anthropology and archeology" in the attack on the Catholic religion. The reviews of the faculty committee thus ignored Letelier's attempts to modernize historical methodology and concentrated on the antireligious nature of a study that questioned the historical accuracy of the Bible. Carlos Risopatrón, head of the Supreme Court, commented in a review inserted between the chapters of *La evolución* when it was first published in the *Anales de la Universidad de Chile* that: "The book titled "The Evolution of History" by Valentín Letelier denies all beliefs of the Catholic Church; it renews all the errors and attacks against its dogmas and teachings, and, in a word, attacks the Catholic Religion which, happily, is that of the state. It is for this reason that it is one of the most prejudicial works for the education of youth and one of the most dangerous works that can be read by adults." The bitterness of this attack may be explained by the fact that it was rumored that Risopatrón was so religious that he was one of the two persons in Chile who consulted his saint faithfully on all matters of importance. The other was the bishop of Concepción. Yet, even moderates and Liberals criticized Letelier's work for similar reasons. Baldomero Pizarro, a lawyer of the Liberal party, commented: "This work ridicules the foundations of Christianity and denies the sacred character of the Old and New Testament. . . . [Pizarro then discussed Letelier's acceptance of Buckle's materialistic view of history.] With this we have arrived at pure materialism, as a few lines before we arrived at atheism. Not even Voltaire arrived at these two extremes!"[38]

Furthermore, Pizarro accused Letelier of violation of the Constitution, which if proven, would have caused Letelier to forfeit any prize money for the work. He argued that the Constitution allowed "the freedom to publish one's opinions in the press, but this liberty should not be abused." Pizarro claimed that Letelier went beyond the limits of free speech by attacking the Catholic faith, which was protected in Article Four of the Constitution. Letelier re-

---

States. When Charles Hodge (1797–1878) wrote *What is Darwinism?* in 1874, he replied, "It is atheism." See R. J. Wilson (ed.), *Darwinism and the American Intellectual* (Homewood, Ill., 1967), 40.

38. Carlos Risopatrón, "Observaciones sobre la 'Evolución de la historia,'" *Anales de la Universidad de Chile* (1900), 728; Virgilio Figueroa, *Diccionario histórico, biográfico, y bibliográfico de Chile* (Santiago, 1931); Baldomero Pizarro, "Informe sobre la Evolución de la historia," *Anales de la Universidad de Chile* (1901), 479–80.

sponded angrily, first criticizing Pizarro for "taking a year to present his report to the University Faculty." Additionally, he recalled that Jorge Huneeus, author of the *Constitución ante el congreso*, had received a university prize in 1879, even though his work had attacked the Constitution itself.[39]

A faculty committee reconsidered Pizarro's report and Letelier's reply and decided to award Letelier the 400-pesos prize. The verdict was not surprising since the new panel consisted of eminent scientists and historians. Although Letelier eventually received his reward, it was to little avail, as his challenge to Chilean historians fell on deaf ears. Scientific or positivistic history, which Lastarria and Letelier had advocated since 1868, had yet to be written. Historians discouraged by both Catholic criticism and the fractured and unenthusiastic nature of Chilean heterodox positivism, never fulfilled the calls for a new history which might aid Chile's future progress. Letelier, discouraged by the reception of *La evolución*, never returned to historical writing.[40]

The response to *La evolución de la historia* also revealed the extent to which Chilean historiography had become politicized during the nineteenth century. Clerical opponents, who had borne the brunt of historical critiques by Barros Arana and Amunátegui, searched for hidden meaning in a historical work before the overt purpose could be accepted. Even a new scientific history was approached with the same suspicion as any work of history written prior to 1900. Therefore, despite the efforts of first Bello and then later Letelier, history was still perceived as a political weapon in the hands of the historian.

---

39. *Antecedentes relativos a la gratificación del primer tomo de "La Evolución de la historia"* (Santiago, 1901), 78–80, 85.
    40. *Ibid.*, 88; Galdames, *Letelier*, Libro IV, Ch. 2 and Ch. 6.

CONCLUSION

IN HIS EARLY YEARS Barros Arana had only one hero—Claude Gay, the astute Frenchman who excited his interest with a multivolume history of Chile. When Miguel Luis Amunátegui criticized Gay's methodology, Barros Arana immediately rose to his defense, claiming that the *Historia física i política de Chile* was "a great work, one of the most notable Chilean histories ever written."[1] Yet, just ten years later, Barros Arana revealed his disappointment with Gay on the occasion of the publication of one of the last volumes of his mammoth work. Although he acknowledged the merits of Gay's considerable research, there was no doubt that he appeared disappointed with the work. Suddenly Barros Arana became grossly offended by Gay's attempts to maintain an acritical posture. Gay claimed that he was presenting all the events of the era in order that the reader might judge for himself the true nature of the epoch under study. Barros Arana countered that the historian who abandoned his main function, that of a judge, revealed a shocking "complacency," which made it impossible for the reader to understand the facts the historian has presented. Barros Arana discovered yet another flaw that appeared still more grievous to him. He found that Gay's pretense of impartiality was mere sham, for he was merely attempting to "disguise his sympathies for the Conservative party and the Constitution of 1833."[2]

1. *Anales de la Universidad de Chile* (February, 1863), 218–23.
2. Diego Barros Arana, *Obras completas* (Santiago, 1905), IX, 100–101.

This abrupt change in attitude is revealing of the change of orientation in historical methodology in Chile in the nineteenth century. In the course of ten years something forced young Barros Arana to abandon Claude Gay's work as a model to be emulated. The changing political conditions in Chile help explain this shift. Before the debates between Church and state over the control of the educational system, Barros Arana remained satisfied with a conception of historical methodology which closely paralleled that of Bello and Gay. By the end of Manuel Montt's term in office, Barros Arana felt compelled to use history as a tool in order to attack the tyranny of the former ruler. Yet his commitment to this new style of history which judged men and epochs of the recent past remained ambiguous. Barros Arana portrayed Montt as a man who betrayed the historian, by hiding and altering documents, rather than a man who betrayed his nation. Later, the National Institute affair erased Barros Arana's hesitancy. Once removed from the rectorship as a result of Conservative intrigues, he released a torrent of anticlerical history unrivalled in the bitterness of tone by anything he had written previously. His short essays depicted a Church and clergy that betrayed Chile both in the colonial and national periods. Although the historian discussed the past, the aura of present disputes haunted the printed page. The text remained a history, but from between the lines emerged a polemic.

Barros Arana was the slowest to reject the historical methodology that Andrés Bello had prescribed in the 1840s. Other historians, including Amunátegui, Vicuña Mackenna, and Errázuriz responded more quickly to threats of political opposition or social ills, and readily abandoned the objectivity that Bello had sought to instill.

The new history of the nineteenth century became functional, designed for use. Although facts might be critically documented and the sources remain above reproach, historians often chose their topics of discussion and assembled their facts with an eye to current social, political, and personal problems. Thus the past became contemporary with the present as politicians and historians, often one and the same, used history in their debates on constitutional issues, Church-state relations, foreign diplomacy, and educational reform in order to support their arguments. While politicians may have rationalized their use of history in this fashion as a means to noble ends, others found the past betrayed by this practice.

Although a few Chileans recognized these abuses of history and attempted to correct them, they unfortunately fell into the same abyss as those they attacked. The Chilean positivists provide a prime example. Lastarria advocated scientific history and used Comtian positivism for support. However, while trying to improve historical methodology, Lastarria also attempted to exalt his personal reputation, and, as a result, produced a memoir of slightly dubious recollections, rather than a historical treatise which might have inspired others to follow in his footsteps. Letelier's similar attempts seemed even more futile, as clerical opponents, hardened by several decades of critical attacks in historical guise, challenged the religious nature of *La evolución de la historia*. Letelier's serious and lengthy tome never pretended to attack religion, but, rather, revise outdated historical methodology. Yet, such a work remained an anomaly in Chile, as covert purpose was often sought before the ostensible message of a work might be accepted.

This polemic tradition never managed to wholly eliminate the dispassionate attitudes advocated by Bello. José Toribio Medina, although a student of Barros Arana and Amunátegui, still bedevils historiographers who attempt to find a philosophy of history or even political motivations in his works.[3] Similarly, Barros Arana, in the midst of his anticlerical histories of the 1870s, might turn to such diverse biographical subjects as Pedro de Valdivia or Christopher Columbus, which bore little relation to his current difficulties.

Yet, the weapon of history was always available, and historians felt no compunction about using it if it served their purposes. The professional skills they had learned independently or in the National Institute or University of Chile rarely hindered them in this practice.

Despite a definite commitment to a functional approach to historical writing, few historians ever admitted that they themselves had abandoned the objectivity that their profession had supposedly demanded. Yet, everyone felt free to criticize this habit among others. Thus Lastarria might attack Vicuña Mackenna or Amunátegui for using history to serve political or personal ends, but he would not admit to the same flaw within himself. This does not appear to be a case of continual self-deception on the part of the historians, since each used the past whenever the situation compelled it, and each recognized the trend among his cohorts.

3. Arthur Whitaker, "Medina's Concept of History," in Maury A. Bromsen (ed.), *José Toribio Medina, Humanist of the Americas* (Washington, D.C., 1960), 69–75.

This refusal to admit to the use of the past for personal purposes can best be seen in the trials of Vicuña Mackenna. As long as the historian maintained a "sacred trust," as a judge or priest, his work would be accepted by the audience. Once the historian lost his carefully cultivated ethos, he would also lose the confidence of his readers and be open to the same criticism as any other political figure. History would thus lose its privileged position of criticism without suspicion or counter-charge. The past could then be interpreted as anyone wished, and the "judge" would become merely an attorney-for-hire. As the century progressed, Vicuña Mackenna's loss of esteem reflected the decline of respect for the historian, as more and more individuals used the past to support their political and social ideals.

As a result, it appears that historians sought to hide the presence of bias or passion by a continual stream of protestations of innocence at the beginning of their historical works. "I am limiting myself to the pure exposition of the facts and abandoning all philosophical judgment to my readers," wrote the cleric José Hipólito Salas. Vicuña Mackenna went even further and compared the role of the historian to that of a priest; Barros Arana compared it to a judgeship. This rhetoric implied the support of the ideals of Andrés Bello, but the content did not. As a result, many nineteenth- and twentieth-century historians have declared the "absolute conquest" of Bello's methods, by taking these protestations as fact. Thus contemporary historians have underestimated this polemical trend in Chilean historiography partially as a result of the nineteenth-century historians' desire to dissemble any appearance of bias on their part.

As the historian became involved in the politics of the emerging nation, he committed his works to achieve his desired goals, whether constitutional reform, inter-American unity, or the patriotic education of Chilean youth. Past and present became inextricably fused in nineteenth-century historical writing, and as a result, the historian rarely retreated to a scholarly cloister during the remainder of his life. Thus, it is no accident that Chile's greatest historians also emerged as their nation's foremost political figures as cabinet ministers, foreign diplomats, and even presidential candidates.

SELECTED BIBLIOGRAPHY

MANUSCRIPT SOURCES

Archivo Nacional de Chile, Santiago, Chile
    Archivo Eyzaguirre
    Archivo Gay-Morla
    Archivo de Don Benjamín Vicuña Mackenna
    Fondos varios

NEWSPAPERS AND JOURNALS

Note: All newspapers and journals published in Santiago, Chile, unless otherwise noted.

La Actualidad, 1861
Anales de la Universidad de Chile, 1843–1900
La Araucana, 1840–1844
La Asamblea Constituyente, 1858
El Comercio de Valparaíso, 1848
El Correo del Domingo, 1862
El Correo Literario, 1864–1865
El Estandarte Católico, 1874–1877
La Estrella de Chile, 1868–1876
El Ferrocarril, 1855–1879
El Heraldo, Valparaíso, 1865
El Independiente, 1871–1876
El Mercurio, 1840–1875
El Museo, 1860–1861
El Museo de Ambas Americas, 1842

El País, 1857
La Philosophie Positive (Paris, France), 1876
El Progreso, 1844–1846
La República, 1866–1878
Revista Católica, 1843–1874
Revista de Santiago, 1872
El Semanario de Santiago, 1842
Sud-América, 1873–1874
La Tribuna, 1849–1851
La Voz de Chile, 1862–1864

BOOKS AND ARTICLES

Alemparte Robles, Julio. *Carrera y Freire, fundadores de la República*. Santiago: Nascimento, 1963.

Alfonso A., José. *La Sociedad de Instrucción Primaria de Santiago de Chile*. Santiago: Casa nacional del niño, 1937.

Amunátegui, Miguel Luis. *Biografías de Americanos*. Santiago: Imprenta nacional, 1854.

———. *Camilo Henríquez*. Santiago: Imprenta nacional, 1888.

———. *Compendio de la historia política i eclesiástica de Chile*. Valparaíso: N. Ezquerra, 1867.

———. *La crónica de 1810*. 3 vols. Santiago: Imprenta de la República de J. Nuñez, 1876.

———. *La cuestión de límites entre Chile i Bolivia*. Santiago: Imprenta nacional, 1863.

———. *La cuestión de límites entre Chile i la República Argentina*. 3 vols. Santiago: Imprenta nacional, 1879–1881.

———. *La dictadura de O'Higgins*. Santiago: Imprenta Barcelona, 1914.

———. *Don José Joaquín de Mora: Apuntes biográficos*. Santiago: Imprenta nacional, 1888.

———. *Don José Joaquín Vallejo*. Santiago: República, 1866.

———. *Don Salvador Sanfuentes*. Santiago: Imprenta nacional, 1892.

———. *La encíclica del Papa Leon XII contra la independencia de América*. Santiago: Imprenta de J. Nuñez, 1874.

———. *Los precursores de la independencia de Chile*. 3 vols. Santiago: Imprenta Barcelona, 1870–1872.

———. *Las primeras representaciones dramáticas en Chile*. Santiago: Imprenta nacional, 1888.

———. "El Templo de la Compañía de Jesús en Santiago de Chile." *Revista de Santiago*, May 15, 1872.

———. *Títulos de la República de Chile a la soberanía i dominio de la estremidad austral del continente Américano*. Santiago: Imprenta nacional, 1855.

Amunátegui, Miguel Luis, and Gregorio Víctor Amunátegui. *De la instrucción pri-*

maria en Chile, lo que es, lo que debería ser. Santiago: Imprenta de Ferrocarril, 1856.

Amunátegui Reyes, M. L. *Don Antonio García Reyes i algunos de sus antepasados en la luz de documentos inéditos*. 5 vols. Santiago: Imprenta Cervantes, 1930.

Amunátegui Solar, Domingo. *Archivo epistolar de Don Miguel Luis Amunátegui*. 2 vols. Santiago: Prensas de la Universidad de Chile, 1942.

———. *El Instituto Nacional bajo los rectorados de Don Manuel Montt, Don Francisco Puente, i Don Antonio Varas, 1835–1845*. Santiago: Imprenta nacional, 1891.

———. *Historia social de Chile*. Santiago: Nascimento, 1932.

Arabena Williams, Hermelo. "Los emigrados argentinos en la cultura chilena." *Boletín de la Academia Chilena de Historia*, VI (1938), 110–29.

Araneda Bravo, Fidel. *El Arzobispo Errázuriz y la evolución política y social de Chile*. Santiago: Editorial Jurídica de Chile, 1956.

———. "Don Ramón Sotomayor Valdés." *Boletín de la Academia Chilena de Historia*, V (1937), 116–33.

Ardao, Arturo. "Assimilation and Transformation of Positivism in Latin America." *Journal of the History of Ideas*, XXIV (1963), 515–22.

Bader, Thomas. "Early Positivistic Thought and Ideological Conflict in Chile." *The Americas*, XXVI (February, 1970), 376–93.

Barnard, F. M. *Herder's Social and Political Thought*. Oxford: Oxford University Press, 1965.

Barros Arana, Diego. *Historia general de Chile*. 15 vols. Santiago: R. Jover, 1884–1902.

———. *Mi destitución*. Santiago: El Ferrocarril, 1876.

———. *Obras completas*. 16 vols. Santiago: Cervantes, 1905–1906.

Barros Arana, Diego, and Miguel Luis Amunátegui. *Nuevo plan de estudios para el curso de humanidades*. Santiago: País, 1857.

Barros Arana, Diego, and José Victorino Lastarria, Domingo Santa María, Marcial González. *Cuadro histórico de la administración Montt*. Valparaíso: El Mercurio, 1861.

Barros Arana, Diego, and Ramón Sotomayor Valdés. *Manifiesto de la oposición de Santiago a la República*. Santiago: País, 1858.

Barros Borgoño, Luis. *Archivo Barros Arana, A través de una correspondencia*. Santiago: Universidad de Chile, 1934.

———. *Archivo Barros Arana: Misión en el Plata, 1876–1878*. Santiago: Universidad de Chile, 1936.

———. *Proemio para la obra de Don Alberto Edwards, "El gobierno de Don Manuel Montt."* Santiago: Nascimento, 1933.

Barzun, Jacques. "Romantic Historiography as a Political Force in France." *Journal of the History of Ideas*, II (June, 1941), 318–29.

Bello, Andrés. *Obras completas*. 16 vols. Santiago: Pedro G. Ramírez, 1884.

Benavente, Diego José. "Don José Miguel Carrera." *Revista Chilena de Historia y Geografía*, XL (1930), 296–310.

Bilbao, Francisco. *Obras completas*. 4 vols. Santiago: Imprenta "El Correo," 1897–1898.

Braun Menéndez, Armando. *Fuerte Bulnes*. Buenos Aires: Fco. de Aguirre, 1968.

Briseño, Ramón. *Estadística bibliográfica de la literatura chilena, 1812–1876*. 4 vols. Santiago: Editorial Universitaria, 1960.

Bulnes, Alfonso. *Errázuriz Zañartu. Su vida*. Santiago: Editorial Jurídica de Chile, 1950.

Burns, E. Bradford. "Ideology in Nineteenth Century Latin American Historiography." *Hispanic American Historical Review*, LVIII (1978), 409–31.

Burr, Robert N. *By Reason or Force*. Berkeley: University of California Press, 1967.

Campbell, Margaret V. *The Development of the National Theatre in Chile to 1842*. Gainesville: University of Florida Press, 1958.

Campos Harriet, Fernando. *Desarrollo educacional, 1810–1960*. Santiago: Andrés Bello, 1960.

Carmona, M. G. *Vicuña Mackenna ante el jurado de Valparaíso*. Valparaíso: El Mercurio, 1861.

Cháneton, Abel. *Historia de Vélez Sársfield*. Buenos Aires: La Facultad, 1938.

Charlton, D. G. *Positivist Thought in France in the Second Empire*. Oxford: Clarendon Press, 1959.

Chiappa, Victor M. *Bibliografía de Don Diego Barros Arana*. Temuco: Imprenta Alemán, 1907.

Cifuentes, Abdón. *Colección de discursos*. Santiago: La Gratitud Nacional, 1897.

———. *Memorias*. 2 vols. Santiago: Nascimento, 1936.

Clark, Robert T. *Herder—His Life and Thought*. Berkeley: University of California Press, 1955.

Clissold, Stephen. *Bernardo O'Higgins and the Independence of Chile*. London: Hart-Davis, 1968.

Collier, Simon. *Ideas and Politics of Chilean Independence, 1808–1833*. Cambridge: Cambridge University Press, 1967.

Comte, Auguste. *The Positive Philosophy*, trans. Harriet Martineau. London: 1893.

Cruz, Domingo B. *El Illmo. Sr. Don José Hipólito Salas*. Santiago: Imprenta Cervantes, 1921.

Cruz, Ernesto de la. *Epistolario de Don Diego Portales*. Santiago: Dir. Gen. de Prisiones, 1936.

Cruz Costa, João. *A History of Ideas in Brazil*. Berkeley: University of California Press, 1964.

Desmadryl, Narciso, ed. *Galería nacional o colección de biografías y retratos de hombres célebres de Chile*. Santiago: Comercio, 1854.

Díaz Molano, Elías. *Vida y obra de Pedro de Ángelis*. Santa Fe, Argentina: Ed. Colgmena, 1968.

Donoso, Armando. *Recuerdos de cincuenta años*. Santiago: Nascimento, 1948.

Donoso, Ricardo. *Hombres e ideas de antaño y hogaño*. Santiago: Ercilla, 1937.

————. *Desarrollo político y social de Chile desde la Constitución de 1833*. Santiago: Impreta Universitaria, 1942.

————. *Diego Barros Arana*. Mexico City: Instituto Panamericano de geografía e historia, 1967.

————. *Don Benjamín Vicuña Mackenna: Su vida, sus escritos, y su tiempo*. Santiago: Imprenta Universitaria, 1925.

————. *Las ideas políticas en Chile*. Mexico City: Editorial Universitaria, 1967.

————. "La labor educativa y literaria de Sarmiento en Chile." *Universidades* (Buenos Aires), I (April, 1961), 17.

Durán Cerda, Julio. *Panorama del teatro chileno, 1842–1959*. Santiago: Editorial del Pacífico, 1959.

Echaiz, René León. *Evolución histórica de los partidos políticos chilenos*. Santiago: Ercilla, 1939.

Edwards, Agustín. *Cuatro presidentes de Chile*. 2 vols. Valparaíso: Imprenta Universo, 1932.

Edwards, Alberto V. *La fronda aristocrática*. Santiago: Editorial del Pacífico, 1972.

————. *El gobierno de Don Manuel Montt, 1851–1861*. Santiago: Nascimento, 1932.

————. *Historia de los partidos políticos chilenos*. Santiago: Editorial del Pacífico, 1949.

Encina, Francisco A. *La cuestión de límites entre Chile y la Argentina desde la Independencia hasta el tratado de 1881*. Santiago: Nascimento, 1959.

————. *Historia de Chile desde la prehistoria hasta 1891*. 20 vols. Santiago: Nascimento, 1942–1952.

————. *La literatura histórica chilena y el concepto actual de la historia*. Santiago: Nascimento, 1935.

————. *Las relaciones entre Chile y Bolivia, 1841–1963*. Santiago: Nascimento, 1963.

Errázuriz, Crescente. *Algo de lo que he visto*. Santiago: Nascimento, 1934.

Errázuriz, Isidoro. *Historia de la administración Errázuriz*. Valparaíso: 1877.

Espinosa, Januario. *Don Manuel Montt, uno de los más grandes estadístas de América*. Santiago: Imprenta Universitaria, 1944.

Eyzaguirre, Jaime. "Una controversia sobre la religiosidad de O'Higgins." *Boletín de la Academia Chilena de Historia*, II (1942), 75–80.

————. *Ideario y ruta de la independencia chilena*. Santiago: Imprenta Universitaria, 1972.

Eyzaguirre, José Ignacio Víctor. *Historia eclesiástica, política, i literaria de Chile*. Valparaíso: Comercio, 1850.

Feliú Cruz, Guillermo. "Andrés Bello y la historiografía chilena." *Mapocho*, IV (1965), 231-63.

————. *Andrés Bello y la redacción de los documentos oficiales del gobierno de Chile*. Caracas: Biblioteca de los Tribunales, 1951.

————. *Barros Arana, historiador.* 5 vols. Santiago: Ediciones AUCH, 1959.
————. *La carrera administrativa de Andrés Bello en Chile.* Santiago: Nascimento, 1966.
————. *Conversaciones históricas de Don Claudio Gay.* Santiago: Andrés Bello, 1965.
————. *Un esquema de la evolución social en Chile en el siglo XIX.* Santiago: Nascimento, 1941.
————. *Historia de la fuentes de la bibliografía chilena.* 4 vols. Santiago: Universidad Católica, 1966.
————. *Historiografía colonial de Chile.* Santiago: Fondo José Toribio Medina, 1958.
————. *El imperio español y los historiadores norteamericanos.* Santiago: Ediciones AUCH, 1960.
Feliú Cruz, Guillermo, and Carlos Stuardo Ortiz, eds. *Correspondencia de Claudio Gay.* Santiago: Ediciones de la Biblioteca Nacional, 1962.
Figueroa, Pedro Pablo. *Diccionario biográfico general de Chile, 1550–1887.* Santiago: Imprenta Barcelona, 1888.
————. *Historia de Francisco Bilbao.* Santiago: El Correo, 1894.
Figueroa, Virgilio. *Diccionario histórica, biográfica, y bibliográfica de Chile.* Santiago: Balcells & Co., 1931.
Frazer, Robert W. "The Role of the Lima Congress, 1864–1865, in the Development of Pan-Americanism." *Hispanic American Historical Review,* XXIX (August, 1949), 319–48.
Fuentealba Hernández, Leonardo. "Filosofía de la historia en Letelier." *Revista Chilena de Historia y Geografía* nos. 127–128 (1959–1960), 313–51.
Fuenzalida Grandón, Alejandro. *Lastarria i su tiempo.* 2 vols. Santiago: Imprenta Barcelona, 1911.
Galdames, Luis. *Valentín Letelier y su obra, 1852–1919.* Santiago: Imprenta Universitaria, 1937.
————. "Crescente Errázuriz como historiador." *Revista Chilena de Historia y Geografía,* LXXII (1932), 22–32.
————. *A History of Chile.* Translated by I. J. Cox. New York: Russell and Russell, 1941.
González Navarro, Moisés. *El pensamiento político de Lucas Alamán.* Mexico City: El Colegio de México, 1948.
Gruner, Shirley M. "Political Historiography in Restoration France." *History and Theory,* VII (1966), 346–65.
Guerra, J. Guillermo. *Sarmiento, su vida y sus obras.* Santiago: Imprenta Universitaria, 1938.
Guirao Massif, Ana. *Historia de la Facultad de Filosofía y Humanidades.* Santiago: Universidad de Chile, 1957.
Guzmán, José Javier de. *El chileno instruído en la historia topográfica, civil, y política de su país.* Santiago: Imprenta Nacional, 1834.
Guzmán Rosales, Miguel, and Octavio Vio Henríquez. *Don Francisco de Paula Taforó*

y la vacancia arzobispal de Santiago, 1878–1887. Santiago: Universidad Católica de Chile, 1964.

Hale, Charles A. "The Reconstruction of Nineteenth Century Politics in Spanish America: A Case for the History of Ideas." *Latin American Research Review*, VIII (1973), 53–73.

Hanisch Espíndola, Walter S.J. "Tres dimensiones del pensamiento de Bello: religión, filosofía, historia." *Historia*, IV (1965), 8–190.

Herder, Johann Gottfried von. *Reflections on the Philosophy of History of Mankind*. Chicago: University of Chicago Press, 1968.

Iggers, George C. *The German Conception of History*. Middletown, Conn.: Wesleyan University Press, 1968.

El Instituto i el Ministro Cifuentes por various alumnos. Santiago: Sud-América, 1873.

Izquierdo F., Gonzalo. *Un estudio de las ideologías chilenas*. Santiago: Centro de Estudios Socioeconómicos, 1968.

Jobet, Julio César. *Doctrina y praxis de los educadores representativos chilenos*. Santiago: Andrés Bello, 1970.

———. *Ensayo crítico del desarrollo económico-social de Chile*. Santiago: Editorial Universitaria, 1955.

Johnson, Douglas. *Guizot: Aspects of French History*. London: Routledge, 1963.

Johnson, John J. *Pioneer Telegraphy in Chile, 1852–1876*. Stanford: Stanford University Press, 1948.

Korth, Eugene H., S.J. *Spanish Policy in Colonial Chile*. Stanford: Stanford University Press, 1968.

Krebs, Ricardo. "La idea de nación en el pensamiento de Bello." *Revista de Historia de América* (Mexico City), nos. 67–68 (1969), 160–74.

Labarca H., Amanda. *Historia de la enseñanza en Chile*. Santiago: Imprenta Universitaria, 1939.

Lasatarria, José Victorino. *Diario político, 1849–1852*. Santiago: Andrés Bello, 1968.

———. *Obras completas*. 15 vols. Santiago: Imprenta Barcelona, 1909.

———. *Recuerdos literarios*. Santiago: Imprenta Barcelona, 1885; Imprenta Barcelona, 1912; Zig-Zag, 1968.

Letelier, Valentín. *De la ciencia política en Chile*. Santiago: Imprenta Gutenberg, 1886.

———. *La evolución de la historia*. 2 vols. Santiago: Imprenta Cervantes, 1900.

———. *El hombre antes de la historia*. Copiapó: El Atacama, 1877.

———. *¿Por qué se rehace la historia?* Santiago: La Libertad, 1888.

Levin, David. *History as a Romantic Art*. Stanford: Stanford University Press, 1959.

Lira Urquieta, Pedro. *José Miguel Carrera*. Santiago: Andrés Bello, 1967.

López, Vicente Fidel. *Manual de la historia de Chile*. Valparaíso: El Mercurio, 1845.

Manuel, Frank E. *The Prophets of Paris*. Cambridge, Mass.: Harvard University Press, 1962.

Martner, Daniel. *Estudio de política comercial chilena e historia económica nacional.* 2 vols. Santiago: Imprenta Universitaria, 1923.

Mellon, Stanley. *The Political Uses of History.* Stanford: Stanford University Press, 1958.

Miliani, Domingo. "Utopian Socialism, Transitional Thread from Romanticism to Positivism in Spanish America." *Journal of the History of Ideas,* XXIV (1963), 523–38.

Ministerio de Educación Pública. *Sarmiento, Director de la escuela normal.* Santiago: Imprenta Universitaria, 1942.

Molina, Raúl A. *Misiones argentinas en los archivos europeos.* Mexico City: Instituto Panamericano, 1955.

Morla Vicuña, C. ed. *Don Miguel Luis Amunátegui.* Paris: Impr. de A. Lahure, 1889.

———. *Estudios históricos sobre el descubrimiento y conquista de la Patagonia y de la Tierra del Fuego.* Liepzig: F. A. Brockhaus, 1903.

Muñoz Donoso, Esteban. *Compendio de historia de América i de Chile escrito para los seminarios i los colejios católicos.* Santiago: El Correo, 1875.

Museo Mitre. *Correspondencia literaria, histórica, i política.* Buenos Aires: Imprenta Coni Hermanos, 1912.

Orgáz, Raúl A. *Vicente Fidel López y la filosofía de la historia.* Córdoba: Imprenta Argentina, 1938.

Orrego Barros, Carlos. *Diego Barros Arana.* Santiago: Universidad de Chile, 1952.

Orrego Vicuña, Eugenio. *Don Andrés Bello.* Santiago: Zig-Zag, 1935.

———. *Iconografía de Vicuña Mackenna.* 2 vols. Santiago: Universidad de Chile, 1939.

Ovalle, Alonso de. *Histórica relación del reino de Chile.* Santiago: Editorial Universitaria, 1969.

Oyarzun, Luis. *El pensamiento de Lastarria.* Santiago: Editorial Jurídica de Chile, 1935.

Palma, Martín. *Reseña histórica-filosófica del gobierno de Manuel Montt.* Santiago: Imprenta Nacional, 1862.

Pérez Rosales, Vicente. *Ensayo sobre Chile.* Santiago: El Ferrocarril, 1859.

———. *Recuerdos del pasado.* Buenos Aires: Fco. de Aguirre, 1970.

Phelan, John L. *The Kingdom of Quito in the Seventeenth Century.* Madison: University of Wisconsin Press, 1967.

Picard, Roger. *Le romantisme social.* New York: Brentano's, 1944.

Piccirilli, Ricardo. *Los López, una dinastía intelectual.* Buenos Aires: Editorial Universitaria, 1972.

Pike, Frederick B. *Chile and the United States, 1880–1962.* Notre Dame: Notre Dame University Press, 1963.

———. "Church and State in Chile and Peru." *American Historical Review,* LXXIII (1967–1968), 30–50.

Pinilla, Norberto. *La generación chilena de 1842.* Santiago: Editorial Manuel Barros Borgoño, 1943.

————. *Panorama y significación del movimiento literario de 1842*. Santiago: Universidad de Chile, 1942.

Pla, Alberto J. *Ideología y método en la historiografía argentina*. Buenos Aires: Nueva Visión, 1972.

Powers, Richard H. *Edgar Quinet: A Study in French Patriotism*. Dallas: Southern Methodist University Press, 1957.

Risopatrón, Carlos, *et al. Juicios sobre "La evolución de la historia" de Valentín Letelier*. Santiago: Imprenta Barcelona, 1901.

Rodríguez Bravo, Joaquín. *Don José Victorino Lastarria*. Santiago: Imprenta Barcelona, 1892.

Rodríguez Velasco, Francisco de P. *Biografía del doctor D. José A. Rodríguez Aldea*. Santiago: Ferrocarril, 1862.

Sacks, Norman P. "Lastarria, un intelectual comprometido." *Revista Chilena de Historia y Geografía*, no. 140 (1972), 153–93.

Salas, José Hipólito. *Memoria sobre servicio personal de los indíjenas i su abolición*. Santiago: Sociedad, 1848.

Santa María, Domingo. *Vida de Don José Miguel Infante*. Santiago: Chilena, 1856.

Sater, William. *The Heroic Image in Chile: Arturo Prat, Secular Saint*. Berkeley: University of California Press, 1973.

Sehlinger, Peter J. "La correspondencia de Don Valentín Letelier." *Revista Chilena de Historia y Geografía*, no. 140 (1972), 194–210.

————. "El desarrollo intelectual y la influencia de Valentín Letelier." *Revista Chilena de Historia y Geografía*, no. 136 (1968), 250–84.

Silva Castro, Raúl. *Antología de cuentistas chilenos*. Santiago: Zig-Zag, 1957.

————. *Don Andrés Bello*. Santiago: Andrés Bello, 1965.

————. *Eusebio Lillo, 1826–1910*. Santiago: Andrés Bello, 1964.

————. "Lastarria, nuestra primer cuentista." *Atenea*, XC (1948), 20–26.

————. *Prensa y periodismo en Chile, 1812–1956*. Santiago: Universidad de Chile, 1958.

Simon, W. M. *European Positivism in the Nineteenth Century*. Ithaca: Cornell University Press, 1963.

Soler, Ricuarte. *El positivismo argentino*. Buenos Aires: Paidos, 1967.

Sotomayor Valdés, Ramón. *Historia de Chile*. 4 vols. Santiago: Estrella de Chile, 1876.

Stuardo Ortiz, Carlos. *El Liceo de Chile*. Santiago: Imprenta Universitaria, 1950.

Van Aken, Mark J. *Pan-Hispanism: Its Origin and Development to 1866*. Los Angeles: University of California Press, 1959.

Vázquez de Knauth, Josefina. *Nacionalismo y educación en México*. Mexico City: El Colegio de México, 1970.

Velásquez, Alberto. *Reseña histórica de la Sociedad de Instrucción Primaria, 1856–1873*. Santiago: Sud-América, 1873.

Vicuña Mackenna, Benjamín. *El castigo de la calumnia*. Santiago: República, 1868.

————, ed. *Colección de ensayos y documentos relativos a la unión y confederación de los pueblos hispanoamericanos.* 2 vols. Santiago: Ferrocarril, 1862.

―――. "Diario desde el 28 de octubre de 1850 hasta el 15 de abril de 1851." *Revista Chilena de Historia y Geografía,* I (1911).

―――. *Diez meses de misión a los Estados Unidos de Norte América como agente confidencial de Chile.* Santiago: Libertad, 1867.

―――. *Discursos parlamentarios.* 3 vols. Santiago: Universidad de Chile, 1939.

―――. *Francisco Moyen o lo que fué la Inquisición en América.* Valparaíso: El Mercurio, 1868.

―――. *El General Don José de San Martín.* Buenos Aires: Fco. de Aguirre, 1971.

―――. *Historia de la jornada del 20 de abril de 1851.* Santiago: Centro Editorial, 1878.

―――. *Historia de los diez años de la administración Montt.* 5 vols. Santiago: Imprenta Chilena, 1862.

―――, ed. *Historia general de la República de Chile desde su independencia hasta nuestros días.* 5 vols. Santiago: Imprenta Nacional, 1866–1882.

―――. *El incendio del Templo de la Compañía.* Buenos Aires: Fco. de Aguirre, 1971.

―――. *La independencia en el Perú.* Buenos Aires: Fco. de Aguirre, 1971.

―――. "Mi defensa ante el jurado de imprenta que tuvo lugar en Valparaíso." *Revista Chilena de Historia y Geografía,* LXX (1931), 30–136.

―――. "Mi diario de prisión." *Revista Chilena de Historia y Geografía,* XVIII (1928), 153ff.

―――. *Miscelanea.* 3 vols. Santiago: El Mercurio, 1872.

―――. *El ostracismo del General O'Higgins.* Valparaíso: El Mercurio, 1860.

―――. *Páginas de mi diario durante tres años de viajes, 1853–1855.* Santiago: Ferrocarril, 1856.

―――. *Vida del General Mackenna.* Santiago, Ferrocarril, 1856.

Vilches, Roberto. "Las revistas literarias chilenas del siglo XIX." *Revista Chilena de Historia y Geografía,* XCI (1942), 325–55.

Villalobos B., Domingo. *Lecciones de la historia de Chile arregladas en círculos concéntricos.* Santiago: Imprenta Cervantes, 1893.

Walker Martínez, Carlos. *Historia de la administración Santa María.* Santiago: El Progreso, 1889.

Woll, Allen L. "The Philosophy of History in Nineteenth Century Chile: The Lastarria-Bello Controversy." *History and Theory,* XIII (1974), 273–90.

Woodward, Ralph Lee, Jr. *Positivism in Latin America, 1850–1900.* New York: 1971.

Yeager, Gertrude Matyoka. "Barros Arana, Vicuña Mackenna, Amunátegui: The Historian as National Educator." *Journal of Inter-American Studies,* XIX (May, 1977), 173–200.

Yrarrázaval Larraín, José Miguel. *La Patagonia.* Santiago: Andrés Bello, 1966.

―――. *El Presidente Balmaceda.* Santiago: Nascimento, 1940.

Zapiola, José. *La Sociedad de Igualdad y sus enemigos.* Santiago: Imprenta Miranda, 1902.

Zea, Leopoldo. *Apogea y decadencia del positivismo en México*. Mexico City: El Colegio de México, 1944.
————. *The Latin American Mind*. Norman, Okla.: University of Oklahoma Press, 1962.
Zegers A., Cristián. *Aníbal Pinto: Historia política de su gobierno*. Santiago: Editorial Universitaria, 1969.

Index